# THE
# INTERSECTION
# OF
# SCIENCE
# FICTION
# AND
# PHILOSOPHY

Contributions to the Study
of Science Fiction and Fantasy
Series Editor: Marshall Tymn

# THE INTERSECTION OF SCIENCE FICTION AND PHILOSOPHY
## _CRITICAL STUDIES_

_Edited by_
## Robert E. Myers

Contributions to the Study of
Science Fiction and Fantasy, Number 4

**GREENWOOD PRESS**
Westport, Connecticut • London, England

**Library of Congress Cataloging in Publication Data**

Main entry under title:

The Intersection of science fiction and
   philosophy.

   (Contributions to the study of science fiction
and fantasy; no. 4)
   Bibliography: p.
   Includes index.
   1. Science fiction—History and criticism—
Addresses, essays, lectures. 2. Philosophy
in literature—Addresses, essays, lectures. I. Myers,
Robert E. II. Series
PN3433.6.I57   1983      809.3'876      82-25162
ISBN 0-313-22493-5 (lib. bdg.)

Library of Congress Catalog Card Number: 82-25162
ISBN 0-313-22493-5

First published in 1983

Greenwood Press
A division of Congressional Information Service, Inc.
88 Post Road West
Westport, Connecticut 06881

Printed in the United States of America

10  9  8  7  6  5  4  3  2  1

**Copyright Acknowledgments**

Grateful acknowledgment is given for permission to use the
following:

Excerpts from *Triton* by Samuel Delany. Copyright © 1976 by
Samuel R. Delany. Used by permission of Bantam Books, Inc. All
rights reserved.

Excerpts from Marge Piercy, *Woman on the Edge of Time* (New York:
Fawcett Crest, 1976). Copyright © 1976 by Alfred A. Knopf, Inc.
Reprinted by permission of Marge Piercy and Alfred A. Knopf.

# Contents

## IV.  Philosophy in *Star Trek* and Problems about Persons

## V.  Alien Perspectives: The Other and the Self

## VI.  Communication: Turmoil and Impact Messages

## VII.  Feminist Science Fiction and Medical Morals

## VIII.  History and Heroes, the Sublime and Changing Theism

# Introduction: Exploring the Intersection

Once upon a time, not too long ago, things seemed to fall into tidy categories. Science fiction was, at best, a strange peripheral pulp, thrown together by incompetent writers and acclaimed by only a few unsophisticated fanatics or fans. Philosophy was, at best, that stuff that was irrelevant for practical purposes and practical persons and that philosophers talked about to other philosophers but nobody else could understand. At that time it was not a compliment to either field to claim that "Science fiction is *the* philosophic literature."

But things change, even well-established popular images. Science fiction has come out of the closet, and philosophy has come down from the "ivory tower." Science fiction has become a clearly recognized and popular genre—a quite respectable one, in some circles. Even sword and sorcery works, which seem to be all action without either significant plot or thought, and the "thud and blunder" products of the youthful genre have been legitimatized as therapeutic escapism. SF (no longer "Sci-Fi") has received attention from literary critics, as well as producers of television series and films. Courses in science fiction have been introduced in high school and college, and many, including some critics, have discovered that SF possesses certain special strengths. Some also have discovered that, although substance and style are not precisely the same in SF as in other forms of literature, there are literary rules involved in its creation and some SF writers are quite competent authors.

Just as the status of the literary maverick has changed, so has the status of the academic maverick. Philosophy, or at least philosophic issues, have become popular concerns. Certain campuses have even discovered that all departments, academic and administrative, operate upon the basis of a given set of assumptions, proceed according to certain paradigms or models, and make decisions and take actions that involve value judgments and have ethical consequences. It is as if *everyone* is now recognized to be part-philosopher—those concerns formerly assigned to the abstract and suspect area of philosophy have become primary for persons in almost all areas of the academy. Major programs that are philosophical in nature have now been adopted as campus-wide priorities. All faculty members are encouraged to assess the ethical and value commitments related to their own fields or disciplines and everyone is urged to teach logic or critical thinking.

Recently, the phrase "applied philosophy" has been established within the discipline of philosophy. An increasing number of persons trained in philosophy bring methods of analysis, logical criticism, constructive synthesis, and criteria evaluation to bear on such areas as business, medicine, journalism, social welfare, environmental and ecological threats, human rights and the rights of future generations, and even the rights of animals. Several philosophy trainees have undertaken special intern services in various governmental agencies, social agencies, legal firms, counselling organizations and law enforcement agencies.

Of course, not everyone is pleased about these changes. Some persons fear that "real SF" will deteriorate now that it has become respectable; they fear that writers who receive acclaim and/or criticism will "play to the critics," thus assuring a loss of the writer's and SF's integrity. Others charge that this concern of philosophy with "applied" areas will produce (or has produced already) "a prostitution of the discipline"; they fear that by becoming popular and everybody's business philosophy and philosophers will lose their integrity and a deterioration of the strict, careful methodology that has been a major characteristic of philosophy and trained philosophers will result.

Although it is too soon to tell if these fears are warranted, the changes themselves have begun and are still evolving on several fronts. Many members of such organizations as the Modern Language Association, the American Association of Philosophy Teachers, the American Philosophical Association, the Popular Culture Association, and the Science Fiction Research Association are involved in initiating, participating in, and supporting program changes and special new sessions to informally discusss and formally "influence" the reassessment and modification of the long-standing tenets of various organizations, graduate programs, journals, and professional committees.

This volume is both a contribution to and a product of these changes and their concomitant attitudinal receptivity or openness. All the contributors to this volume enjoy reading SF; they are critical appreciators of the genre, and about half of them are professors of philosophy. The others are associated with high schools, institutes or universities in the areas of English, the social sciences, linguistics, futurism, and the medical humanities. Thus, they bring different backgrounds, training, and professional skills to bear on the critical elaboration and examination of the philosophical problems and values within science fiction stories, novels and series. Starting from different perspectives, they meet at the intersection of science fiction and philosophy.

Colin Wilson, in the "Prefatory Note" to *The Philosopher's Stone*—a book termed "a science fiction novel of inner space"—writes:

Most of my contemporaries seem to feel pretty strongly that the activities of thinking and novel-writing are incompatible, and that to be interested in ideas reveals a deficiency in the creative faculties. And since the critics also like to foster this idea—perhaps out of a kind of defensive trade-unionism—it seems to have achieved the status of a law of contemporary literature.

But I enjoy ideas. And this seems to give me a rather odd perspective on modern literature. . . . Mr. Osborne once said his aim was to make people feel. I think they feel too much. I'd like to make them stop feeling and start thinking. [New York: Warner Books, 1977, 2d ed., pp. 17-18.]

The intersection of science fiction and philosophy begins with the ideas and concepts within science fiction that are philosophically interesting, in the sense that they initiate thought and critical examination of the concepts, basic assumptions, and consequences that follow from them. Although science fiction and philosophy are not identical, some of their concerns and methodological techniques intersect. The essays in this volume explore aspects of this intersection.

The first task in a critical study of this intersection is to develop a set of working definitions. It is deceptively easy for all specialists to adopt the jargon of the specialized area but while this may serve as a kind of shorthand for communication within a given field, it limits communication to only specialists within that field. In an attempt to overcome this problem, we have tried to exclude jargon from the essays in this volume. Where specialized terms are retained, we have tried to provide an appropriate translation. This seems consistent with one major goal of this volume, namely, to "bridge" concerns in fields that are often construed and maintained as separate. Each contributor is aware of the need for and of the effort required to "dejargonize" these works. Even so, it may be helpful to identify briefly philosophy's primary areas of inquiry and the technical terms it employs.

The traditional subdivisions within philosophy are: axiology, or the general theory of value; epistemology, or the theory of knowledge; metaphysics, or the study of the basic constituents and categories of reality; history of philosophy, or the study of major historical philosophic thought systems and paradigms; logic, or the rules for correct reasoning in inductive and deductive procedures and the means to avoid incorrect reasoning or fallacies; and various "philosophy of" studies, for instance, philosophy of science, philosophy of history, of religion, of education, of medicine, or art, in which the basic assumptions or principles of a given field are identified, analyzed, and critically assessed.

Each of these subdivisions includes several more areas of concerns. Axiology usually is divided into ethics and aesthetics. Epistemology includes questions on the possibility of knowledge and its nature, the degree of certainty, the problem of error, the kinds of knowledge, and the nature of and criteria for truth. Metaphysics can deal with such problems as the relation of appearance and reality, the ultimate nature of reality, the categories we use to order and interpret what we understand to be real (their meaning, implications, and justifications), and the implications of major models or paradigms that have been adopted to explain the order of reality, or world views (*Weltanschauungen*). The history of philosophy would include also the consequences and impact of these thought systems and paradigms on persons and institutions, as well as their strengths and weaknesses. Logic is both a subdivision of study and the principal method of analysis used to elaborate and examine the other subdivisions and fields.

We all live and attempt to carry out our daily activities and responsibilities within some interpretive conceptual framework or *schema*. These schemata consist of the assumption sets or the presuppositional concept structures that we use to interpret or evaluate our experience, value judgments, goals, priorities, and successes or failures. A schema enables us to "make sense" of our world, our experience, and ourselves.

One may not be immediately aware of the schemata upon which the values, practices, and goals of the culture or society in which one lives are based or even what they presuppose. At the unreflective, uncritical level in which most daily activities are conducted, we are seldom aware of such underlying presuppositions. John Dewey suggested that thinking begins only when habitual behavior no longer functions effectively, that is when something "doesn't work" any longer. When our habitual practices and meanings do not effectively interpret our world, our experiences, or ourselves, we may be led to detect and then to examine the schemata that were subtly impressed upon us. A confluence of unexpected events that "just don't make sense" and upset habitual aplomb may be the occasion for critically examining the content and merit of a *schema*; in a crisis some conceptual cornerstones of the *schema* may crumble.

In the absence of a crisis, a good deal of reflective thinking is needed to recognize the existence of an interpretive conceptual framework. To detect the existence of one's own schema and its constituent parts (sometimes termed "paradigms," metaphysical foundations, or world view) usually demands considerably more effort. Some persons, by temperament or professional interest, are inclined to investigate these areas; others are not. Indeed, under normal circumstances probably most of us are not inclined to invest much effort in digging out and examining what is so far removed from "practical life," for we do not see the need for such work. Some seem to deny that such schemata exist as the basis for what we do, say, value, believe, or for what we consider as "real" and "unreal." Since our language and its meanings derive from our conceptions of "the real" and "the unreal," that is from our interpretive schema (which is often unexamined and/or undetected) and the network of values and meanings implied by and built upon it, it is not surprising that adaptive thinking to new situations is difficult and that the attempts to communicate between persons (let alone cultures and nations) is often frustrating.

One continuing task of philosophy—the traditional understanding of philosophy—is the detection and critical examination of these schemata, the relation of the constituent concepts to one another, and the implications or consequences that follow from the adoption of given schemata. This process may begin with our ordinary experiences and beliefs and proceed to an analysis of what these presuppose, thus going from common sense to schemata. Alternatively, philosophers may set up a schema that differs in significant aspects from the one adopted by most persons and *then* trace the implications of this "new" or altered schema, contrasting those with actual practices. These critical and speculative procedures involve epistemology, a modified metaphysics and logical analysis, axiology, and "philosophy of" a number of areas, the foundations of which form a part of, or follow from, that schema. Dominant methodology and the criteria for truth, evidence, and certainly, value and goals, are all inescapably involved.

Part I, "Philosophy, Science Fiction, and Cosmic Views of Value," serves a double function. In their respective chapters, Philip Pecorino and Alexandra Aldridge provide carefully examined, working definitions of philosophy and science fiction and sketch the contributions each of these areas can make to the other when they are in the appropriate relationship. In addition, both Pecorino and Aldridge mention several issues or points of intersection that are developed at length by other writers in later sections, for example, time-space, models and metaphors, and the impact of Cartesian dualism.

Time and space are fundamental concepts in our thought models; the particular forms of these models and the metaphors we select for them significantly influence the way we think about our world, others, and ourselves. In Part II, "Space-Time and Time Travel: Metaphors, Models, and Implications," Gilbert Fulmer and Lee Werth rigorously examine several of the problems involved in our models of time and space. They explore the adequacy of certain models or metaphors and the implications that follow, or do not follow, from certain presuppositions.

Part III focuses on particular parts of the space-time world and challenges two widely held notions. In "Nature through Science Fiction," Frans van der Bogert claims that the definition of science fiction as "the elaboration of human responses to innovations in science and technology" is too narrow, as it does not include any of the several types of "nature" science fiction. In "Teleology of Human Nature *for* Mentality?" Rosemarie Arbur challenges the widely held "Western bias" that the final cause, the end or goal, of human evolution is pure intellection, which she finds to be a one-dimensional mental abstraction model that distorts any proper notion of "the-whole-person."

Certainly these warnings are appropriate for our era: we must be more sensitive to nature, to the fact that we are a part of a greater ecosystem and that "human nature" or "being a person," a whole person, consists of more than cognitive activity. These concerns raise again the complex questions involved in trying to explain what it is to be human or to be a person, and how one knows and responds to "the other," to that which is not the self that I am.

Part IV, "Philosophy in *Star Trek* and Problems about Persons," offers two aspects of this complex question and the issues related to it. Dorothy Atkins does not deny the need for a balanced portrait of human nature, but she explains that an identifiable body of science fiction already presents a balanced and optimistic view of what it is to be human. Richard Double presents a negative thesis, namely, there are no persons, and in defending it, he calls into question the adequacy of at least two major theories of what it is to be a person.

As humans, we seek to learn about ourselves from the responses, in words and actions, of others. At the same time, we are greatly concerned with individuality, with difference. If the other, whether another human being or a non-human being or entity, is not-me, it is different, that is "the other," what is to me "alien." If that difference is total, we seem to face an insurmountable epistemological problem. How can we relate cognitively or affectively to what is "alien" unless there is some point of commonality, some basis of similarity? How, without such a common point of reference, could we hope to establish a basis for communication?

In Part V, "Alien Perspectives: The Other and the Self," Ted Krulik explores how we humans may be seen and understood by aliens, aliens who are becoming residents in our "environment." Paul Rice examines how we can "see," "say," and understand the alien "self" and the alien perspective. His literary and linguistic analysis has an expositional relevance for the alien perspectives cited and elaborated by Krulik.

Part VI, "Communication: Turmoil and Impact Messages," carries the epistemological analysis still further and focuses on particular difficulties in communication and culture. Adam Frisch examines the works of several science fiction writers who have portrayed in their works the impact that technology has made on human abilities to communicate. Joann P. Cobb discusses a story by Ellison as a paradigm of the "structural imagination" in which the writer not only informs but also evokes a response from the reader's heart (feelings) by making the medium into the message. Through Ellison's writing, the reader learns, feels, and experiences the consequences of the loss of "human values."

Part VII, "Feminist Science Fiction and Medical Morals," examines the ability of science fiction to portray the need for "human values" and to provide guidelines for moral decisions in medicine. Ann Hudson Jones identifies the ethos of our culture as composed principally of sexist, racist, and authoritarian attitudes. These attitudes motivate actions that deprive a significant number of human beings of their basic dignity.

Through a blend of factual events and science fiction scenarios, Jones assesses the ethics of medical practice, which she views as "a microcosm of our culture," and calls for ethics over ethos.

David White examines the merit of one of the most common arguments used to oppose medical innovations. According to White, science fiction stories have special qualities that enable them to assist in making decisions, particularly about medical innovations.

Part VIII, "History and Heroes, the Sublime and Changing Theism," concerns the philosophy of history, aesthetics, and philosophical theology. In a broad sense, each of these chapters is historical. William Schuyler examines historical modes, modes of recording events and the activities of persons involved in them. Bart Thurber presents a brief history of "the sublime" and then traces its essential contribution to the rise and historic development of science fiction, science, and the technological perspective in the modern period. Robert Pielke examines similar thematic challenges, ranging from feminist theology and science fiction to culturally and historically developed concepts of deity. He suggests that science fiction may be capable of providing a mythology for the "new" world view of science and technology that pervades our historic era.

This volume does not cover the whole range of science fiction, and it does not cover in depth the whole range of philosophy. Rather, it was meant to be a beginning exploration of the intersection of science fiction and philosophy. Dozens of science fiction works are mentioned in the following essays, as are many works by philosophers, social critics, literary critics, scientists, and others. Within the sections of this book are discussions of, and implications for, aspects of metaphysics, cosmology, ontology, teleology, epistemology, logic, aesthetics, and ethics, as well as the philosophies of history, of society and politics, nature and human nature, literature, language and communication, religion, symbol and myth, and personal identity. We hope that the journey through these pages will be as worthwhile to our readers as the process of thinking, writing and preparing this volume has been to each of us.

# 1

# Philosophy, Science Fiction, and Cosmic Views of Value

Is science fiction distinct from fantasy and other more traditional types of fiction? According to Philip Pecorino, science fiction is a special type of prose narrative that is concerned with speculation about possibilities; when it reaches its philosophical stage, SF's central focus is on the exposition and investigation of values and philosophy. Considered as an art form, the message, or matter, of science fiction is more important than its medium, or form. It deals with ideas and creates images or an imagistic cosmos for the interpretation of reality.

Pecorino traces the major developments of philosophy from the pre-Socratic adoption of a special elements-metaphor to interpret reality through contemporary strands of emphasis and points out the discipline's two continuing tasks: analysis and speculation. While philosophy is more coherent and logically rigorous than science fiction, Pecorino believes that it is in speculative activity that the disciplines meet most clearly. Indeed, he suggests that science fiction has become popular because it provides the kind of speculative activity that philosophy should provide but has not. In his view philosophy has dwelled too much on the analytic task and too little on the speculative task. It has invested too little effort in examining the speculative problems arising from human experience and in proposing systems of thought that might bring a sense of meaning to the range of human experience.

Alexandra Aldridge also distinguishes science fiction

from the traditional modern novel and in her essay elaborates on the place of science and scientific presuppositions in science fiction. She holds that the utopian/dystopian variety of science fiction is science fiction at its best and that it serves to register newly emerging values. In her view it functions as "a kind of fictive seismograph" of not yet institutionalized social change.

Science fiction, Aldridge explains, attempts to dramatize a cosmos or a cosmic point of view, ranging over expanses of time and space. This implies an ordered system of ideas, a world view (*Weltanschauung*). Obviously, a world view involves sets of values, space-time theories, ecological and sociopolitical structures and models, and metaphors through which a culture and its people can interpret its world, cosmos, and way of life.

Citing liberally from the works of Mary Shelley, Ursula Le Guin, and others, Aldridge demonstrates that SF can dramatize aspects of cosmic views as models or paradigms of space-time, mechanistic physics, struggles to replace culturally dominant but seemingly unsatisfactory models, and several other value problems. She elaborates upon the attempt by Le Guin's character to make the General Temporal Theory meaningful and thus to achieve the goal of uniting or reconciling the theories of sequency and simultaneity. Were this to occur in a fictional future, perhaps we would have a model for overcoming, in a real future, the economic, political, social, and psychic disorder found in our world. Perhaps, since humanistic utopians and social critics tell us "the materials for transformation exist," the transformation from disorder and dividedness to wholeness can occur—perhaps.

# 1

## Philosophy and Science Fiction

### PHILIP A. PECORINO

"I love you sons of bitches," Eliot said in Milford. "You're all I read anymore. You're the only ones who'll talk about the really terrific changes going on, the only ones crazy enough to know that life is a space voyage, and not a short one, either, but one that'll last for billions of years. You're the only ones with guts enough to really care about the future, who really notice what machines do to us, what wars do to us, what cities do to us, what big, simple ideas do to us, what tremendous misunderstandings, mistakes, accidents, and catastrophies do to us. You're the only ones zany enough to agonize over time and distances without limit, over mysteries that will never die, over the fact that we are right now determining whether the space voyage for the next billion or so is going to be Heaven or Hell."

Eliot admitted later on that science fiction writers couldn't write for sour apples, but he declared that it didn't matter. He said they were poets just the same. . . .

*God Bless you, Mr. Rosewater, or Pearls Before Swine*
Kurt Vonnegut Jr.

For most philosophers, science fiction has three strikes against it: it deals with science; it is fiction; and even more it is science fiction. Although science fiction often deals with important issues in valuable ways, few philosophers consider it an appropriate media for conveying ideas, a valuable source for significant issues, or an effective means for encouraging reflection. Yet reflections on the nature of both science fiction and philosophy and their possible interrelation may open the way to a new consideration of science fiction.[1] Such reflections necessarily involve an examination of the relationship of philosophy to art and literature and a discussion of the issues that belong to the philosophy of value. In so doing, it is hoped that misconceptions can be rectified and the basis for more fruitful interaction between philosophy and science fiction can be established. By speculating about present trends and future possibilities science fiction can offer much to philosophers, and philosophy can offer much to science-fiction writers in terms of understanding the interrelations, extensions, and implications of ideas, concepts, and visions. Through philosophy, science-fiction writers are likely to produce more critical and subtle executions of its art form and, through an appreciation of science fiction, philosophers may become more willing and able to speculate on issues of truly human concern.

## Science Fiction

We are making the future. . .
and hardly any of us troubled to
think what future we were making.
And here it is!

*When The Sleeper Wakes*
H. G. Wells

Since the end of World War II, science fiction has enjoyed a constant popularity. While science-fiction movies, television series, magazines, and paperback novels are the most obvious signs of its surge in popularity, science fiction itself has never been satisfactorily defined. Theodore Sturgeon, a noted science-fiction author, has defined science fiction as speculative fiction that deals with science. However, this definition is inadequate, for it suffers from vagueness, and it does not at all answer the question, "What is and is not science fiction?"

H. Bruce Franklin has adopted a more comprehensive yet critical approach.[2] Noting that all fiction seeks to describe present reality but different types of fiction do so from different viewpoints, he divides fiction into four general types:

1. Realistic fiction—a description of present reality by the production of a counterfeit of that reality

2. Historical fiction—a description of present reality by the production of a counterfeit of that reality's history

3. Science fiction—a description of present reality in terms of a credible, hypothetical invention, past, present, or, most usually, future, extrapolated from that reality

4. Fantasy—a description of the present reality in terms of impossible alternatives to that reality.

In this view, science fiction is concerned primarily with extrapolation from the present reality. But this extrapolation must be seen as possible or else the work is in the realm of fantasy and is not science fiction at all. For instance, if a writer in 1981 writes a story in which Mars is depicted as having an atmosphere similar to Earth's the work would be fantasy because it is contradictory to scientific knowledge. If, however, the author portrays a planet with an atmosphere similar to Earth's in another galaxy, the work may well be classified as science fiction. There is, then, a dividing line between science fiction and fantasy.

If science fiction is not fantasy, it also is not realistic fiction in Franklin's sense of the word. To be science fiction there must be speculation as science fiction is an extrapolation from the present reality. If a writer in 1981 writes a story involving laser technology or a story in which a city is destroyed by an atomic weapon, it is not science fiction. Fifty years earlier either story would have been science fiction because either would have been a speculation on future possibilities, but in 1981 the stories are either realistic fiction or historical fiction since the element of speculation beyond present scientific knowledge and technology has been almost totally eliminated.

Beyond extrapolated possibilities, science fiction, as its name implies, somehow must be related to science. As science is responsible for the most rapid advances in constructing the world in which we presently live and will live tomorrow and as science fiction is concerned with extrapolated future possibilities, science fiction must be concerned with "science," if it is concerned about the future of human experience. "Science" here is taken to signify that body of systematic knowledge, including hypotheses, theories, and laws, that has been built up through the work of numerous scientists who pursue the common goal of a more accurate understanding of the universe. As such, there are three levels: pure science, applied science, and technology. Pure science can be exemplified by a research scientist studying micro-organisms in the blood; applied science by the doctor who is treating the patient with a blood disease, and technology by the drug that is used in the treatment. One or more of these levels of science is present in most science fiction, but the way in which they are treated differs with the tone or intention of the works.

Isaac Asimov has noted that there are three types of science fiction: 1) adventure oriented, 2) technology oriented, and 3) socially oriented. To these three types, there may be added a fourth—the philosophically oriented. Science is treated differently in each of these types of science fiction. The adventure type is usually close to fantasy because it often includes implausible events and/or situations. The adventure story usually can be reduced to a simple clash between a hero/heroine and a villain/villainess, that is, good and evil, in simplistic terms. In adventure science fiction, science is usually just an embellishment to the story, superimposed to keep the reader interested. There are numerous adventure stories of this type in the comic strips and on television. *Buck Rogers, Flash Gordon*, the many stories of Edgar Rice Burroughs, and now the film saga, *Star Wars*, are fine examples of the adventure type of science fiction.

In the technological type of science fiction, science usually is seen as a value unto itself and not as a means to an end. These works are often referred to as "gadget" stories because they are concerned primarily with presenting new technological devices to further embellish the simple adventure story. The vast majority of all science fiction is a combination of adventure and "gadget" stories. The elements of these stories are familiar to all and include the hero or heroine, the villain or villainess, invaders from outer space who are usually BEMs (bug-eyed monsters), and an imposing array of ray guns, heat waves, space ships, and so forth. Superior gadgets usually allow the "good guys" to triumph. There are times when it is not a scientific gadget but a scientific theory that is the focus of the story. For example, there are numerous stories dealing with time and relativity theories.

It is in the third, the socially oriented types that the real cultural and philosophical importance of science fiction emerges. These science-fiction works focus on the implications of technological progress for society in general rather than on technological advances, gadgets, or theories. Science in these works is viewed as a means to an end. The works themselves display and explore varying views on the value and role of science, especially technology. A fine example of socially oriented science fiction is Isaac Asimov's novel, *I, Robot*, which considers the sociological implications of employing robots in nearly every area of society. The work explores the values and attitudes of a technologized future society in which humans are becoming less and less important to the maintenance of society. It is in this process of exploring values and attitudes that science fiction becomes vitally important.

In philosophical science fiction, the exposition and investigation of values and philosophy become the dominant themes of the works. Works in this classification either expose a certain philosophical tradition through the story or criticize such a philosophical tradition by showing its failures. Perhaps the two definitive examples of philosophical science fictions are Olaf Stapledon's *Last and First Men* and *Star Maker*. The first work traces mankind from the twentieth century to its end millions of years later on Neptune as the sun begins to die. *Star Maker* is the story of one man's journey from Earth to the farthest reaches of the cosmos, where he is confronted by the Star Maker, "the eternal and perfect spirit which comprises all things and all times." It is, in fact, an exposition of the cosmology and anthropology of process philosophy. In the preface to *Last and First Men*, Stapledon writes, "To romance of the far future, then, is an attempt to see the human race in its cosmic setting, and to mould our hearts to entertain new values."[3] Stapledon labels his work "an imaginative construction of possible futures." It is in the philosophical form that science fiction attains its highest level of artistic achievement. Science fiction in these works becomes a vehicle for the exploration of values as well as an exposition of possible alternatives for the future. Among contemporary novels some of the works of Stanislaw Lem display this philosophical character.

These four types of science fiction have been presented here as if they were clearly defined entities that are mutually exclusive. This is not the case at all. All four may be present in a single work, although this is exceedingly rare. Almost all science-fiction novels have elements of the first two types, many today have elements of the third, and some are philosophically oriented. What is inherent in all four is speculation; this speculation usually comes about as a result of the author's attempt to answer one of three possibilities: what if. . .if this goes on. . .and if only. . . .[4] Thus, the science fiction writer wonders what past trends have conditioned the present or what the future will be like if certain trends continue or what would happen if certain important trends were altered or reversed.

If science fiction is as rich and important as this essay presents it to be, why does it not enjoy more critical acclaim? In order to consider this issue, it is necessary to appraise science fiction as art. In order to do this, it is necessary to distinguish between the medium of science fiction and its message between its process and its substance.

For the most part, science fiction has been regarded as poor literature. With certain exceptions, this is true; most science fiction *is* stylistically primitive, that is the syntax and writing style are not as developed as those of other forms of fiction. The sentence structure is simplistic, usually composed of many declarative sentences piled on top of each other. Science fiction authors usually do not display any great virtuosity with such literary techniques as symbolism, allegory, or metaphor. Because most science fiction is based on action to keep the story moving, the characters are usually one dimensional and unmemorable. The emphasis is on the plot, the action, for science fiction writers are more concerned with the ideas embodied in their stories than the manner in which they present them. Thus, the medium of the story, its process, is fairly primitive.

The critical importance of science fiction as art, however, lies not in its process but rather in its substance. The author is concerned with the relationship of ideas, with extrapolated possibilities, with the patterns important in a society. If the importance of art is seen to lie in its offering of images to help form an interpretation of reality, then science fiction is important as an art form. It is, however, an art form often conspicuously lacking the refinements that appeal to aesthetic sensibility. The strong point of science fiction as art lies in its substance, in its offering of images to aid in an interpretation of reality and its presentation of possibilities that force us to remember we are shaping the future and should be conscious of its possible consequences for humankind.

Science fiction, then, is that class of prose narrative that concerns itself primarily with extrapolated possibilities. It is not fantasy because the extrapolations are seen as being possible; it is not realistic fiction because it utilizes extrapolation and speculation. Science fiction exists in a temporal perspective: what was science fiction in 1900 may well be realistic fiction or fantasy if written today. Science fiction creates extrapolated possibilities that are a combination of present trends and the author's critical imagination.

## Philosophy

In philosophical discussion, the merest hint of dogmatic certainty as to the finality of a statement is an exhibition of folly.

Alfred North Whitehead

Like science fiction, philosophy too is in need of a definition, and like science fiction, such a definition is not easily obtained. Philosophers not only disagree over such a definition but revel in and pride themselves on their disagreements. In the most general sense of the term, many people define philosophy as a personal attitude toward life and the universe, but it is more than that. It begins in wonder, doubt, and curiosity and results in a method of critical thinking and reasoned inquiry. Philosophy is an intellectual activity that tries to view life in all its relationships. Speculative philosophy, especially, is an attempt to formulate a worldview that is consistent with both science and human experience. It is an attempt to better understand reality as it exists now, and as it may exist in the future. It is important to realize as Titus writes, that "philosophy is willing to look beyond the actualities to the possibilities."[5] Thus, in its broadest sense, philosophy attempts to integrate all of man's knowledge and set forth a comprehensive view of the universe and of life and its meaning, while maintaining a critical stance toward that view.[6]

With this as a starting point, it is possible to consider how several philosophers have defined philosophy. In the first chapter of *Process and Reality*, A. N. Whitehead describes his notion of philosophy:

Philosophy is the welding of imagination and common sense into a restraint upon specialists, and also into an enlargement of their imaginations. By providing the generic notions, philosophy should make it easier to conceive the infinite variety of specific instances which rest unrealized in the womb of nature.[7]

Speculative philosophy is the endeavor to frame a coherent, logical, necessary system of general ideas in terms of which every element of our experience can be interpreted.[8]

Thus, in Whitehead's description of philosophy, in general, and speculative philosophy, in particular, there is an intrinsic relationship between philosophy and imagination. It is the role of philosophy to provide the generic notions that guide the artist. The artist in turn creates images of the "specific instances" that are seen to be possible. Philosophy is also concerned with interpreting experience, that is exhibiting the fullest meaning of events and ideas in their relationship to other events and ideas. It is interesting to note that Whitehead sees philosophy as enlarging the imaginations of specialists, for enlarged imaginations can only result in a wider range of possibilities to be placed at the disposal of the society in general. To Whitehead, then, philosophy is the organization of a given world in such a way as to make evident the intensity of contrast; this intensity of contrast is affected by the introduction of novelty into the society. It is the role of the artist, the force of imagination, to present novel images that aid in an interpretation of reality. These images are then judged by philosophy according to their comprehensiveness and relevance.

In distinguishing between two elements of philosophy, the analytic and the interpretive, John E. Smith offers a more precise definition of philosophy in his book, *Reason and God*.[9] The analytic is the critical portion of philosophy, semantics, linguistic analysis, and so forth; speculative philosophy belongs to the interpretive element. The same distinction is made by John Dewey in *Democracy and Education*:

Philosophy thus has a double task: that of criticizing existing aims with respect to the existing state of science, pointing out values that have become obsolete with the command of new resources, showing what values are merely sentimental because there are no means for their realization; and also that of interpreting the results of specialized science in their bearing on future social endeavor.[10]

Thus, Whitehead, Smith, and Dewey have all distinguished two elements of philosophy, the analytic or critical, and the speculative, or comprehensive. This distinction is important to an understanding of the relationship between science fiction and philosophy.

Dewey further explores the nature of philosophy in his *Reconstruction in Philosophy*. Quoting William James, he notes that " 'philosophy is vision' and its chief function is to free men's minds from bias and prejudice and to enlarge their perceptions of the world around them."[11] This is similar to Whitehead. Dewey goes on to say that philosophy may proceed down a path wherein it becomes a systematic endeavor to see and state the constructive significance for the future of man issuing from the revolution wrought primarily by the new science; provided we exercise resolute wisdom in developing a system of beliefs-attitudes, a philosophy, framed on the basis of resources now at our command.[12]

Inherently, then in the formulation of a speculative philosophy that interprets all the elements of one's experience coherently is the vision to shape future events so as to include that which a person values as good. This reiterates the Titus quotation at the beginning of this section concerning philosophy's willingness to look beyond actualities to possibilities.

## Philosophy and Science Fiction

> We do not merely have to repeat the past, or wait for accidents to force change upon us. We use our past experiences to construct new and better ones in the future. The very fact of experience thus includes the process by which it directs itself in its own betterment.
>
> John Dewey

By tracing the history of speculative philosophy, it is possible to see why science fiction emerges when it does and to explore the relationship between philosophy and science fiction.

In the beginning of Western philosophy the central concern was to derive from nature the root metaphor to interpret the nature of reality. Thus, in the Milesian school of philosophy, Thales, Anaximander, and Anaximenes sought to derive a root metaphor for the interpretation of reality from the four recognized elements: earth, air, fire, and water. Pythagoras, Heraclitus, and Parmenides sought to refute past speculations and to derive new interpretations of the nature of reality. In doing so, they were attempting to formulate a system of thought that would explain human experience. This is speculative philosophy.

Plato carried on this task of speculation. It can be said in fact that the *Republic* is the oldest example of science fiction known for Plato speculated in exactly the same way as many science fiction writers do today. He investigated trends that were active in his day and speculated on what would happen if they continued, were altered, or were reversed. In the fifth book of the *Republic*, Plato's speculation even included eugenics, a subject that is becoming increasingly controversial today because of advancements in the technology of genetic engineering and reproduction.

After Plato, speculation declined. Aristotle did not speculate as much as he classified. The emphasis in philosophy shifted slightly from interpretation to analysis. With the growth and widespread acceptance of the hellenized Judeo-Christian world view, speculation suffered a premature death. During the Middle Ages the hellenized Judeo-Christian world view was so ingrained in the fabric of society there was no speculation on future possibilities at all. Philosophy was concerned with filling in the picture of things known. While in Greece, speculation on possible future alternatives was inherent in philosophy until the death of Plato. During the Middle Ages the accepted interpretation allowed for no alternatives to the future. There was only one possible future and that was the future of linear Judeo-Christian history.

The birth of the "new science," as Dewey called it, altered all that. A chronological investigation of utopian fiction and science fiction reveals a revitalization of speculation that corresponds to the beginnings of modern science. The hellenized Judeo-Christian world view was shown to be grossly inaccurate in many of its assumptions and the result was a search for a new interpretation of reality. The controversy between creation and evolution, although arriving late in the breakdown of the old order, is a fine example of why speculation was resurrected. When evolution became a viable theory, men could no longer believe that a humankind, created by God at a given instant in time, would always remain the same, and the floodgates of speculation on past and future evolutions flow open. It would be difficult to find today a science-fiction anthology that did not include at least one selection concerned with the evolutionary process. In fact, one of the finest science-fiction narratives ever written, Olaf Stapledon's *Last and First Men*, is concerned with just that—possible future evolutions involving humankind.

It is possible that science fiction is so popular today because too much philosophical energy has been directed toward the analytic task of philosophy and not enough toward the speculative task. Scientific advancements constantly raise more and more possibilities that need to be explored and judged. Today's science fiction incorporates these advancements and shows the kind of future they may form. In its advanced forms, science fiction fulfills the function of Dewey's social philosopher, one who " 'solves' problems by showing the relationship of ideas."[13]

The relationship between science fiction and philosophy reflects the relationship between art in general and philosophy. The first part of this paper dealt with science fiction as an art form and concluded that the artistic importance of the genre lay in its ability to create images to aid in an interpretation of reality. This is the crux of the artistic-philosophic relationship. Art is the representation of a critical imagination that sees a present reality and speculates on the past and possible futures of that reality. These images then are offered to the judgment of philosophy, which ought to be in contact with all sources of information in a society and which should judge the adequacy and applicability of the images in relation to the reality they are attempting to interpret. The images are then either accepted or modified or rejected. This is the interaction between the philosopher and the artist. Science fiction may be philosophically oriented, but it is not philosophy, for it cannot judge the adequacy and applicability of its own images, which must be tested by concrete experience and judged by philosophy. Science fiction, as an art form, offers images from the lowest level of conscious activity to be tested in experience and judged by philosophy at the highest level of reflective thought. By exploring the type of world that is shaped by philosophy, these images may well include a criticism of certain philosophies.

Like philosophy, science fiction has its origin in wonder, doubt, and curiosity. Some humans wonder, doubt, and are curious and reflect these feelings by producing a work of art. Others have the same feelings but their speculation is more controlled, complex, and developed and result in a speculative philosophy. This is the difference between a Stapledon and a Whitehead. *Star Maker* is an aesthetic exposition of process philosophy, but it is not as comprehensive, sophisticated, logically coherent, or as adequate as Whitehead's most complex essay, *Process and Reality*, which is itself imperfect. Herein lies the reason that even the greatest works of art are not philosophy.

Even so, it is today's science fiction that fulfills the current need for a revised interpretation of reality. If philosophy is viewed as composed of two elements, the speculative and the analytic, science fiction is related to the speculative element insofar as it is primarily concerned with extrapolated future possibilities and it offers up images to aid in an interpretation of the nature of reality. It can be said that science fiction is one part of the telescope that enables philosophy to look beyond the actualities to explore the possibilities for the future of the human race.

But science fiction lacks the logical coherence and consistency that is the basis of speculative philosophy. Whereas philosophy is essentially self-critical, science fiction must be tested in experience and judged by philosophy. The vital importance of science fiction in a world that science is changing daily lies in its attempt to view human beings in their cosmological setting, clothed in their greatest successes and most ignominious defeats. Realizing this, perhaps philosophers can share the feelings for science-fiction writers that Kurt Vonnegut's socially minded humanitarian character, Eliot Rosewater, expresses when he exclaims, "I love you sons of bitches." After all, science-fiction writers provide not only philosophers but all humankind with images, stories, questions, quandaries, and future possibilities that serve as the foundation and provocation for what is properly described as philosophical reflection.

## Notes

1. The development and expression of the ideas contained in this paper have been greatly assisted by John Hurley, who shared my interest in and appreciation of science fiction as a source of wonder, the birthplace of philosophy.

2. H. Bruce Franklin, *Future Perfect: American Science Fiction of the Nineteenth Century* (New York: Oxford University Press, 1966), p. 3.

3. Olaf Stapledon, *Last and First Men* and *Star Maker* (New York: Dover Publications, Inc., 1961), p. 9.

4. J. O. Bailey, *Pilgrims Through Space and Time: Trends and Patterns in Scientific and Utopian Fiction* (New York: Argus, 1947), p. 12.

5. Harold H. Titus, *Living Issues in Philosophy*, 4th ed. (New York: American Book Co., 1964), pp. 6-7.

6. Ibid., p. 96.

7. Alfred North Whitehead, *Process and Reality* (New York: The Free Press, 1969), p. 21.

8. Ibid., p. 5.

9. John E. Smith, *Reason and God* (New Haven: Yale University Press, 1961), p. xii

10. John Dewey, *Democracy and Education* (New York: Macmillan Company, 1916), p. 329.

11. John Dewey, *Reconstruction in Philosophy* (Boston: The Beacon Press, 1948), p. 21.

12. Ibid., p. xxxiv.

13. Ibid., p. 192.

## 2

# Science Fiction and Emerging Values

*ALEXANDRA ALDRIDGE*

In the *New York Review of Books* a few years ago, Michael Wood dismissed what he called science fiction's "favorite alibi": the claim, implicitly made as earl as H. G. Wells and overtly expressed by such critics as Robert Scholes, that "the genre helps us to meet our sudden tomorrows." Scholes had stated in *Structural Fabulation* that "to live well in the present, to live decently and humanely, we must see into the future." Wood countered, "It seems more likely that to live at all in the future, we need to see into the present."[1]

Let us assume with Wood, that the futures offered by science fiction are rarely reliable as short-term forecasts, much less prophecies; that projected uses of technology depend on variables inaccessible to human foresight; and most importantly, that science-fiction writers are limited by the terms of their zeitgeist. Even the works of so successful a forecaster as H. G. Wells become, over time, increasingly appreciated as social criticism—admonitions to his heedless contemporaries.[2] Dystopic stories such as *When the Sleeper Wakes, The Time Machine,* and *The Shape of Things to Come* document the worst fears of Wells's progressivist generation. While they may not "see into" any future that has come to pass, they dramatize the potential consequences of large-scale social and political neglect and offer alternatives to the collapse of civilization within the world view of post-Victorian England.

This is not to say that some scenarios, for example, those predicated on ecological or nuclear disaster, could never occur. And certainly the continued existence of some social engineering trends that were first exposed by Aldous Huxley and George Orwell cannot be denied. But science fiction, particularly of the utopian/dystopian variety, is better understood and appraised as a register of newly emerging values.[3] In that sense, it often serves as a fictive seismograph of not altogether visible social change before that change becomes institutionalized. In the past decade, writers have recorded again and again the widely felt longing in our time to abandon a world view founded on scientific rationalism and the desire to replace it with a new humanism or neo-romanticism, based on a holistic or visionary scientific world view. The scientific conceptualization that appears in Ursula Le Guin's much acclaimed utopia *The Dispossessed* (1974) can be related to recent speculations by a group of philosophical futurists. But first, a few points of clarification about science and the novel are necessary.

What are the distinguishing features of science fiction? How does it differ from the traditional modern novel? Certainly reading *Brave New World* is not like reading *Madame Bovary* or *The Great Gatsby*. The SF novel represents an effort to dramatize a cosmos or a cosmic point of view. A cosmic point of view is one that ranges over vast expanses of time and space, as in Olaf Stapledon's *The Star Maker* and Wells's *The Time Machine*. But a cosmos, in the less grandiose sense, suggests an ordered system of ideas. The creation of a cosmos is an attempt to transmit a holistic view, one that is recognizable, yet in some way alien to the world we know (Suvin's "cognitive estrangement").[4] This is particularly true of utopian and dystopian science fiction, which constitutes the most serious work in the genre. While individual experience in a fragment of a historically familiar world constitutes the principal subject matter of the traditional modern novel, in SF individual experience recedes into the background.

Not only does individual experience recede, but often the background itself, the setting and/or objects, mechanisms, and techniques become the real subject and the focus of our attention. In *Brave New World*, what remains more memorable than the personal crises of Bernard Marx or Helmholtz Watson or Lenina Crowne are the essential props of their world: the Bokanovsky process of ectogenic reproduction; a genetically programmed caste system of Alpha plus intellectuals and Epsilon minus morons; neo-Pavlovian conditioning and hypnopaedia whereby children of each caste are prepared scientifically for life in a futuristic London. As David Samuelson tells us: "Things will be more important than people, the brain will predominate over the heart, ideas more than experience, will be basic to setting, character and plot."[5]

Modern science fiction evolved from the introduction into literature of a kind of scientific perspective, which coincided with the rise of science in the sixteenth and seventeenth centuries. The utopias of that period (*Utopia, The New Atlantis, Christianopolis, City of the Sun*) were written in the spirit of the new scientific rationalism; they were attempts to construct a harmonious order, a perfectly efficient social system. Thus, to the modern reader they exhibit a machinelike quality. Even sexual relations, which, however reluctantly, are usually accounted for, are seen as a function of reproduction, or of manly needs, that must be met in the same way that a sensitive engine requires regular tune-ups.

Other progenitors of the genre include the pseudoscientific voyage fantasies of the seventeenth century: Kepler's *Somnium* and Bishop Godwin's *The Man in the Moon*, which, in a giddy way, make use of Copernicus' astronomy, Galileo's telescopic instruments, and Newton's priciples of gravitation. Protoscience fiction employed the fantastical, the magical, and the supernatural, which is not surprising since primitive Western science also had a certain fraternity with alchemy, necromancy, sorcery—the quasi-magical transformational researches of the late Middle Ages and early Renaissance. There even appears a kind of ur-science fiction in the eighteenth-century mystery story, particularly the Gothic novel. Hugh Walpole's *Castle of Otranto*, is the prototype, crammed with ghostly visitations and titillating images of death.

It is Mary Shelley's *Frankenstein* (1817) that contains both the murderous thrills of the Gothic novel and the first significant extrapolation from scientific (really, pseudoscientific) thinking. What makes Shelley's novel singularly important in the history of science fiction is her depiction of the promise that science has made to humanity and the absolute belief of the scientific community in the fulfillment of that promise. Victor Frankenstein's mentor extols the scientist as a miracle maker whose powers seem inherited from his sorcerer predecessors: "They penetrate into the recesses of nature, and show how she works in her hiding places. They ascend to the heavens: they have discovered how the blood circulates, and the nature of the air we breathe. They have acquired new and almost unlimited powers. . . ."[6]

From the moment Frankenstein asks himself, "Whence did the principle of life proceed?" he lets nothing emotional or philosophical interfere with finding the answer. Neither his protracted absence from home and family nor the unpleasant necessity of pillaging charnel houses distresses him. He barely gives a thought to the social implications of generating life. His only doubts are methodological. Should he attempt to create a being like himself "or one of simpler organization?" How can he cope with "the minuteness of the parts?"

Throughout the course of her novel, Shelley criticizes the scientific world view for its lack of responsibility and absence of human-centered values. Scientific authority is the ultimate authority and the scientific method, characterized by efficiency and detachment, is the divine tool for discovering and possessing "real" (scientific) knowledge. The creature we have come to imagine after Boris Karloff is a distorted reification of the pursuit of science for its own sake. By inventing its creator, Victor Frankenstein, the Faustian seeker indefatigably pursuing "the cause and generation of life," Shelley was not condemning scientific research as forbidden knowledge. Instead, she did for her contemporaries what modern utopian/dystopian science-fiction writers often do: she alerted them to the social dangers contained in a newly forming mythos.

Shelley's early warnings of the potential dangers and philosophical limitations built into the scientific world view were reinstated in science fiction at the end of the nineteenth century with the dystopian stories of H. G. Wells. As many critics have observed, virtually every major science disaster scenario of the twentieth century has its origins in a theme created by Wells, from world holocaust (*The Shape of Things to Come*) to authoritarianism in the scientifically managed state (*When the Sleeper Wakes*).[7] Some of the most highly regarded science fiction of the 1950s and 1960s dealt with the Wellsian theme of technological progress outstripping human wisdom—Ray Bradbury's *Martian Chronicles* (1950), Arthur C. Clarke's *Childhood's End* (1953), Walter M. Miller's *Canticle for Leibowitz* (1959), and Kurt Vonnegut's *Cat's Cradle* (1963).

Wells's technological critique and his reservations about collective wisdom affected the values of succeeding generations and still remain an influence.[8] The most widely discussed science fiction of recent times, however, seems, once again, to come from a feminine imagination that is, most of all, obsessed with the dehumanization inherent in a mechanistic concept of science and whose social criticism locates the ultimate motives for moral choice in the scientific world view. In *The Dispossessed*, Ursula Le Guin, like Mary Shelley, focuses directly on the relationships between scientific conceptualization and social values. It should be noted that both Shelley and Le Guin have produced exceptionally popular science-fiction novels that, although somewhat amateurishly written, are teeming with ideas that reflect the romantic counterargument to the scientific rationalism of their respective times.

It seems probable that so much has been said about Ursula Le Guin's work recently because she is among the few contemporary writers of utopian science fiction to attract a large reading public hungry for a sense of vision and affirmation, for some relief from the spate of dystopias that have coincided with the bleak outlook of literary modernism.[9] One of the principal occupations of Le Guin readers has been to determine the exact nature of her philosophical stance. How do we characterize her world view? Is she a romantic (her own label)? Is she a romantic in the Taoist's sense of the world as organic, in their emphasis on the oneness of the universe? Is she a romantic in the modern anarchist's belief that individual enrichment can only exist in human-scale organizations where people are regulated by internal code rather than impersonal law? Does the romantic in her, which assumes a unity between the individual soul and the cosmos as well as the uniqueness of self, lead her to depict the ideal political system as an anarchy, where, theoretically, this romantic individualism can be best expressed?

I would answer yes to all the preceding questions. But in thinking about her rendering of the relationship between a world view and the ideologies and institutions engendered by that view, I keep returning to her metaphor for the basic unity of the universe in *The Dispossessed*, what her scientist-hero calls a "General Temporal Theory." This formulation would unite two accepted theories in physics and thereby provide a means for instantaneous contact among estranged peoples. Moreover, it is implied in the novel that a new conceptualization of nature and the natural world would change the shape of human consciousness from a disposition toward the linear and fragmented to a preference for holistic thinking. A new mode of perception would breed, in turn, a new ethos and a more humanistic set of institutions. As overly ambitious as that may sound as a framework for social change, Le Guin shares this set of assumptions with a group of philosophical futurists who were writing within the same five-year period, among them: Theodore Roszak (*The Making of a Counter Culture* [1969]), William Irwin Thompson (*At the Edge of History* [1971] and *Passages About Earth* [1973] ), E. F. Schumacher (*Small is Beautiful* [1973] ), Robert Pirsig (*Zen and the Art of Motorcycle Maintenance* [1974]), Ernest Callenbach (*Ecotopia* [1975]), and Fritjof Capra (*The Tao of Physics* [1975]).

In the early 1970s when Le Guin was writing *The Dispossessed*, these thinkers were, to a large degree, responsible for the popular dissemination of what has become a commonly held notion among futurists, including readers and writers of science fiction.[10] That is, they have assumed, as did the generation of Alfred North Whitehead, Bertrand Russell, and Aldous Huxley, that the scientific world view formed three centuries ago is "the cosmology underlying all our mental processes."[11] Fritjof Capra explains this position in a way so representative of this belief that it is worth quoting at length:

The birth of modern science was preceded and accompanied by a development of philosophical thought which led to an extreme formulation of the spirit/matter dualism. This formulation appeared in the seventeenth century in the philosophy of René Descartes who based his view of nature on a fundamental division into two separate and independent realms: that of mind, and that of matter. The "Cartesian" division allowed scientists to treat matter as dead and completely separate from themselves, and to see the material world as a multitude of different objects assembled into a huge machine. Such a mechanistic world view was held by Isaac Newton, who constructed his mechanics on its basis and made it the foundation of classical physics. From the second half of the seventeenth to the end of the nineteenth century, the mechanistic Newtonian model of the universe dominated all scientific thought. . . .As a consequence of the Cartesian division, most individuals are aware of themselves as isolated egos existing "inside" their bodies.

The fragmented view is further extended to society, which is split into different nations, religions and political groups. The belief that all these fragments—in ourselves, in our environment, and in our society—are really separate can be seen as the essential reason for the present series of social, ecological, and cultural crises. It has alienated us from nature and from our fellow human beings. It has brought a grossly unjust distribution of natural resources, creating economic and political disorder; an ever-rising wave of violence, both spontaneous and institutionalized, and an ugly, polluted environment in which life has often become physically and mentally unhealthy.[12]

Through this associative mode of thinking, Capra travels from Cartesian/Newtonian dualism to its reflection in the isolated ego, which leads to the condition of national, racial, and ethnic fragmentation and alienation from nature and from our fellow humans. In turn, these qualities are the cause of an inequitable distribution of wealth, cultural disorder and ecological crises, and a life that is, in general, physically and mentally unsalutary. Humankind's current "unnatural" posture, characterized by what Robert Pirsig calls "subject-object dualities," is,

Capra feels, traceable to the world view effected by mechanist physics. Although Le Guin does not depict precisely the same chain of interrelated conditions, the more Earthlike of her two societies is meant to be seen as the outcome of a similar series.

Her protagonist, Shevek, having come from "an experiment in nonauthoritarian communism," finds the value system on Urras shockingly inverse to his own. Instead of shared goods, shared space, shared labor, and the mutual concern encouraged on Anarres, he discovers that competing egos, elitism, conspiracy, and factionalism in the form of rival individuals and rival nation states are the norm. In place of the Spartan life-style associated with a hostile environment, he sees the privileged class of Urras consumed by artifice, "the women in full gowns that swept the floor, their breasts bare, their waists and necks and heads adorned with jewelry and lace and gauze, the men in trousers and coats or tunics of red, blue, violet, gold, green, with slashed sleeves and cascades of lace, or long gowns of crimson or dark green or black that parted at the knee to show the white stockings, silver-gartered."[13] To Shevek the Urrasti's alienation from their fellows is signified by a rage for privacy: private rooms, private baths, private homes, private families, with the rich maintaining themselves through a rigid class structure.

In the end, Capra's "economical and political disorder" materializes on Le Guin's Urras as violent revolution after a show of despair and deprivation among the lower classes. Although an ecological crisis has been averted in this society (at the expense of strict taxation and inequity), life is still described as physically and mentally unhealthy. Alcoholism, overeating and indolence are common among the rich; the dominance of men over women is practiced as in an Islamic state; and people live according to codes (women's place, aristocratic duty, the superiority of one person or people to another) that strike Shevek as unwholesome. The settlement on Anarres originally was meant to correct this ethic of waste, inequity, and fragmentation, but over the centuries Anarresti idealism developed into dogma, the struggle for survival stifled initiative, and the humane social order became increasingly bureaucratized. Neither Anarres nor Urras is a model society. The reader comes to understand that Le Guin's subtitle, "An Ambiguous Utopia," suggests that Anarres has not fulfilled its utopian promise because of its deliberate and bitter resistance to the love of beauty and ideas that constitute the other side of Urrasti materialism.

The hero's moral mission, then, is to reestablish the broken connection with Urras, to be an "unbuilder of walls" (in Le Guin's overworked rhetoric), to unify the two peoples, and even to open communications among all "the nine Known Worlds." If the problem is fragmentation on every level of experience, the resolution lies in unification, also on every level of experience—between peoples, between persons, between man and nature, between sides of self. Shevek's determination to complete the General Temporal Theory is clearly offered as a metaphor for unification as well as the practical means to instant harmony. To stop there, however, is to see less than the author intended.

It is important to understand that the General Temporal Theory is more than a metaphor for healing social wounds. The fundamental building block of both her moral idealism and social criticism lies in her rendering of the scientific world view common to Urras and Anarres— one principally lodged in "sequency" physics (mechanist physics). The seminal passages on sequency occur two-thirds of the way through the novel. We learn from Shevek, who attends a party on Urras held by that "body profiteer," Vea, that time flowing, the passage of time, time as a linear succession of moments, is not a "physically objective phenomenon, but a subjective one." His Urrasti adversary, however, replies: "But the fact is that we experience the universe as a succession, a flow. In which case, what's the use of this theory of how on some higher plane it may all be eternally coexistent?"[14] Shevek then tries to explain the difference between sequency theory (linear time, time flowing) and simultaneity through the analogue of time as experienced differently by the conscious and unconscious mind. The unconscious, for example, has little sense of time flowing while it dreams, events are not necessarily linked to discernible causes, while the experience of "time flowing" during waking reality can be explained as a creation of consciousness.

What has all this to do with either the uninspiring materialism of Urras or the bureaucratized, imperfect anarchism of Anarres? The leaps from a scientific world view to social criticism are ambiguous in Le Guin who is first a writer of fiction and next an ideologue or a moralist. A more explicit connection between the scientific world view and the current social condition can be found in the futurist, William Irwin Thompson, who also wrote in 1973-74 (*The Dispossessed* was published in 1974). Thompson's work helps to clarify her position.

Thompson, an anti-institutional historian, is, like Le Guin, a romantic—a kind of twentieth-century transcendentalist. Like the generation of Blake, Wordsworth, and Coleridge, he seems to believe that nature, the physical universe, the visible world, is merely the perceivable outer form of the cosmos. This cosmos contains spirit and mystery, the various manifestations of godliness. By apprehending nature in a special way, by opening our minds, by moving beyond rational processes to the intuitive, the imaginative and unconscious, or unselfconscious, we may come into contact with the spiritual dimensions of the cosmos.

Thompson outlines the tenets of his neoromantic revolt in *Passages About Earth*, which offers the following argument: Western individuation, which began in the Renaissance, has culminated in categorical psychology, in the dominance of the social science perspective, and, for individuals, in alienation and narcissism. This situation requires a new cosmic mythology, which will move beyond the individual as a separate reality, toward what Marshall McLuhan calls "psychic communal integration." Thompson is quick to explain that he does not wish to suggest the loss of personhood, which a Sovietization or bureaucratization of humanity engenders. Such a loss would be the inevitable consequence of applying strictly linear, mechanistic, empirically oriented, excessively rational criteria to social organizations.

In Thompson's view (and here we return to the spirit of Shevek's speeches on time at Vea's party) we have passed through the period of individuation which began during the Renaissance and ended in twentieth-century alienation. Analogously, we've passed through a period of diachronic science (the natural world conceptualized in terms of a linear, sequential progression through time). The advanced frontiers of physics have been characterized for some time by synchronic conceptualization (the perceiver and the perceived impact on one another). "To explain this," Thompson says, "consider music: the family dog listening with us to Bach on the phonograph hears the sounds, the successive pulses of noise through serial time; but he cannot perceive the fugue. He is perceiving sounds diachronically, and knows only their vanishing; when the music is gone, it is gone; we, however, are perceiving the sounds synchronically as music; when the music is finished, it is gathered up into resolved form; it is consummated in pure consciousness."[15]

It is this consummation into pure consciousness that Shevek refers to at Vea's party. He attempts to relate the mental analogue to the simultaneity theory by saying that a baby has no concept of time and does not understand the difference between yesterday and tomorrow. The unconscious dream world of the adult also violates time sequences, superimposing separate events and mixing up cause and effect. In myth and legend, "once upon a time" is a vague notion of no time in particular. It is only the conscious mind trained to observe the principles of reason and order, Shevek argues, that experiences time in a strict sense. This is why, "when the mystic makes the reconnection of his reason and his unconscious, he sees all becoming as one being, and understands the eternal return."[16]

Shevek then attempts a vague and partial reconciliation between sequency and the simultaneity theory as applied to ethics when he states that responsibility, for example keeping a promise, involves a sense of time as a succession of moments: now and then, cause and effect, means and end. We need complexity (simultaneity theory applied) so that the model of the cosmos is as inexhaustible as the cosmos itself. This complexity should include creation as well as duration, beginning as well as becoming and ethics as well as geometry.[17] Le Guin, however, is better at describing the social consequences of mechanist physics than projecting the effect a visionary science would have on the moral order.

Until Shevek's completion of the General Temporal Theory, which reconciles sequency and simultaneity, both Urras and Anarres have held to sequency physics. The linear and compartmentalized thinking made authoritative by the established scientific world view has bred "hard facts" and "practical living" values—the common flaw in both worlds. It is this common flaw that allows Shevek's mother on Anarres to condemn her son on legalistic, rather than humanistic, grounds: once an Anarresti leaves his planet he cannot return because no "foreigners" are allowed admission. In turn, on Urras, Shevek's opponent at Vea's party dismisses the simultaneity theory because "it has no practical application, no relevance to real life. Unless it means we can build a time machine!"[18] Thus Shevek's genius, his originality, his inclination to think from some unique source of self rather than from current ideology or myth ostracizes him inside the bureaucratized setting of Anarres and prompts the Urrasti to see him only for his use value.

The ascription of "hard facts" values and use-values to a mechanist world view is stated more directly by Theodore Roszak, another widely read futurist, who wrote a few years before the publication of *The Dispossessed*. His thesis in *The Making of a Counter Culture* is that "the paramount struggle of our day" is against an "ideologically invisible" enemy, the technocracy. Roszak defines the technocracy as "that society in which those who govern justify themselves by appeal to technical experts who, in turn, justify themselves by appeal to scientific forms of knowledge. And beyond the authority of science, there is no appeal."[19] He considers this to be essentially a psychological problem, not a political one. Therefore, if we want to revolt against the technocracy and technocratic imperatives we need to engage in a revolution of consciousness. To do this, however, we must first understand that the source of the technocracy lies in the dominant scientific world view and that mechanist world view is our most penetrating contemporary, sociocultural myth.

Thus it becomes Shevek's challenge to shatter what Roszak likes to call the "myth of objective consciousness" with a nonmechanistic interpretation of the physical universe. Such an interpretation will change the shape of the social imagination and lead the collective consciousness to value both linear and holistic thinking. Shevek's own consciousness, particularly the nature of his moral perceptions, are a register of the social ideal implicit in the General Temporal Theory. In effect, he represents the so-called new man, the humanistic embodiment of a scientific abstraction. The implications of the General Temporal Theory are at work in the reiterated journey and return theme with its temporal as well as spatial meanings. Shevek has been indoctrinated by Odo's paradox, "To be whole is to be part/True journey is return," and he incorporates that concept into a view of history as eternal recurrence. "You are our history," he tells the Urrasti. "We are perhaps your future."[20] The settlers of Anarres have chosen to have only the future, but because the future becomes the past, the past becomes the future.[21] Past and future, as seen from both the linear and eternally coexistent prospects of consciousness, offer a basis for that loyalty, for example, that asserts past and future are bound into a continuity by time and thus provide the root of human strength.[22]

After his scientific breakthrough, Shevek easily conceptualizes in sequency and simultaneity terms without actually *using* those terms. This becomes particularly evident when he reprimands the Terran ambassador for her lack of utopian faith:

> You don't understand what time is. You say the past is gone, the future is not real, there is no change, no hope. You think Anarres is a future that cannot be reached, as your past cannot be changed. So there is nothing but the present. . . .But it is not real, you know. It is not stable, not solid—nothing is. Things change, change. You cannot have anything. . . .And least of all can you have the present, unless you accept it with the past and the future. . . .Because they are

real: only their reality makes the present real. You will not achieve or even understand Urras unless you accept the reality, the enduring reality, of Anarres.[23]

Just as Mary Shelley introduced the popular science of her time into her novel to produce an unforgettable image of the scientific world view gone wrong, Le Guin creates a memorable impression of the social values to be expected from a more complex and hopeful scientific picture. Probably Le Guin's best achievement has been her dramatization of the new humanism. She offers a model character for the future, a voice, which, although it sometimes speaks in sententious tones, delivers the message that there is no formula, no set of rules for making us whole or perfect or happy. There is the chance, of course, that even this open-ended kind of thinking can become a new orthodoxy. The utopian ideals of "transformation," "new consciousness," and "holism" espoused by so many humanist futurists and science-fiction writers over the past decade are beginning to sound a little thin. But rightly understood, Le Guin's story is inconclusive. The materials for transformation exist; the process remains agreeably unknown.

## Notes

1. Michael Wood, "Coffee Break for Sisyphus," *New York Review of Books* (October 2, 1975), p. 3.

2. It is true that Wells had an astonishing record for technological prediction: aerial warfare, the atomic bomb, the express technology of World War I (predicted in the nineteenth century)—trench warfare, tanks, and Zeppelins. But his lasting legacy was to the generation of Aldous Huxley, Orwell, and Zamiatin in the form of social criticism. See, for example, Mark Hillegas, *The Future as Nightmare* (New York: Oxford University Press, 1967), W. Warren Wagar, *H. G. Wells and the World State* (New Haven: Yale University Press, 1961), and Alexandra Aldridge, "Scientising Society: The Dystopian Novel and the Scientific World View" (Ph.D. diss., University of Michigan 1978), chap. 2. Moreover, the futures Wells dramatized, particularly in his numerous utopias, became material for the dystopian scenarios of the aforementioned fiction writers. It is these futures that most of the world has made an assiduous attempt to avoid.

3. I'm using the terms utopian and dystopian in a broad sense here to describe any science-fiction scenario that projects a reasonably complete picture of an "ideal" or "nightmare" society with the goal of using that scenario to make social criticism.

4. See Darko Suvin's well-known essay, "On the Poetics of the Science Fiction Genre," *College English* 34, no. 3 (1972): 372-82.

5. David Samuelson, "Studies in the Contemporary American and British

Science Fiction Novel" (Ph.D. diss., University of Southern California 1969), p. 51.

6. Mary Shelley, *Frankenstein* (1817; reprint ed., New York: Dell, 1975), p. 46.

7. See, for example, Hillegas, *Future* and Wagar, *H. G. Wells*.

8. See note 2.

9. Le Guin criticism has almost become a subsidiary industry of current science fiction and utopian criticism. Aside from recurrent allusions to her work in recent criticism of feminist utopias and new wave science fiction, she is a frequent subject for MLA panels, utopia conference papers and meetings of the Science Fiction Research Association. The Le Guin material in this essay is drawn from my remarks at the SFRA meeting in New York, June 1980. For some particularly good recent Le Guin criticism, see *Science Fiction Studies* 7, pt. 1 (March 1980), which contained a special section "Science Fiction on Women— Science Fiction by Women." Also see *Alternative Futures* 4, nos. 2-3 (Spring/Summer, 1981)—a special issue entitled "Women and the Future." Other contemporary utopian writers who have attracted a large reading public are: Robert Pirsig, Ernest Callenbach, Marge Piercy, and Doris Lessing.

10. For a critical analysis of philosophical futurism in the 1970s, see Alexandra Aldridge, "Popular Futurism: Soft Thinking in Hard Times," *Michigan Quarterly Review* 20, no. 3 (Summer 1981): 284-93.

11. E. A. Burtt, *The Metaphysical Foundations of Modern Science*, 2d ed. (1924; reprint ed., New York: Doubleday, 1954), p. 17. Also see Alexandra Aldridge, "Brave New World and the Mechanist/Vitalist Controversy," *Comparative Literature Studies* 17, no. 2 (June 1980: 116-32.

12. Fritjof Capra, *The Tao of Physics* (New York: Bantam Books, 1975), pp. 8–9.

13. Ursula Le Guin, *The Dispossessed* (New York: Harper & Row, 1974), p. 20.

14. Ibid., p. 194.

15. William Irwin Thompson, *Passages About Earth* (New York: Perennial Library, 1973, 1974) pp. 95-96.

16. Le Guin, *The Dispossessed*, p. 194.

17. Ibid., p. 198.

18. Ibid., p. 194.

19. Theodore Roszak, *The Making of a Counter Culture* (New York: Anchor Books, 1969), p. 8.

20. Le Guin, *The Dispossessed*, p. 66.

21. Ibid., p. 78.

22. Ibid., p. 292.

23. Ibid., pp. 304-5.

# II

# Space-Time and Time Travel: Metaphors, Models and Implications

Time and space are fundamental categories for interpreting the perceptions and basic concepts present in our thought models. The way we think about and come to understand our world, others, ourselves, and our experiences may be determined to a large degree by the metaphors that we adopt for time and/or space.

Gilbert Fulmer brings together three special ideas or concepts: cosmology, the nature and creation of the universe; time travel, a continuing theme in SF stories; and a creator, as the major orthodox monotheistic religions define their God. He discusses the philosophical problems associated with time travel, including the problems of causal loops, an unchangeable past, a notion of time as "flowing," and the possible distinction between the "external" time and "personal" time of the time traveler.

Using the modern scientific belief that the universe had a distinct (temporal) beginning, Fulmer explores the orthodox religious thesis that its beginning was the act or product of a creator-God. Fulmer then assesses critically the implications of the hypothesis that the creator-God could be a time traveler.

Lee Werth lists and examines a series of metaphors for time, such as, wheel, river, light. After noting that to take these metaphors literally produces logical inconsistency, Werth proceeds to "unpack" the metaphors, pointing out their logical similarity. Time metaphors seem to be considered essential in understanding history, which, as well as personal and object existence, is usually construed as occurring through time, usually designated as past, present, or future.

Through his philosophical analysis, Werth shows why several of the time metaphors are appropriate and examines the nature of time and its relation to human experience. Having formulated and evaluated certain conditions that are applicable to both metaphor and reality, he proposes what he believes to be a more adequate paradigm: time as a filmstrip. As a model or paradigm, it is defensible in relation to contemporary physics and has the value of explaining seeming inconsistencies in our talk about time. In fact, the paradigm even seems to make sense of such things as the mystical experience of transcending time and the notion of free will.

# Cosmological Implications of Time Travel

*GILBERT FULMER*

The idea of time travel has become a topic of philosophical inquiry, as well as a standard plot device in science fiction. Its logic has been examined in a number of articles in the professional philosophical literature, leading, as usual, to considerable disparity of opinion.[1] The burden of this essay, however, is not to illuminate the idea of time travel itself, but rather to consider certain implications that might be thought to follow from it in the area of cosmology—the attempt to explain the nature and origin of the universe.

Before beginning this task, though, I must explain how I conceive time travel, and make clear some logical implications that must be accepted if it is a possibility. To travel in time, in my view, would be to arrive at some past or future time at which one would not otherwise be found. For example, I might enter a time machine (time machines seem usually to be envisioned as resembling tiny taxicabs!) and set the controls for the future, thus avoiding the necessity of living through those years to the date that has been selected. Thus, if I live to 1985, I will be able to "travel" to 1985; but only as the years pass and that time becomes the present. If time travel were possible, however, I could depart now (1983), and find myself in 1985 with no or only a negligible elapsed subjective time. If the "trip" as perceived by the traveler were instantaneous, then I would be no older after activating the controls than before, though I would then be in 1985; and my watch would record no lapse of time either. If the trip does take some subjective time, then both my perceptions and my watch would record it. But of course the time so recorded would be far less than the actual intervening years.

Conversely, time travel as conceived here would permit travel to the past—something which is not otherwise possible at all. I would enter the machine, set the controls for, say, 1977, and activate them. Upon emerging from the machine, my perception and watch would record the same small or non-existent elapsed time, but then I would be in the selected time of the past.

Time travel, then, requires the separation of what David Lewis has called "personal" and "external" time.[2] Personal time is that which is associated with the individual: his perception of duration, his aging and metabolic processes, and his own watch. External time is that of the world as a whole; it grows continuously older, as measured by any ordinary chronology. Normally, personal and external time are synchronized; but in time travel the traveler's personal time would be different from external time. In travel to the future, the traveler's personal time would show only the duration of the trip to have elapsed, while the external time elapsed would be the "length" of the trip in calendar time. Similarly, in travel to the past, the traveler's personal time would show a forward progress of time: that is, the traveler would grow continuously older; but he would be at an earlier point in external time.

Time travel would also imply reverse causation. That is, travel to the past would require that an earlier event (the arrival of the time traveler at his destination) be caused by a later event (his activation of the time machine at the time of departure). Some philosophers have argued that reverse causation is logically impossible in itself, and that time travel is therefore also logically impossible. Reverse causation certainly seems impossible for those of us who have no time machines, and this impossibility may make it seem a part of the concept of causation that effects must follow (or at least be simultaneous with) their causes. But our intuitions on such matters are obviously formed by our experience, and sometimes more extensive experience forces us to revise our intuitions. Modern science, especially relativity theory, affords many examples of this: relativistic cosmogony, for example, offers us a universe that is *finite* in extent, yet *unbounded*; that is, no part of it is on the edge! Perhaps the idea of reverse causation also requires only revision of our intuitions.

Next, it must be recognized that time travel would not involve changing the past. The notion that it would has presented many of the most serious obstacles to the idea of time travel in the minds of many thinkers. For, they have argued, what *has* happened *has* happened. Not even God, it is often argued, could make it true now that I had eggs instead of cereal for breakfast this morning. I fully agree that the idea of changing the past is logically incoherent, and, therefore, the act logically impossible. But this is no objection to time travel, for time travel does not require the possibility of changing the past.

The idea that a traveler to the past could change the past is associated with the idea that time travel would somehow cause the past to be repeated. Suppose, for example, that Smith has a time machine, and resolves to change the past. In 1972, just before the first Arab oil embargo, Smith turned down an opportunity to buy some oil leases at a price that he now realizes was a mere pittance. Can he do so? No, for the past cannot be changed. The Smith of 1983 did not present the Smith of 1972 with the needed knowledge. There was only one 1972, it occurred some eleven years before Smith acquires his time machine, and in that year Smith did not buy the oil leases. Nothing can now change that fact.

It is not that there is some arcane force which prevents time travelers from changing the past. Some science fiction suggests that time travelers to the past must be hedged about with all sorts of restrictions on what they may do, to prevent them from changing the past in some trivial way that would radically alter reality in the present. But this is a confusion by authors who have supposed that time travel repeats the past. The powers of a time traveler in the past are no different from those he has in his own time. The Smith of 1983 is not imprisoned in some invisible cocoon that prevents him from contacting his earlier self in 1972; it is just that he did not do so, for any number of possible reasons, but they must have been perfectly ordinary reasons unrelated to the fact that he was a traveler in time. Perhaps he missed his bus, perhaps the phone was busy, perhaps he couldn't get past the receptionist to the inner office. We do not know why he did not tell his earlier incarnation to buy the leases, and we do not need to know. The offer was refused and the Smith of 1983 is the poorer for it; time travel makes no difference.

The final implication of time travel is one that is relevant to the cosmological inquiry of this essay. It is that time travel would make possible closed causal loops, in which the later event is caused by the earlier event, and the earlier by the later. Such loops are radically counter to ordinary intuitions, of course; yet once again we should not rely too complacently on intuitions that have been formed in the absence of time travel. The standard version of the closed causal loop is, of course, the man who returns to the past and fathers a child who grows up to be himself—thus becoming his own father. Surely this seems impossible!

But if time travel is possible, I think causal loops also must be possible. And if the impossibility of causal loops is to be used as an argument against the possibility of time travel, then the impossibility of the loops must be shown independently. Yet, in the preceding example, each event has a perfectly ordinary cause: our traveler decides, say in 2000, to travel back in time to 1930. While in that year he meets a woman; one thing leads to another, and a child is born. The child grows up and in 2000 decides to travel back in time. . . .It makes no difference in 1930 that he is a traveler from the future; this renders him neither sterile nor impotent, nor less subject to the attractions of a woman. His ability to travel to 1930 from 2000 is assumed with the initial acceptance of time travel.

It is the idea of such causal loops that gives rise to the investigation of the possible cosmological implications of time travel. The most fundamental of all cosmological questions is that of the origin of the universe itself. Until quite recently, the scientific view was that the universe had no origin, but had existed from all eternity and was infinitely old. This view was opposed by religious thinkers, at least Judeo-Christian ones, who held that the universe had a distinct beginning, as stated in the first sentence of the Bible: "In the beginning God created the heavens and the earth."[3] This belief seems to have been considered more pious, since, unlike the scientific view, it provided a specific role for a Creator.

In the last few decades, however, the scientific view has changed. The so-called Big Bang theory of the origin of the universe is now all but universally (!) accepted by knowledgeable astrophysicists. According to this theory, the present universe began in a colossal explosion some fifteen or so billion years ago, when all matter was condensed into a relatively small area, at unimaginably high temperatures—the so-called "cosmic egg" of neutrons. All the matter in the present universe has come from these neutrons. Hydrogen (the simplest element, whose atom consists of a single proton and a single electron) can be formed by splitting a neutron into one electron and one proton. At temperatures above 10 million degrees Centigrade hydrogen can be converted into helium (two electrons, two protons, and two neutrons) in a process called "fusion," which generates enormous quantities of energy. Our sun and other stars shine with energy from the fusion reaction. All the heavier elements have been generated by the recombination of hydrogen at successively higher temperatures, that is, in the interiors of giant stars, and in the explosions of stars called novas and supernovas.[4]

Religionists were not slow to point to the supposed similarity between the Big Bang theory and the religious belief in a beginning of the universe in time. Some even claimed that their beliefs had received the support of the best scientific thinkers of the day. No less an authority than Robert Jastrow has written, "For the scientist who has lived by his faith in the power of reason, the story ends like a bad dream. He has scaled the mountains of ignorance; he is about to conquer the highest peak; as he pulls himself over the final rock, he is greeted by a band of theologians who have been sitting there for centuries."[5]

The suggestion that Genesis was really about the Big Bang all along has been justly pilloried by Isaac Asimov.[6] With his usual rapier wit and steely logic, Asimov points out that, even if Genesis really was about the Big Bang, no one realized it until the Big Bang had been discovered scientifically! In other words, the biblical creation story sat around for some 3,000 years, and never served as the source of the information it was intended to convey.

I might also note that it seems suspiciously convenient that Jastrow discovers in the Big Bang confirmation of the predominant religious thought of *his own society*. Innumerable cultures past and present have held that the universe came into existence at some point in time; how does the Big Bang theory uniquely confirm the story of Genesis? If any known religion were to be regarded as confirmed by contemporary astrophysical theory, it certainly would seem to be sun worship, for the scientific account summarized above makes it clear that it is the stars which have been the mechanism for the synthesis of nearly all the elements in the universe.

Since it would seem that the universe did have a beginning, it is possible to hypothesize that it was the product of intelligent creation and that time travel was the mechanism by which it was created. It can be hypothesized that the Big Bang was caused by a time traveler (or by more than one) who journeyed to the past for that purpose. Of course, there is no evidence for this hypothesis; but it does have the merit of explaining in a comprehensible way the apparent anomaly of an original beginning.

I will argue, on the contrary, that the time traveler hypothesis provides no appreciable support for the religious view of the universe. In Judeo-Christian theism God is held to be a personal being, animate like ourselves. He is said to be unique. He is said, moreover, to be incorporeal (at least in theologically sophisticated versions). He is said to be eternal. He is said to be infinitely powerful, wise, and good. And he is said to be supernatural, in the sense of being wholly independent of the natural order which in turn is wholly dependent on him, since he created the physical universe and the laws that describe it *ex nihilo*.

The time traveler hypothesis suggests that some intelligent being or beings, having presumably discovered the Big Bang from the same sort of evidence we did, perceived the necessity of bringing it about. He/she/it/they therefore traveled backward in time and did whatever was necessary to initiate the Big Bang. It is true that we have not the faintest idea of how the Big Bang was brought about; but then we have no idea how to go traveling in time, either. If we let things like this bother us this book would not exist. At least in principle it seems possible to suppose that a sufficiently advanced science could solve the technical problems.

The most immediate thought is that the time traveler(s) must have originated in the far distant future because of the immense scientific and engineering difficulties apparently required for such a task. This involves, however, the wholly unsupported assumption that the Big Bang was caused by human beings. But the size of the universe is beyond the reach of the imagination. Current estimates put the "diameter" of the universe at 10 to 20 billion light years, although it is important to understand that this does not mean the distance from edge to edge, since there are no edges. And the number of stars is estimated to be something like $10^{22}$ (a "1" followed by 22 zeros). Moreover, contemporary astrophysical theory holds that planets probably develop naturally in the process of the development of a star, so that many or most stars should have planetary systems. Finally, there are both theoretical and experimental reasons for believing that life should emerge quite naturally under conditions resembling those on the primordial earth. All this makes it seem overwhelmingly probable that many other intelligent species have existed, do exist, and will exist elsewhere in the universe, although almost certainly none exist at the present time in our own solar system.

George Abell has attempted to estimate the number of alien civilizations that could reasonably be expected to exist in our own galaxy at the present time.[7] Making certain plausible, although controversial, assumptions, Abell concludes that "the number of planets *in our own galaxy* on which intelligent, communicative beings of some description have evolved at some time or other would lie in the range of 100 million ($10^8$) to ten billion ($10^{10}$)."[8] Abell confines his discussion to our own galaxy because he is considering the possibility of communication with alien races, and even the mind accustomed to science fiction may balk at the suggestion of communication between galaxies. For our purposes, however, this restriction is unnecessary, for there is no reason to suppose that the time traveler(s) we are hypothesizing originated in this particular galaxy. Since current estimates put the number of galaxies in the universe at about $10^{11}$, and since our own seems to be about average in size, we must multiply Abell's estimates by the latter figure to obtain an estimate of the number of intelligences that have evolved in the 15 or 20 billion years since the Big Bang. This gives a range of $10^{19}$ to $10^{21}$ as the number of intelligent species that have existed or now exist.

But our hypothesis must take us even farther, for there is no reason to suppose that the time traveler(s) originated in any time up to the present; it could just as well be in the far future. Unfortunately, to make possible any estimate of the total number of candidates for the time traveling creator(s), we must make some guess about the total age the universe will reach, and thus the total time available in which evolutionary processes could produce intelligent species that could discover time travel. And any estimate on this subject will be even more uncertain than the foregoing ones. For scientific cosmogonists do not even agree about whether the universe will go on expanding forever, or whether it will reach a point of maximum dispersion, and afterward collapse back into a new primordial fire ball. If the latter belief is correct, then the length of time available is finite; but any estimate made here will be guesswork. Let us arbitrarily suppose that the universe has now passed 1 percent of its total duration; this gives a total age of approximately 2,000 billion ($2 \times 10^{12}$) years. Thus our final estimate of the total number of intelligent species that might have brought about the Big Bang must be the number estimated to have already come into existence, multiplied by one hundred. This calculation results in an estimate between $10^{21}$ and $10^{23}$—which should make it clear that we cannot assume that it is our own distant descendants who must have done the creating.

Let us now consider how much and in what ways the time traveler hypothesis coincides with the traditional Judeo-Christian concept of God. The time traveling creator(s) would, on this hypothesis, be personal. That is, any such being(s) would be conscious and rational, at least in the sense of possessing goals and the capability of selecting the means to attain them, since the hypothesis itself ascribes to the traveler(s) the purposive act of traveling back in time to initiate the Big Bang. In this one sense, then, the hypothesis preserves the essentially animistic view of theism, in which the universe was brought into existence by the conscious act of a personal being or beings.

However, in Judaism, Christianity, and the even more aggressively monotheistic Islam, God is said to be unique. The time traveler hypothesis does not demand this: the creating personal agent could have acted alone, or the project could have been a group effort. It may be tempting to suppose that such an undertaking required the efforts of many members of the species; but this temptation should be resisted, for this notion stems entirely from the unfounded notion that the time traveler(s) resembled human beings. A universe as large as this one is likely to have spawned wildly diverse life forms; and it may be that the time traveler(s) were (are/will be) so advanced that the job was easily performed by a single one of them.

Or again, our very notion of individual identity arises in part from our own physical nature; it is possible that there are life forms elsewhere to which such a concept of identity could not be applied. Perhaps, for example, a species exists in which physically discrete organisms combine from time to time like bees in a hive, but in such a way that the aggregation has intellectual powers not present in the component parts. Perhaps further this aggregation is only temporary, and different aggregates form for different purposes. If our time traveler(s) were such a collective entity, the proposition that the Big Bang was the work of an individual personality would be not so much false as meaningless.

Next, God is said to be incorporeal. No less a personage than Billy Graham has remarked, "The Bible declares that God is. . .a Spirit—that He is not limited to body; He is not limited to shape; He is not limited to boundaries or bonds. . . .The Bible tells us that because He has no such limitations He can be everywhere at once, that He can hear all, see all, and know all."[9] Of course, the time traveler hypothesis has nothing to say about the corporeal or incorporeal nature of the hypothetical traveler(s). If there can be and are (or were or will be) bodiless intelligent beings in the universe then they could have created it as well as corporeal ones—provided only that they were able to manipulate matter in some ways. While all of the life forms we know of are corporeal, and we know of no scientific laws by which incorporeal ones could evolve, it may be that they have or will; and so again, it is wise not to assume too much.[10] Thus the incorporeality of the creator(s) is neither supported nor undermined by the hypothesis.

Next, God is said to be eternal. This property is one that need not, and probably would not, be possessed by the creator of the universe according to our hypothesis. Since (as we will see) any time travelers must necessarily be a part of the natural order, it seems altogether probable that, whatever the nature of the life form, members of that species come into existence by processes at least analogous to those we term biological. And, although it is not biologically necessary, death serves an evolutionary goal in allowing new species to replace old. Thus, it would seem likely that any organism that was the product of the evolutionary process would be mortal, rather than eternal.

Here again, however, we risk being misled by parochialism. For, whatever its evolutionary value, death is usually viewed with distaste by the organism that is dying; and it is not parochial to suppose that that distaste would be shared by any product of the evolutionary process: for organisms lacking it would probably perish quickly and drop out of the gene pool. Moreover, a species with the technological ability to travel in time and create universes *might* have conquered death for its own members. So the question of the time traveler(s)' immortality is left open: the creation might have been performed by either a mortal or an immortal individual or group. Indeed, the universe may have been created by a member or members of a species that long ago became extinct, in which case the created order has been simply proceeding ahead under its own steam.

The issue of attributing infinite power, wisdom, and goodness to the creator of the universe was canvassed quite thoroughly two centuries ago by David Hume, and it is doubtful that I can say anything here that will go much beyond his arguments. It is never legitimate to infer the operation of an infinite cause from the observation of a finite effect, Hume reasoned, for it is only legitimate to ascribe to the cause a degree of power sufficient to bring about the effect and no more.[11] Hume's example is as illuminating today as when he wrote. Imagine that we are presented with a balance scale which is half covered by an opaque screen so that we can see only one arm and one pan. The visible pan is raised and holds a one-pound weight. All we can properly infer is that the hidden weight is heavier than one pound. It may be two pounds, or ten, but we have no grounds for thinking so. Similarly, when we ask what power was required to create the universe, the only justifiable answer must be: whatever power was required. It is a perhaps curious consequence of contemporary scientific cosmogony that the universe is finite, containing "only" some $10^{22}$ stars (though cautious astronomers recognize that in such calculations being wrong by a factor of a few million is a small matter). Now, this number is very large and so is the universe, but as Hume was astute enough to see, "large" is not "infinite": you can't get to infinity by counting up. Therefore, the universe could have been created by a finite power, and we have no right to ascribe infinite power to the creator(s).

(For all of that, the job may not have been so big as we suppose. Some very advanced being might have found the creation of the universe a challenge scarcely worthy of its attention. And it could also be that some relatively minor action was all that was necessary, after which natural processes took over in somewhat the same way that an enormous avalanche may be started by a mere shout.)

Precisely the same arguments apply to ascribing infinite wisdom to the time traveling creator(s). Some considerable amount of wisdom—or, more precisely, technological capacity—must presumably be possessed by anyone capable of such things. But there are no grounds whatever for supposing it to be infinite.

The ascription of infinite goodness also must fall by the wayside. As we are engaged in trying to infer the properties of the cause of the universe from observations of its own properties, we can only infer that the creator(s) resembled the creation. And the universe, from our standpoint, clearly contains both good and evil: natural beauty and (occasional) human virtue must be balanced against natural disaster, disease, and (all too frequent) human wickedness. If this observation constitutes the evidence for the moral character of the being or beings who brought the universe into existence, the only conclusion warranted is that he/she/it/they was/were/will be good enough to produce the good—and evil enough to produce the evil.

However, we must here depart slightly from Hume's analysis of the argument from design. For in that theological context it was supposed that the divine creator was omnipotent, and thus able to create any sort of universe which it was logically possible for him to create. Consequently it seemed just to lay the evils of the world at his door, since he could have prevented them if he chose.

Our situation, however, is different. The time traveling creator(s) need not be supposed to have infinite power; therefore the hypothetical creator(s) cannot automatically be held responsible for all the evils in the world, since having the power to avert an evil is a necessary condition of being responsible for its existence. Indeed, if we adhere to the hypothesis in its most plausible form, the task force assigned to create the universe probably could have had no way of knowing of the evils to be suffered by human beings fifteen billion years in the future—unless it happens that they were human themselves. But if the number of intelligent species produced during the life of the universe is really in the range of $10^{21}$ to $10^{23}$ it is quite likely that many of *them* suffer evils of which *we* know nothing. Under these circumstances, it is probably unfair to blame the evils of the universe on its hypothetical creator(s).

On the other hand, it may be that the universe was created by a member or members of a species that we, if we knew them, would judge to be prodigiously evil. That they created the universe in which we dwell is not necessarily to their moral credit; they may have been motivated solely by self-serving considerations. After all, they dwell (or did or will dwell) in the universe too. It is even possible that members of that race greatly regret the fact that the universe they produced has produced other intelligences such as our own. Thus, the time traveler hypothesis licenses no conclusions about the moral character of whoever created the universe.

Finally, God is said to be supernatural. That is, he is said to have created the material universe and the natural laws that describe it *ex nihilo*, and consequently he is said to be wholly independent of the natural order, which in turn is wholly dependent on him. But the time traveler hypothesis cannot support this contention. In fact, I think we have warrant to conclude not only that that being (or those beings) could not have been supernatural, but also that no supernatural being whatever has existed or ever could exist. This is because the concept of a supernatural agent is logically incoherent, rather like the concept of a square circle. No figure ever has been drawn or ever could be drawn that is both truly square and truly circular. Any figure that meets one criterion must *ipso facto* fail the other. This is not the result of deficiencies in draftsmanship, which might be overcome by more ingenious artists, but of a conceptual impossibility that follows from the meanings of the concepts of roundness and squareness. And so there can be no square circles. There can be no supernatural agent for a similarly conceptual reason: anything that is an agent must *ipso facto* fail to be supernatural.[12]

Etienne Gilson, a respected contemporary Roman Catholic philosopher and historian of philosophy, described the Christian philosophy of the Middle Ages as follows:

Everywhere in medieval philosophy the natural order leans on a supernatural order, depends on it as for its origin and end. . . . The very physical world, created as it is for God's glory, tends with a kind of blind love towards its Authors; and each being, each operation of each being, depends momentarily, for existence and efficacy, on an omnipotent conserving will.[13]

More recently a distinguished British Anglican commentator has written, "all teaching of Christian revelation deals with the breaking-in of the greater supernatural order upon our more limited finite world."[14] And "the truths of Christian revelation, one and all, put this life decisively within the framework of a bigger one; and the Christian mind, thinking christianly, cannot for a moment escape a frame of reference which reaches out to the supernatural."[15]

Thus, if the supernaturalistic view of the universe offered by traditional theism is to be supported by the time traveler hypothesis, that hypothesis must require that the time traveling creator(s) be supernatural. If this is not possible, then the creator(s), like ourselves, must be a part of the natural order. And if this is so, then the world must ultimately be viewed in naturalistic, not animistic, terms.[16]

To show this it will be necessary to develop an account—brief and incomplete—of explanation in terms of natural, or scientific, law. Such explanations involve subsuming the event explained (the explanandum) under a more general law or set of laws (the explanans) in such a way that the explanandum can be inferred from the explanans. To use a simple example, let us undertake to explain the generally southward flow of the Mississippi River. The explanans will include two sentences:

1. Water flows downhill.
2. The land is progressively lower in elevation along the southward path of the Mississippi from Minnesota to the Gulf of Mexico.

The explanandum that follows is:

3. The Mississippi River flows southward.

So formulated, as Charles G. Hempel has remarked, "the explanation is an argument to the effect that the phenomenon to be explained. . .is just what is to be expected in view of the explanatory facts cited."[17] In general, then, an explanation in terms of natural laws consists of showing that the explanation is an example (or class of examples) of a more general law that includes the explanandum and other phenomena as well. The more general law is natural if and only if it states the way things happen in the universe, independently of any conscious agent's will. Thus, the fact stated above that water flows downhill is a natural law, while the fact that John always chooses apple rather than cherry pie is not.

If any agent can perform any act whatever, it must be a natural law in the above sense that events follow his will. If I raise my arm, it is a natural law that when I will my arm to rise, it does so. (*Ceteris paribus*, of course: the arm must not be strapped down, paralyzed, etc.) Applying this principle to any hypothetical creator of the universe (the traditional deity or a time traveler) we see that any agent having the power to create must do so by virtue of a natural law. Thus, even if some conscious agent created the material universe and all the *other* natural laws in it, there must be at least *one* law that he/she/it did not create: his/her/its power to make events occur. The fact that events occur as the creator(s) will(s) them, cannot be the result of the creating will, because to make it a fact that events occur as he/she/it wills them would be to make events occur! Thus, even if there were a creator or creators of *most* of the universe, he/she/it/they nonetheless would be dependent on at least one natural law—and thus would not be supernatural.

Nothing in the foregoing argument turns on whether the suppositious creator was the traditional God or a time traveler: neither could be a supernatural agent, for being an agent precludes being supernatural. Thus, it cannot be true that the natural order can be explained in animistic terms as wholly the result of a supernatural Mind or minds; the universe must ultimately be as it is for reasons of natural law. And so even if the Big Bang was induced by one or more time travelers, the supernatural order envisioned by such theists as Gilson and Blamires, and indeed all traditional Jews, Christians, and Muslims, does not exist. The conclusion, it seems to me, has been established: however promising it may seem at the outset, the time traveler hypothesis gives no significant support to traditional theism.

Time travel cannot give us God.

## Notes

1. For example, Larry Dwyer, "Time Travel and Changing the Past," *Philosophical Studies* 29 (1975): 341-50; Paul Horwich, "On Some Alleged Paradoxes of Time Travel," *Journal of Philosophy* 72 (1975): 432-44; David Lewis, "The

Paradoxes of Time Travel," *American Philosophical Quarterly* 13 (1976): 145-52; Gilbert Fulmer, "Understanding Time Travel," *Southwestern Journal of Philosophy* 11 (1980): 151-56; and Fulmer, "Time Travel, Determinism, and Fatalism," *Philosophical Speculations in Science Fiction and Fantasy* 1 (1981): 41-48.

2. Lewis, "The Paradoxes of Time Travel."

3. Gen. 1:1.

4. An excellent brief summary of current scientific cosmological thought may be found in Preston Cloud's *Cosmos, Earth, and Man* (New Haven: Yale University Press, 1978), pp. 25-29.

5. Robert Jastrow, *God and the Astronomers* (New York: Norton, 1978), p. 116. Dr. Jastrow is the director of the Goddard Institute of Space Flight in New York City.

6. Isaac Asimov, "Science and the Mountain Peak," *The Skeptical Inquirer* 5 (Winter 1980-81): 42-51.

7. George Abell, "The Search for Life Beyond Earth: A Scientific Update," in *Extra-Terrestrial Intelligence: The First Encounter* ed. James A. Christian (Buffalo, N.Y.: Prometheus Books, 1976), pp. 53-71.

8. Ibid., p. 59, emphasis added.

9. Billy Graham, *Peace With God* (New York: Doubleday, 1953), p. 29.

10. I have said that there is no positive *scientific* evidence that incorporeal intelligence is impossible. There may be, however, *philosophical* reasons to deny that it is possible. Many contemporary philosophers, influenced by the work of Ludwig Wittgenstein, Gilbert Ryle, and others, have concluded that the concept of a bodiless intelligence is logically incoherent, and that there could therefore be no such being. I am strongly inclined to accept this view; but I will not discuss it here, since it has no bearing on time travel.

11. David Hume, *Dialogues Concerning Natural Religion*, ed. Norman Kemp Smith (Oxford: Oxford University Press, 1935).

12. I have argued this point previously in "The Concept of the Supernatural," *Analysis* 57 (1977): 113-17, and in "Animistic and Naturalistic World Views," *Religious Humanism* 11 (1977): 36-39.

13. Etienne Gilson, *The Spirit of Medieval Philosophy*, Gifford Lectures, 1931-32 (New York: Scribner's, 1940), p. 364.

14. Harry Blamires, *The Christian Mind* (Ann Arbor, Mich.: Servant Books, 1978), p. 68.

15. Ibid., p. 69.

16. This conclusion is the upshot of my article "Animistic and Naturalistic World Views."

17. Carl G. Hempel, *Philosophy of Natural Science* (Englewood Cliffs, N.J.: Prentice-Hall, 1966), p. 50.

# 4

## Siddhartha and Slaughterhouse Five (A New Paradigm of Time)

### LEE F. WERTH

The past and future are present even now.

This assertion, if taken literally, is logically inconsistent, and only an inhabitant of Kurt Vonnegut's Tralfamadore would find nothing odd in it. The Tralfamadorian, in fact, would not even find the assertion profound. From his[1] perspective, it merely belabors the obvious. As Billy Pilgrim writes:

The most important thing I learned on Tralfamadore was that when a person dies he only *appears* to die. He is still very much alive in the past, so it is very silly for people to cry at his funeral. All moments, past, present, and future, always have existed, always will exist.[2]

Here again is a claim that, if taken literally, is logically inconsistent, but it continues to appear in literature. Hermann Hesse writes:

Siddhartha's previous lives were also not in the past, and his death and his return to Brahma are not in the future. Nothing was, nothing will be, everything has reality and presence.[3]

What is there about these equivocations on tense that is genuinely significant? The past, present, and future cannot coexist literally. Are we trying to hide from impending death by embracing an absurdity? Is time truly an enigma?

Certain metaphors for time appear again and again in the works of diverse cultures, and in unpacking these metaphors, in understanding their similar logic we can come to understand why they are appropriate and even more important, we can learn more about the nature of time and its relation to human experience.

To begin, there are the many variations of the "wheel" metaphor. T. S. Eliot speaks of the "still point of the turning world."[4] Jorge Luis Borges quotes from the twelfth-century French theologian Alain de Lille (Alanus de Insulis): "God is an intelligible sphere, whose center is everywhere and whose circumference is nowhere."[5] And there is Borges's own employment of the sphere metaphor in his discussion of time:

> We might compare time to a constantly revolving sphere; the part that was always sinking would be the past, that which was always rising would be the future; but the invisible point at the top, where the tangent touches, would be the extensionless present.[6]

We are also told that a Buddhist treatise of the fifth century illustrates the same doctrine with a chariot wheel which rolls on only one point.[7] One might understand the biblical passage about Ezekiel's wheel in a similar manner.

There are also many variations of the "river" metaphor. T. S. Eliot, interplaying the river with the sea, employs water metaphors in his third quartet, "Dry Salvages." Rivers flow; the sea, although active, does not; and ragged rocks appear. Sometimes, as in the philosophy of Henri Bergson and the physics of Newton,[8] the river is without banks and without bottom. In Borges's "The Garden of Forking Paths," the river of time has tributaries, confluences, and a delta.[9] A river is also very much in evidence in *Siddhartha*, but in this work the voices of the river and the reflections on its surface are also important.

Light too has its role in repeated metaphors for time. White light can be fragmented into a rainbow, the colors of which were intrinsically present all along. Mirrors reflect different images, depending upon position or perspective, and those who look into them can see different images, although they are looking in the same mirror. Lights, used in traveling at night, illuminate successively different things in the surroundings, but these things remain present even before and after they are illuminated.

Of course, there are other metaphors for time: grains of sand, necklaces, coils and self devouring snakes, Chinese boxes that nest inside of one another, phonograph records, music, and the various Phoenix myths.

Nevertheless, I suspect Borges is correct in saying that "it may be that universal history is the history of different intonations given a handful of metaphors."[10]

Time metaphors, no matter how varied, have a similar but not identical logical structure. Each has its indigenous advantage or advantages and successfully represents some feature or features of temporality. For example, presentness and its transitory character might be emphasized; alternatively, the eternal order of events might be drawn to our attention. The better metaphors, for example, the wheel, fulfill more than one task. Yet the wheel metaphor entails a fatalistic view of human choice, a destiny to be endlessly repeated, eternal recurrence, unless the metaphor is altered or elaborated upon. (We shall return to this free will issue later.)

While each metaphor could be the subject of lengthy logical analysis, present purposes are better served if the predominate features of the various metaphors are revealed. In this manner it is possible to present in terms of contemporary science a model of time that renders intelligible what, if taken literally, is unintelligible in *Siddhartha, Slaughterhouse Five*, T. S. Eliot's *Four Quartets*, and Borges's story, "The Garden of Forking Paths." As a philosopher I am obliged to state literally what a poet may state metaphorically or allegorically. (Even a scientific or philosophical theory may be thought by some to be a metaphor, but if so, it is a metaphor in a different sense.)

The time metaphors symbolize two conditions: (i) a serial continuum of coexisting elements that constitute a permanent and unchanging order; (ii) a relationship of this series to ourselves, or to something, a relationship that changes at each instant, thus giving rise to the transiency and flux of human experience (or the world). If for some reason, the river metaphor omits banks and bottom, as does Bergson's and Newton's, the second condition is violated. To the extent that the metaphor remains intelligible, we are implicitly adding ourselves as the fixed point by which the river flows.

Philosophers who argue that reality is itself static and immutable argue that the first condition characterizes ultimate reality. They may call reality "pure being," "being *qua* being," which is *per se* immutable. Being may also be called God. Such being is a repository of all information and all truth. The emphasis upon the first condition is known as Platonism. Since ultimate reality is thought to be unchanging, time is said to be unreal.

Philosophers who argue that reality is itself dynamic and everchanging argue that the second condition characterizes ultimate reality. Time is said to be real as is the transition from possibility to actuality. Things are said to originate and terminate. In this view there is perpetual becoming. The serial continuum of elements in condition one is understood to be the order of the successive states of the world, only one of which is actual and present and is to be instantaneously replaced by its successor.

It is a mistake to emphasize either of the two conditions as somehow more fundamental than the other. Moreover, by clarifying the conditions many seeming paradoxes can be avoided. In particular, a clarification of condition one avoids the paradox of arguing that past, present, and future exist all at once or simultaneously. Coexisting *elements* of a continuum should not be confused with *events* which are said to be past, present, and future.

A clarification of condition two reveals that it is not paradoxical to speak of past, present, and future events even though, as Augustine and others have argued, the past no longer exists, the future does not yet exist, and the present is a boundary of null duration, a mere relation between terms (past and future) that do not exist, and hence time cannot be real.

The clarification of both conditions will, if successful, eliminate the source of philosophers' perplexities about time, but there is still the task of rendering time travel intelligible and that of providing a rational explanation for mystical experiences. These three tasks, however, are basically the same. To explain how one is aware of any time as the present time is also to explain how it is possible to be aware of "another" time as the present time or, for that matter, to be aware of every time as the "present" time.

Perhaps the most powerful metaphor for time is that of a filmstrip. The strip itself should not be confused with a series of events. Every frame coexists with the other frames that comprise the filmstrip. The filmstrip itself is a series that satisfies condition one, even though, strictly speaking, the filmstrip as a discrete set of frames does not comprise a continuum. Condition two is met upon projection of the filmstrip. One frame at a time is "brought to life"; successively different frames in being projected give rise to the action on the screen or the movie as a series of *events* in time, as opposed to a static order of coexisting frames.

The analogy fails only because we understand the frames of the filmstrip to coexist in the sense that they exist at the *same* time, whereas the serially ordered elements of condition one coexist *nontemporally*; they do not coexist at the same time. The serially ordered elements of that continuum represent the *possibility* of a temporal ordering, but they are no more temporally ordered than a series of integers. If five is the successor to four, this is not usually thought to mean that five is later than four. The integers coexist together nontemporally. It is a mistake to equate the concept of existing at every time with the concept of existing nontemporally. For temporal relations to have meaning, there must be an appeal to a change of some sort. If we consider a static series of elements (condition one) and introduce no other consideration, we cannot speak intelligibly of temporal relations. A serial order can be understood as a temporal order only after we introduce a state-change of some sort. Hence condition two must be met before time concepts can be rendered intelligible. When the filmstrip is projected, we can use the terms "earlier" and "later" meaningfully. While the movie is projected, there is the frame that constitutes the specious present. The other frames coexist on the filmstrip as permanent possibilities for projection.

In the terms of this account, it is not that time is unreal; it is simply that time is logically derivative. That is, the two conditions must be satisfied for temporal relations to be possible. There must coexist (nontemporally) those elements that are the possibilities for diverse experiences. As we change our relation to the set of coexisting elements, as we "project" different ones upon the "screens of our consciousness," as we experience first this, then that, we can temporally relate our experiences, and in so doing we construct a temporal series. We then consider the objects we experience to exist in time and formulate the notion of a physical event. Yet the only genuine change that is logically required is the change from one experience to another. It does not follow that the physical world changes simply because our experiences change. We do not believe that railroad tracks converge in the distance or that people shrink as they move away from us. Yet, we somehow have failed to consider that *all* physical change may be appearance only and that the physical world itself may not change, even though our experience of it changes. The physical world may be as static as the frames of a filmstrip when these frames are considered in terms of condition one, that is, in terms of one another. In other words, the physical world may itself change no more than a series of integers, yet the relationship between the physical world and ourselves is everchanging (condition two) and thus our experience is everchanging. It is this fundamental change that gives rise to time. It does not take time; it "generates" time. Time is real but logically derivative.

We understand from the film analogy that all the information on the filmstrip remains unaltered. At the movie's end the filmstrip does not end, its frames do not cease to exist. We know the frames can be rearranged so that the end precedes the beginning. In fact, any arrangement that is necessary to satisfy the requirements of Eliot's *Burnt Norton*, Vonnegut's *Slaughterhouse Five*, or Hesse's *Siddhartha* is possible. A film loop can be constructed. A series of frames can be cut out and cause precognition to occur. Sections can be superimposed. Every frame can be superimposed which would be analogous to a mystical experience: seeing everything happen, which is to see nothing happen—the void the Buddhists speak of when one becomes aware of everything "at once," which is to obviate change and, therefore, time.

We can now correlate the terms of the film metaphor of time with those of contemporary space-time theories. Unlike Newton's account of absolute time, Einstein-Minkowskian space-time is congenial to this account of time. If we construe a physical object as a four-dimensional solid, as we can in the relativistic account, then we can regard three-dimensional intersections of that four-dimensional object as the "frames of the filmstrip." A sequence of such three-dimensional intersections, if we are aware of them one at a time, would account for our experience of a seemingly three-dimensional physical world in process, a world which, since it is four-dimensional, is not truly in process but only appears to be. We may regard ordinary consciousness as sequentially intersecting the four-dimensional, static human body along its world-line in order to bring to life (bring to the "screen of consciousness") different three-dimensional states. In this way one seems to oneself a two-legged creature who is moving about.

This same model allows for what Vonnegut speaks of as the Tralfamadorian view, a view in which we appear to be elongated tubes. Our time becomes a spatial dimension to them; our long life appears to them as our long body. The Tralfamadorians, however, can selectively view different areas of the four-dimensional world. They tell Billy Pilgrim to attend to what is pleasant just as we try to look upon pleasant scenery, but the total scenery is exactly what it is and remains unchanging. Hence the only freedom possible for the Tralfamadorians is the freedom to "look" away from that which is unpleasant. Four-dimensional objects do not change.

Whereas it is possible to construe a four-dimensional object as somehow "growing" and including ever more space-time loci, and to use this growth to explain why we are aware of what we *now* are aware of, that is, to construe our four-dimensional body as growing longer and having a lengthening world-line, Vonnegut does not explore this possibility. Indeed, it would be a barrier to his story if a four-dimensional body were capable of change as a *four*-dimensional body. Why would Billy get "unstuck in time?"

As all of Billy's body exists in space-time as a static entity, there is no reason in principle why Billy should not experience *any* "time," at least any particular intersection across the world-line of his four-dimensional body, as the *present* time. In this respect at least, Vonnegut's account shares the position of Adolf Grünbaum who argues that no nonarbitrary and mind independent status can be granted the present moment.[11] Something is present because we experience it as present. Billy has the habit of becoming "unstuck in time," his consciousness randomly intersecting his four-dimensional unchanging body, thus making him experience himself as a three-dimensional person whose experiences are disjointed, he's young, he's old, sick, well, and so forth. Yet, the nontemporal coexistence of all the three-dimensional intersections that comprise his four-dimensional body allows for the possibility of Billy's consciousness "projecting" them. We do not want to know how Billy can experience the so-called future and past, but rather why of all the possible three-dimensional sections of his four-dimensional body, he should experience the ones he experiences. Why has he become erratic in his projection sequences? Even the Tralfamadorians seem to have an ordering principle: their interests and likes determine which four-dimensional expanses they view. They are not "unstuck in time" even though their experiences are rather like looking at a four-dimensional slide show. Perhaps the question should be turned about: why shouldn't Billy project at random? Indeed, why do we whose experience is ordinary, project sequentially along the world-lines of our four-dimensional bodies? Without some understanding of the "mechanism" of our consciousness becoming aware of different three-dimensional intersections, we cannot answer the question.

It is, in fact, the very question we cannot answer that provides a rational basis for Hesse's account of a mystical experience in *Siddhartha*. If in principle any three-demensional intersection is available as a potential object of consciousness, the question becomes not why are we aware of *this* intersection *now?* But rather, why aren't we aware of *every* intersection, that is, why should we experience the change from one experience to another? In principle, we can be aware of everything. Of course, if we were to be aware of all intersections, we would have unchanging experience, and time (or temporal awareness) would cease. We are to believe that it is our moral defects, our ignorance, our desires for specific things that limit our consciousness to particular things at particular places and times. If we were to cease striving for particulars, we would have a different sort of awareness in which we would be aware of everything; such an awareness would not be of things but of the activity of consciousness being aware of reality in total. Exactly the nature of that reality is left unstated in Buddhist accounts. Reality doesn't have a nature; even if it were to have a nature, we could hardly describe it in ordinary language which is suited to the expression of what appears to us to be a three-dimensional world in process.

A major issue remains: how are we to understand free will? On the Buddhist account freedom is not the freedom to choose this or that. It is instead the freedom from having to choose this or that. The mystic's world, which is not a world of particulars, is also not a world in which particular choices can be made. To choose is to render a possibility actual; choosing is an inextricably temporal concept. In the sense already stated, the mystic transcends time in his all-encompassing experience. He is free from choice.

However, we may sympathize with Billy and the Tralfamadorians. If we are forced to project along the world-line of our lives and even if the projection is not of each successively ordered three-dimensional intersection, as long as we are limited to the one-dimensional world-line of our four-dimensional body, we must (to use the earlier metaphor) either watch the same movie again and again (it is not clear whether we would be aware of the repetition) or cut and splice as we like but never add or change a frame. It is a poor freedom we are offered. If we know the end of a movie we may not wish to see it again; we crave novelty and see ourselves as creating order, not as the passive spectators of order already given. Even reshuffling is not enough. Tralfamadorians are aware of all of finite space-time (presumably it is finite but unbounded, which is in keeping with the general theory of relativity), but surely even the pleasant regions will lose their charm, given that both they and we are said to live forever, to endlessly experience.

In Borges's story "The Garden of Forking Paths" time is construed as a river that branches. Reconvergences are possible but not necessary. Hence, time branches outwardly into novelty. The branches of time are the result of choices that are made. Borges argues that it is not that one of several possibilities is actualized when one makes a choice but rather that every possibility is actualized every time a choice is made. Obviously a contradiction arises if I am said to choose all of several mutually exclusive alternatives. Borges avoids the contradiction by arguing that a branching time would allow each of the possibilities to be actualized on a separate branch of time. He thus supplies the logical separation required to avoid a contradiction. Since each alternative is actualized on a separate branch of time, no contradiction obtains. Hence, whenever mutually exclusive alternatives arise, time branches.

By modifying Borges's concepts, it is possible to introduce greater freedom into Vonnegut's account. Let us reject the notion of time as flowing and branching like a river yet retain the notion of a branch "time." The four-dimensional static body of Billy Pilgrim might be construed as having branches off the world-line. The branches would also have branches. It is not that the static four-dimensional body is branching. It is not in process. It is simply that it has branches. (It is as though a filmstrip had branches.) Thus Billy's consciousness is not restrained to projecting three-dimensional intersections confined to a four-dimensional body with merely two temporal ends. The branches on his treelike four-dimensional body afford his consciousness the opportunity to make choices. If he chooses to drop out of college, there is that route or branch that if projected would provide Billy the sequence of experiences that comprise the life of a drop-out. (I have deliberately avoided the use of the expression "would have provided" since Billy, if "unstuck in time," may well drop out next time he faces the same choice, the next time his consciousness intersects at this particular fork of his four-dimensional static body.)

Unfortunately, to be precise we now have to construe Billy's static body as five-dimensional. There are the three spatial dimensions that provide the body with its length, width, and breadth, and there are the two "temporal" dimensions that provide the world-line with the logical possibility of being forked. The "temporal" dimensions are not in time. They simply locate the series of elements that on projection (intersection by consciousness) provide successive human experiences of an apparently three-dimensional world in process. That series of experiences (as opposed to the coexisting elements) is in time; it is the experiencing that generates the one-dimensional time series. Experiencing is temporalizing. In construing Billy's body as having branches we have not made time more than one dimensional. We have, however, escaped from the fatalism that results if Billy's nontemporal body is unforked.

One more move is needed to give Billy his freedom. Even a forked body would allow only a limited number of choices. If Billy can return to an earlier choice, he can soon exhaust all the possibilities of his life unless the number of branches is infinite at the various forks. Why not?

There are many variations on this model. It can accommodate reincarnation, backwards causation, and "time" loops. I offer it as a toy for devotees of metaphysical fiction and as a punching bag for academic philosophers. One learns much in play and in combat.[12]

## Notes

1. Tralfamadorians have five sexes. Hence to say "he or she" or "his or her" is to engage in sexism.

2. Kurt Vonnegut, Jr., *Slaughterhouse Five* (New York: Dell Publishing Co., 1968), pp. 26-27.

3. Herman Hesse, *Siddhartha* (New York: A New Directions Paperbook, 1951), p. 110.

4. T. S. Eliot, "Burnt Norton," *Four Quartets* (New York: Harcourt, Brace & World, Inc., 1943), p. 5.

5. Jorge Luis Borges, "The Fearful Sphere of Pascal," *Labyrinths* (New York: New Directions Publishing Corporation, 1962), p. 190.

6. Jorge Luis Borges, "A New Refutation of Time," *Labyrinths*, p. 233.

7. Ibid.

8. Henri Bergson, "An Introduction to Metaphysics," in *Problems of Space and Time*, J.J.C. Smart (New York: The Macmillan Co., 1964), pp. 143-44. Isaac Newton, "Mathematical Principles of Natural Philosophy," in *Problems of Space and Time*, J.J.C. Smart, p. 81.

9. Borges, "The Garden of Forking Paths," *Labyrinths*, pp. 19-29.

10. Borges, "The Fearful Sphere of Pascal," *Labyrinths*, p. 192.

11. Adolf Grünbaum, "The Status of Temporal Becoming," *Annals of the New York Academy of Science* 138 (1967): 374-95.

12. For an account of how the present model relates to the paranormal phenomenon of precognition, see Lee F. Werth, "Normalizing the Paranormal," *American Philosophical Quarterly* 15, no. 1 (January 1978). For an account of its relation to Tantric time concepts, see Lee F. Werth, "Tachyons and Yogons," *Darshana International* 18, no. 1 (April 1978).

# III

# Nature, Human Nature and Teleology

Frans van der Bogert insists that science fiction is as much a literature of nature as it is a literature of science and technology. The more common definition of SF as human responses to technological and scientific innovation is much too narrow, according to van der Bogert; according to his view, SF is more appropriately and adequately defined as the account of human responses to involuntarily suffered changes in the total environment. Citing several examples, he suggests that "the fiction of evolution" is one type of SF story that increases the sensitivity of its readers to nature and their place in nature. Other types include "disaster fiction," and "invasion fiction," which enable their readers to realize how much human existence depends upon the forces and balance of nature and a "liveable" balance among species. These stories and the broad type of "ecofiction" (dealing with some subtle or major alteration in the larger ecosystem) deal not with changes in science and technology but with changes in the basic structures of nature and the relation between nature and culture. Since these SF stories make us more aware of our dependence on nature and show us features of our own "human nature" by displaying the nature of other beings ("aliens" or proto-humans composed, and/or behaving, differently), they provide us with the kinds of insights that we must have as we become increasingly dependent upon maintaining our existence as a part of, rather than in masterful disregard for, our larger ecosystem.

Rosemarie Arbur is especially moved by what she feels is our peculiar bias for human beings in relation to other beings and the goals we accept for fulfilled humanity. She challenges the belief that human beings should evolve toward a progressively higher and purer mentality. She develops a forceful challenge to this belief through a blend of scientific studies, aesthetic and linguistic studies, science fiction stories, and philosophico-humanistic argument.

Arbur points out that even philosophy (literally, love of wisdom) should be construed to mean an involvement of the whole person, not just intellect. Contrary to the belief that humans are at the top of the evolutionary-ecological ladder because of their ability to think abstractly, she argues that being human involves "much more than abstract thought (science) and its physical application (technology)."

Arbur explains how our preconceptions arose, their basis in reading the past, the present, and the future, how SF and technology tend to mirror and reinforce these misconceptions, and how a teleology for mentality arose. Some SF stories, she insists, illuminate the dangers present in this notion of evolutionary progress. The special aesthetic qualities of science fiction make it an appropriate art form for speaking effectively to the whole being.

After citing several SF stories and other studies that at least raise the possibility that other species may be more highly but differently developed, Arbur suggests that our bias, carried to its logical conclusion, may be disastrous to "human nature" and to individuality. We may be moving toward an end of higher mentality, but science fiction warns us, according to Arbur, that such an evolution is decidedly deficient, for it ignores other aspects of the whole being.

# 5

# Nature through Science Fiction

*FRANS VAN DER BOGERT*

In *New Maps of Hell*, Kingsley Amis defines science fiction as:

that class of prose narrative treating of a situation that could not arise in the world we know, but which is hypothesized on the basis of some innovation in science or technology, or pseudo-science or pseudo-technology, whether human or extra-terrestrial in origin.[1]

Definitions always run the risk, on the one hand, of being too general to be informative, and on the other, of being overly restrictive. Amis's definition is too restrictive in at least one respect: by placing the stress it does upon the element of scientific or technological innovation, it excludes those forms of science fiction that depend on other kinds of changes in the familiar. Amis recognizes this narrowness in his own definition, for he appends to it "a couple of codicils," describing those narratives that could be added on the grounds that they appeal to the same interests as science fiction narrowly defined. These are stories about prehistoric man, stories based on some change or disturbance or local anomaly in physical conditions, and stories that take as their theme changes in the political or economic realm.[2] In restating his description of the genre in terms general enough to include these types of stories, Amis says:

Science fiction presents with verisimilitude the human effects of spectacular changes in our environment, changes either deliberately willed or involuntarily suffered.[3]

Changes that are suffered rather than willed include not only the unintended effects of scientific and technological change but also those alterations that come about by entirely natural means. Therefore this description of the genre differs significantly from the earlier quoted and better-known definition.

I think that science fiction may be characterized as a "literature of nature" as well as a literature of science and technology. Stories about human responses to involuntarily suffered change are as correctly thought of as "typical science fiction" as stories about scientific and technological innovation. This is not to replace one oversimplification with another, for a preoccupation with scientific ideas need not be incompatible with an interest in nature. Science is a study of the natural world, and to imagine a different science is to imagine a nature that is at least known differently from that which is familiar to us. Technology is also natural in the sense that it is compatible with, and makes use of, the fundamental principles of science. Because technology is the basis of human economies in that it provides us with the means to cure for ourselves the fundamental necessities of life, an imagined change in technology is not only a change in what we picture as the natural capabilities of the human race but also a change in our picture of the relationship between civilization and environment.

Any literature of science and technology, then, is necessarily a literature of nature. But often a preoccupation with nature is explicit as well as implied in science-fiction stories. While Amis dismisses stories about prehistoric man as "numerically insignificant" and seems to regard it as something of an accident that they are regarded as science fiction at all, these stories become more significant when it is realized that they may be grouped with other examples of what might be called the "fiction of evolution."[4] In the fiction of evolution, imagined variations are made in the story of human development or the details and contexts of this development are filled in to achieve some dramatic effect.

H. G. Wells's *The Time Machine* falls into this category. Wells's time traveler to 802,000 A.D. discovers that two distinct species of "human" beings have been differentiated in the intervening years by the inexorable forces of natural selection. The traveler's gradual realization that the Eloi are not the sole inheritors of the human condition is accompanied by extended reflection on the relationship between nature and human life:

Things will move faster and faster toward the subjugation of Nature. In the end, wisely and carefully we shall readjust the balance of animal and vegetable life to suit our human needs. . . .But with this change in condition comes inevitably adaptations to the change. . . .Under the new conditions of perfect comfort and security, that restless energy, that with us is strength, would become weakness. . .in a state of physical balance and security, power, intellectual as well as physical, would be out of place.[5]

In *Metamorphoses of Science Fiction*, Darko Suvin has observed that Wells depicts the future in his novel by reversing one aspect of the orthodox Darwinist and Huxleyan account of the development of species. Wells has associated a forward motion in time with a movement backward along the phylogenetic series: "The Time Traveller's futures are a. . .progressive series of devolutions."[6] Instead of moving upward into a position of greater humanness and dominance over nature, humanity has mutated into something that possesses the characteristics of animals:

Gradually, the truth dawned on me: that Man had not remained one species, but had differentiated into two distinct animals: that my graceful children of the Upper World were not the sole descendants of our generation, but that this bleached, obscene, nocturnal Thing, which had flashed before me, was also heir to all the ages.[7]

Although the development of technology is responsible in part for the fate of mankind, Wells has a more important point to make. A limited mastery over his environment has not exempted technological man from the principles of evolutionary development. The world of the future is free of noxious weeds, undesirable insects, and disease, but it has spawned a new and tragic form of parasitism: mankind itself, freed of the challenge of an external wildness, has generated a new kind of wildness from within itself by developing into prey and predator. The "graceful children" of the future are human cattle, and the nocturnal apelike Morlocks are more accurately described as human carnivores than cannibals.

Like *The Time Machine*, Edmond Hamilton's "Devolution" postulates a world in which the most significant differences from the familiar are imposed upon humanity by the action of natural forces rather than science and technology. Near the end of the story, one of Hamilton's aliens says:

This world is a world of deadly horror: A world that somehow damages the genes of our race's bodies and changes them bodily and mentally, making them degenerate further each generation.[8]

One of the human protagonists responds in horrified disbelief:

We humans aren't the product of downward devolution, we're the product of ages of upward evolution! We must be, I tell you! Why, we wouldn't want to live. I wouldn't want to live, if that other tale was true. It can't be true![9]

Since the theory of evolution was itself received with the same horror, this part of Hamilton's story might be considered a parody of that reaction, but at the same time, it suggests that the belief in evolution can assume the character of dogma, thus providing some of its adherents with illegitimate and insecure grounds upon which to base their confidence in the meaningfulness of human life.

Stories concerning evolution may also be found in the second category of narratives that Amis added to his original definition. These stories place human beings in unusually challenging situations and are "based on some change or disturbance. . .in physical conditions." Among these Amis lists examples of what might be called "disaster fiction," such as Fred Hoyle's *The Black Cloud* and John Christopher's *The Death of Grass* (*No Blade of Grass*).[10] In these stories, humanity is threatened by natural events that significantly alter the conditions of its existence. This type of narrative fosters an awareness of the vulnerability of civilization when it is considered in relation to the immensity of the surrounding universe. It makes explicit the extent to which our survival depends upon nature's gifts. In *No Blade of Grass*, Christopher imagines a virus that attacks all the members of the grass family. As a result a good percentage of the world's population starves to death and a bitter struggle breaks out among the survivors. Besides informing the reader of the familial relationships that exist between various members of the plant kingdom, the novel makes its readers aware of the extent to which human destiny is interconnected with that of the grasses.

Still another large category of nature-oriented science fiction, which is not separately recognized in Amis's discussion, is "invasion fiction," stories about conflicts between our own species and alien life forms. When the aliens are of higher intelligence, these narratives may have more to do with the struggles between individuals or societies than with conflict between humanity and nature. Sometimes they are modernized versions of conflict with the gods. When, however, the aliens with which human protagonists have to contend are more like terrestrial animals, plants, or microorganisms than other human beings, the stories belong to that class of science fiction in which a preoccupation with nature is visible.

*The Body Snatchers*, by Jack Finney, incorporates all three themes: evolution, disaster, and invasion.[11] In Finney's story earth has been invaded by organisms that have an unlimited capacity to imitate other life forms, including human beings. Gradually the hero and heroine discover that their friends, relatives, and acquaintances are being replaced by nearly identical duplicates that differ from the original persons only in their lack of human emotions. It is hypothesized that the invading organisms are "space spores," germs of material that drift through space until they accidentally strike a world which can support their development:

What happens when an ancient planet finally dies? The life form on it must reckon with and prepare for that fact—to survive. . . .in a sense of course, the pods are a parasite. . . .But they are the perfect parasite, capable of far more than clinging to the host. They are completely evolved life; they have the ability to reform and reconstitute themselves into perfect duplication, cell for living cell, of any life form they encounter in whatever conditions that life has suited itself for.[12]

Like many other science-fiction stories, Finney's shows the strong influence of the Darwinian revolution. By imagining an organism that is an even better mimic than our species, it threatens to overturn the view of Renaissance Humanism, which held that Man is superior to other animals because he is able to take on the character of any other animal. The pods leave the planet Earth only when the hero and heroine set fire to a field filled with developing pods. Humans, it turns out, are also aggressive competitors capable of protecting their living places. It should be noted, however, that both the 1956 movie version of the novel and the 1979 one changed Finney's ending. The battle with the invaders is unresolved at the close of the earlier movie, and at the close of the later movie the pods score an apparent victory. It is tempting to hypothesize that these changes reflect general trends in public attitudes toward nature as well as the decisions of particular producers, directors, and writers. Dousing the menace with gasoline and setting it afire was a pest-control method more convincing in the 1950s than today.

In disaster and invasion stories, the threat that arises to the survival of a culture or species may be the result of events over which human beings have no control. But sometimes human beings themselves accidentally set into motion events that take on the character of a disaster or an invasion as they develop. On the surface, these stories may appear to fit neatly into Amis's definition of science fiction, because the changes that initiate the action in these narratives are technological. In these stories, however, nature responds to human tampering. That artificially induced radiation engenders mutated varieties of plants and animals, for example, provides the generative idea for many stories which could not be written only around radiation-producing technology. These stories may be described as "ecofiction," that is, the fiction of ecology, even though many of them were written before the concept of ecology had become fully explicit.

In H. G. Wells's novel *The Food of the Gods*, a growth-promoting material called "Heraklophorbia" escapes into the environment. Suddenly, the human protagonists find themselves battling immense wasps, earwigs, chickens, and the like. In the end, the disappearance of ordinary sized humans seems inevitable, as children fed Heraklophorbia grow into giants, and magnified rats are as much an accepted fact in southwest London "as tigers in the delta by Calcutta."[13]

Harold L. Berger has argued in *Science Fiction and the New Dark Age* that much of science fiction, instead of being proscience and protechnology, is skeptical of scientific and technological progress.[14] His belief that science fiction has from its very beginnings contained such a skeptical streak is borne out by an examination of the fiction of Wells. Long before people were worrying about the adverse effects of environmental pollution by toxic chemicals, nuclear wastes, or engineered viruses, Wells wrote about unpredictable environmental changes brought about by the creation of an apparently benevolent material.

The range of works in the "ecofiction" category is quite broad and includes works far more realistic than Wells's fantasy. John Brunner's *The Sheep Look Up* presents us with the depressing spectacle of a world gradually dying a death of a thousand cuts.[15] One small incident after another adds to the cumulative chaos of the world's ecology. The hope that rests on the charismatic leader, Austin Train, is disappointed when Train is cut off from national exposure, first by presidential order and then by a well-placed bomb that brings the roof of the television studio down upon him.

In Brunner's not so hypothetical society, economic and political forces cannot easily accommodate ecological imperatives, and those who would defend nature against human ravages are actively suppressed by the government. A happier future is pictured by Ernest Callenbach's *Ecotopia*, a story about a secessionist state in the Northwest that withdraws from the less enlightened part of the country to form a polity founded upon the "survivalist" principles of zero (or negative) population growth, a steady state economy, recycling of nearly all waste, and maximal use of renewable resources.[16] The narrator of the story, William Weston, is a newspaper reporter and much of the novel consists of his columns describing the society and technology of the new country. Although his reports are packed with detailed descriptions of technological innovations, nature is an omnipresent object of concern. The Ecotopians have replaced the automobile with mass transit systems and bicycles, provided free by the government. Houses are built from biodegradable plastic, and energy is generated from solar, geothermal, and other relatively nonpolluting sources. Unlike the hero of Brunner's novel, Weston is allowed to find a place healthy enough to raise bright and sane children and to spread the news about the Ecotopian solution.

So far, the fiction of evolution, disaster fiction, invasion fiction, and ecofiction have been discussed only as forms in which the generative ideas of science fiction are not alterations in science or technology but rather changes in the fundamental facts of nature or in the relationship between culture and nature. But there is also something called "human nature," which is related closely to the physiochemical, biological, and behavioral properties of our own bodies. Some science fiction falls into a category that might be called "fiction of alien (or other) persons," intelligent beings whose natures differ from our own. These persons may have nonhuman ancestors, be mutations derived from human stock, or may be even entirely artificial beings. When the fiction of alien persons deals with non-artificial (that is, "natural") persons, it is a form of nature literature, insofar as it explores the relationships between the natural aspects of personhood and its "mental" or "spiritual" features.

In *Brave New World*, Aldous Huxley shows us a society in which many so-called natural functions of human beings, such as procreation and child-rearing, have been standardized or replaced by assembly-line operations.[17] "Wild" human nature, as personified in the Indians of the reservation and in John, the protagonist of the novel, is contrasted to human nature both bred and engineered. In the new world's assembly plant, things go according to "Our Ford"; human nature is bent and directed into forms that are amenable to the imperative to produce and consume. Because a love of nature does not stimulate either production or consumption, infants are conditioned not to like roses. Drugs are employed to control sexual activity and to ensure that it takes place only under approved conditions. Where the forces of evolution have produced two "human" races in Wells's *The Time Machine*, Huxley's engineers have made five and written five scripts for their behavior. Like Wells, Huxley suggests that all the wildness can't be taken out of human nature and that if it could the result would be morally doubtful.

Frank Herbert's *Hellstrom's Hive* describes a mutated strain of human beings who are in many respects like those of *Brave New World*. But the dominant metaphor in Herbert's book is the beehive, while in Huxley's it is the automobile factory. The humans of *Hellstrom's Hive* have been infused with the spirit of insect life. By quoting texts on Eastern philosophy, ecology, and "hive philosophy," Herbert makes us empathize more fully with the outlook of the hive people than we do with the Controllers of Huxley's society. While highly unnatural in that it deviates from the human norm, the behavior of the hive people remains natural in other senses. Huxley imagines humans stripped of their naturalness; Herbert imagines an "unnatural" combination of animal and human natures, a human nature possessed by the power of nature or merged into it.

The path to species extinction begins with the proud belief that in each individual there is a mentalistic being—an *ego* or personality, spirit, anima, character, soul, or mind—and that this separated incarnation is somehow free.[18]

Besides denying these "myths" about human nature, and calling into question the idea that we are related to the natural world as spirits are related to bodies, the "hive philosophy" quoted here suggests that if we were not human, if our perceptions were not blinded by a raging individualism which makes it impossible for us to engage in self-sacrificial acts, the world of nature would seem different to us. To the "wild" individualist the powers of nature threaten to destroy personality or freedom; nature is viewed as an antagonist that must be subdued. To the hive people, nature is something into which a successful being melts: personality and individual freedoms are discarded as obstacles to full functioning, adaptation, and survival:

Hellstrom knew he took an unhealthy enjoyment in the possession of a distinct name and an Outsider-like identity, but most of the Hive's workers were free of this bondage.
*I am a transitional form*, he told himself, *and someday I will be obsolete.*[19]

Ursula Le Guin's *The Left Hand of Darkness* describes a race of androgynous individuals who only become "sexed" during a short period of receptivity similar to heat. The novel is full of nature imagery. Fictional excerpts from the race's philosophy and mythology are used to indicate some of their attitudes toward nature. In their creation myth, which begins with "nothing but ice and the sun," the first event is the opening by the sun of a great crevasse. "In the sides of this crevasse were great shapes of ice, and there was no bottom to it."[20] Creation here is analogous to the appearance of a "sexed" nature out of an undifferentiated one.

At the end of Le Guin's novel, the Earthman who has spent so much time among these aliens now must look at his fellow terrestrials with new eyes:

But they all looked strange to me, men and women, well as I knew them. Their voices sounded strange, too deep, too shrill. They were like a troupe of great, strange animals, of two different species; great apes with intelligent eyes, all of them in rut, in kemmer. . . .[21]

It is this vision of our own species as something alien that Suvin believes is one definitive property of science fiction. Borrowing from Bertolt Brecht, Suvin offers the following definition of "estrangement": "A representation which estranges is one which allows us to recognize its subject, but at the same time makes it seem unfamiliar."[22] While one may not agree with Suvin's definition of science fiction as literature combining the elements of estrangement and cognition, it is certainly correct to see certain science fiction works this way.

Hal Clement's portrait of our own planet as a bleak and incredibly cold world whose surface holds great oceans of a toxic and explosive substance is yet another estranging vision of nature and human nature. *Iceworld* is told from the point of view of Mercurians to whom hydrogen oxide presents many hazards. When Clement has one of his Mercurians describe its dangers, he is presenting us with a different, estranged view of our world.

> "It's a liquid—see how the reflection at the edge trembles in the air currents!"
> "So what?"
> "The only liquid I've encountered on this planet behaved an awful lot like that queer oxide we found on Four—the one that nearly froze my feet. I saw some before here, and dipped a handler in it; the stuff vaporized instantly, and it was minutes before I could put a tentacle in the sleeve again. I think it's that heat-drinking stuff—hydrogen oxide."[23]

When the Mercurians bring a sample of the material into their ship for testing, it explodes with great violence.

While Le Guin's portrayal of humans as oversexed aliens leads us to a reexamination of our beliefs and attitudes about sex and sexuality, a reassessment that may well be painful, Clement's estranged vision of hydrogen oxide (that is, water) as pure poison may be therapeutic, for it offers us a certain degree of security. If we can live in an environment that is toxic to other life forms, it may be a testament to our own powers of adaptation and survival.

Science-fiction stories based upon alterations in the familiar world of nature often embody our currently accepted beliefs about nature and the social and technological forms that define our past and present relationships with it. *Ecotopia*, for example, contains reasonably accurate accounts of alternative energy sources, low-impact lumbering practices, organic farming and gardening, and recycling. While the novel is no substitute for textbook studies of these subjects, it certainly can reinforce textbook presentations. *No Blade of Grass* contains information about the taxonomy of grasses, their importance to nutrition, and possible substitutes for the grasses in the human diet. But teaching us facts about nature is not the only sort of teaching science fiction provides, nor the most important of its teaching functions. Philosophers of science point out that science orders facts by subsuming them under generalizations, theories, and hypotheses. Logic and methodology do not provide infallible means for discovering generalizations, theories, and hypotheses, although they can contribute guidelines for testing the adequacy of such proposals. The development of generalizations, theories, and hypotheses requires the use of a creative imagination to delineate, explore, and flesh out possibilities.

Imagination is not only needed to envisage and articulate possibilities but also to plan intelligently for the future. The philosophical theory of probability and decision-making identifies as rationally sound a choice which maximizes the likelihood of desirable states of affairs and minimizes that of undesirable ones.[24] Catastrophic outcomes need to be avoided more scrupulously than ones that are not so terrible; sometimes a long shot is worth betting on, if the payoff is sufficiently high. While in games of chance, we usually can assign numerical values to various payoffs, thus making it easy to compare relative values, it is much more difficult to assign values to situations that may result in the world around us. A skilled pilot keeps dangerous reefs and safe harbors in mind, even while studying the waters lying immediately ahead. But which reefs are really dangerous, and which harbors are truly safe? Vicariously experiencing possible worlds through dreams, fantasies, fables, and fiction enables us to explore our feelings about them, to see if what seems attractive or repulsive on first impression is really that way. Fiction writing demands that an imagined future be peopled with actors and that these actors live through a series of events. Fictional futures are therefore in some respects more fully detailed than the abstract extrapolations of futurologists. Fiction and philosophy arrive at knowledge in very different ways, yet the knowledge that science fiction offers, may rightly be called "philosophical" as it pertains to possible as well as actual situations.

To imagine nonhuman views of nature is connected with the development of a critical awareness of the possible limitations of a human perspective. This type of science fiction is philosophical in yet another sense. Western philosophy is derived in part from the self-critical inquiries of Socrates, who supposedly took as one of his principal maxims the advice of the Delphic Oracle, "Know Thyself."[25] For Socrates, a full self-knowledge involved an awareness of one's radical ignorance. Other philosophers in the skeptical tradition have agreed that our perceptions, drawn from our senses, give us an extremely biased and narrow understanding of reality. Fiction encourages us to ask if our beliefs and feelings about nature are objective enough to be shared by beings with different bodies and psychologies. When science fiction goes beyond the simple picturing and evaluating of possibilities to the invention of nonhuman views of familiar objects, it forces us to become more aware of the conditions and limitations of our powers of perception and cognition.

## Notes

1. Kingsley Amis, *New Maps of Hell: A Survey of Science Fiction* (New York: Harcourt Brace and Company, 1960), p. 18.

2. Ibid., p. 24.

3. Ibid., p. 26.

4. Ibid., p. 24.

5. H. G. Wells, *The Time Machine*, in *Seven Science Fiction Novels of H. G. Wells* (New York: Dover Publications, 1950), pp. 26-28.

6. Darko Suvin, *Metamorphoses of Science Fiction: On the Poetics and History of a Literary Genre* (New Haven: Yale University Press, 1979), p. 233.

7. H. G. Wells, *The Time Machine*, p. 39.

8. Edmond Hamilton, "Devolution," in *Before the Golden Age: A Science Fiction Anthology of the 1930's*, Book 3, ed. Isaac Asimov (New York: Doubleday and Company, 1974, Fawcett Publications, Inc., 1975), p. 278.

9. Ibid.

10. Fred Hoyle, *The Black Cloud* (New York: Signet Books, 1969). John Christopher, *No Blade of Grass* (New York: Avon Books, 1957). Christopher's novel was originally published in England under the title, *The Death of Grass.*

11. Jack Finney's *The Body Snatchers* first appeared in serial form in *Collier's Magazine* in 1954. It was published as a book in 1955. The first movie edition of the story, *The Invasion of the Body Snatchers*, was released by Allied Artists in 1956. A newer version of the movie appeared in 1978, released by United Artists. A "revised and updated edition" of the book was published by Dell Publishing Co., in 1978. All page references are to this most recent edition. Although the latest edition of the book has been retitled as *The Invasion of the Body Snatchers*, I have used the earlier title in my own text.

12. Jack Finney, *The Invasion of the Body Snatchers* (New York: Dell Publishing Co., 1978), p. 173.

13. H. G. Wells, *Seven Science Fiction Novels of H. G. Wells*, p. 747.

14. Harold L. Berger, *Science Fiction and the New Dark Age* (Bowling Green, Ohio: Bowling Green University Popular Press, 1976). See especially chapter one, "The Threat of Science."

15. John Brunner, *The Sheep Look Up* (London: Brunner Fact and Fiction, Ltd., 1972; New York: Ballantine Books, 1973).

16. Ernest Callenbach, *Ecotopia* (Berkeley, California: Banyan Tree Books, 1975; New York: Bantam Books, 1977).

17. Aldous Huxley, *Brave New World* (Garden City, New York: Doubleday, Doran and Co., 1932; Perennial Classics, Harper & Row, 1969).

18. Frank Herbert, *Hellstrom's Hive* (New York: Bantam Books, 1972), p. 288.

19. Ibid., p. 303.

20. Ursula K. Le Guin, *The Left Hand of Darkness* (New York: Ace Books, 1969), p. 237.

21. Ibid., p. 297.

22. Suvin, *Metamorphoses of Science Fiction*, p. 6.

23. Hal Clement, *Iceworld* (New York: Ballantine Books, 1977), p. 189.

24. See, for example, Rudolf Carnap, *Logical Foundations of Probability*, 2d ed. (Chicago: University of Chicago Press, 1962), pp. 252-70. A more elementary treatment of this topic is found in Brian Skyrms, *Choice and Chance: An Introduction to Inductive Logic*, 2d ed. Belmont, Calif.: Dickenson Publishing Co., 1975), pp. 153-55.

25. Plato, *Charmides*, in *The Dialogues of Plato* (London: Oxford University Press, 1892), pp. 164d-165a. Other appeals to this maxim, which was inscribed upon the entrance to the Delphic Oracle, are found in *Phaedrus*, p. 230a; *Philebus*, 48c; and *Protagoras*, 343b.

# 6

# Teleology of Human Nature *for* Mentality?

*ROSEMARIE ARBUR*

Aristotle's *Poetics*, though probaby a compilation of his students' notes, still remains a valuable guide for defining and formulating literary theory. According to the ancient Greek authority, literature artfully and verbally represents human action by imitating what is, what was, and what could or should be. Science fiction belongs in the last of these categories. It presents us with a speculative, probable *could* and, insofar as all literature is thematic to some degree, it provides approximations of the probable in order for us to learn or to form judgments about whether or not the *could* is *should*. If it is, the theme becomes a kind of guide; if the *could* is *should not*, the theme becomes a clear admonition.

We turn to ancient Greek civilization for a definition of philosophy as well: literally, it is the love of wisdom. If we are not thoroughly cynical, committed to dicta which tell us of the innate depravity of the genus *Homo*, we must regard wisdom as a good and regard love as an equally good appetitive orientation or instinct. This statement in itself poses serious questions, for neither love nor wisdom is entirely cognitive or intellectual. Instead, both love and wisdom refer to the result of our being hylomorphic entities. Human beings do not have a *dual* nature— half-animal and half-spiritual or - intellectual—but rather a nature arising from an inextricable bonding of "heart" and "head," of feeling and thought, of instinct and intellection.

To love wisdom (to be a philosopher) involves, then, much more than a reasonable, deliberate approbation of what is logical, intelligible, and valid, despite the affinity that Western cultures have for rationality. It involves a desire to know (in almost the biblical sense) what is true, and the truth desired embraces the perceptual as much as the conceptual. "To love wisdom" involves the whole person.

One serious question suggested by our preoccupation with reason is: "What, if not our ability to think abstractly and then embody such abstract thought in previously nonexistent physical forms, puts us atop this planet's ecological pyramid?" I do not presume to know the answer, but I trust my feeling that "human" means much more than abstract thought (science) and its physical application (technology).

Those who write science fiction have addressed that question more frequently than a casual reader may realize. With all that is possible and even remotely probable available to them as subject matter, science-fiction writers create verbally existent worlds and universes limited only by "laws" extrapolated from those which science has abstracted from the workings of the universe and world we know. Thus, a work of science fiction may be about almost anything not explicitly forbidden by known "laws of nature." Since we humans are very nearly obsessed by the mystery of our own nature, it is hardly surprising that many works of science fiction inquire thematically about the nature of humankind.

While the nature of humanity is a favorite object of philosophical speculation, this essay will examine only two of its fundamental aspects. One—that we are certainly not angels but are somewhat more than beasts—not only affects how we manage the processes of perception and conception but also, since we take pride in being thinking creatures, determines our interpretations of ourselves as a species. This aspect, which I mention first, is simply the applicability of Heisenberg's Principle to human knowing: just as the instrument of measurement intrudes upon what is being measured and so precludes absolute exactitude, our preconceptions and prejudices about ourselves make all our observations about humanity to some degree inaccurate. Thus, however objective we try to be, we are deflected from the truth by the very "instrument" that seeks it.

The second aspect of the nature of humanity is the focus of this essay: we perceive in time past (and so acknowledge temporality), then conceive in time present what we—and all that impinges upon us—will be like in the future. Aware of change, we seek some beginning. Convinced by fossil records that those who were almost certainly our ancestors were less advanced, three million years ago, than we are now, we postulate a continuation of the process we call human evolution. Unsatisfied by causes (like random genetic mutation) that apparently resulted in what we are today, we demand some final cause, some end: we make up teleology.

Since the future cannot be mapped by any means we use to map the past—in fact, cannot be mapped at all—we are left with unproven theories of probability and our human proclivity for speculation. We make up science fiction.

Earlier I implied that we as a species take pride in our ability to think abstractly and rationally. We delight in our exercises of reason: "I think, therefore I am," "Plato is a man / All men are mortal / Therefore,. . ." and even such deductions as "My car will not start; the engine doesn't turn over; the headlights won't go on; I must have a dead battery." Because of the practical implications of this reasoning, because we can often determine the solution to a problem solely by the use of our minds, many persons regard the ever greater exercise of reason as an improvement, as a positive step on our evolutionary path.

The ascendancy of science fiction as a literary movement coincides with the ascendancy of technology. Earlier in this century, when principles of science were applied to everyday life with increasing frequency, the proponents of such application believed that the resulting "labor- and time-saving" devices would free us from physical labor so that we could "move ahead" more swiftly. They envisioned a future that would make possible increasingly greater use of the mind. As the discovery of fire for cooking saved our ancestors hours of chewing, hours to be spent developing skills that derived from thinking, so would technological automation grant us extra time to evolve intellectually. The brilliant future awaiting us would be the result of enhanced intelligence.

We have no time machines to take us to the future; we simply cannot know if our evolution as a species is actually headed toward ever increasing mentality, nor can we know that this hypothesized teleology is wholly beneficial. We do, however, have works of science fiction to read, and they are of inestimable value. Like all literary works they please, delight, and entertain us at the same time that they impart knowledge, provide new ideas, educate (or, at least, present interesting situations in answer to both writers' and readers' "what if's").

As literature, science fiction engages the reader's emotions as well as intellective processes. While one might intellectually shrug off a forthright expository examination of the dangers of overpopulation, John Brunner's *Stand on Zanzibar*, because it is literature and thereby affective, is not so easy to dismiss. A well-written work of science fiction has aesthetic (as opposed to anaesthetic) qualities, and at least two of these paradoxically support one another.

One meaning of *aesthetic* I have used above: it is the quality that enables a work of art to affect or move the person who reads it. Thus, reading about a probable human development as it is embodied in a novel is being caught up in the more than just intellectual meaning that the work presents. Because of this aesthetic quality, the science-fiction novel elicits a real emotional response.

The complementary aesthetic quality is what we mean when we speak of "aesthetic distance." The feelings are there and we cannot escape them, but, because we know that we are reading about instead of living through the fictional incidents, we can back off emotionally and examine the emotional and intellectual reactions that the novel evokes. Because of these complementary aesthetic qualities and because much science fiction is a make-believe time machine, those who would inquire into the teleology of human evolution can find few, if any, better means.

To examine the ways by which science fiction approaches the possibility of evolution-for-mentality is essentially an examination of the "thematic statements" generated by the interaction of various literary elements that constitute the science-fiction works. What a given work "says" about the notion that *H. sapiens* is evolving increasingly better ways of thinking and reasoning is the work's relevent theme. As we examine a number of science-fiction works, we can recognize and differentiate three basic thematic attitudes: the naive, the admonitory, and the retrospective.

Naive in this context is almost synonymous with innocent. Works with this thematic orientation—many of them written within ten or fifteen years of Hugo Gernsback's first publication of *Amazing* in 1926—very frequently emphasize a "sense of wonder." They portray a future in which a mentally advanced human race is responsible for awe-inspiring accomplishments. Such works seem thematically to confuse knowledge of the good with morally good behavior—just as the ancient Greeks did.

Influenced by the promises of contemporary technology, science-fiction writers and their readers naively postulate futures in which mentality overshadows everything else. If there is a problem, some fictional scientist will think up a solution; if there is an extra-terrestrial enemy, the humans of the future will overcome it because of their evolved intellectual prowess. Even if our brains should enlarge themselves according to the evolutionary plan and become so massive that atrophied human bodies cannot support their weight, well, the minds inside those massive brains will have devised mechanical vehicles to house and support the brains and to perform the physical functions we now entrust to our skeletal and muscular systems.

The admonitory thematic attitude is practically the obverse of the naive one, probably because science fiction which embodies it has generally been written more recently, after the promises of technology have been realized—to humanity's dismay. $E = mc^2$ may have *promised* a virtually limitless and beneficial source of energy, but in practice the equation conjures up images of mushroom-shaped clouds, craters where cities are now, and misshapen children whose mothers' milk contained a bit too much strontium 90.

Influenced by the fearsome results of their contemporary technology, writers and readers of admonitory science fiction also postulate futures in which mentality overshadows everything else. If the humans of the future denude our planet of its forests, they will do the logical thing: find another world with forests—Le Guin's Athshe is one example—and clear-cut them. These logical humans will pay no heed to such a world's native inhabitants because the "natives"—like Le Guin's "creechies" who make no false distinctions between "heart" and "head"—will no doubt be considered different and therefore inferior. If, in a work that has an admonitory theme, there is a problem like an abundance of disease-transmitting mosquitoes—some fictional scientist will solve it not by importing little larvae-eating fish but by saturating the environment with some poison like DDT. Having seen the results of such problem-solving on our own planet, science-fiction writers warn us by destroying entire ecosystems on their fictional worlds.[1]

The retrospective thematic attitude exists as a result of readers' and writers' looking back on what seemed to be naive science fiction and finding in it real tension and ambiguity. Stanley Weinbaum's "Martian Odyssey" (1934), as it is read today and perhaps as it was read when it was first published, is a good example. Superficially, the story is an entertaining tale of an adventure-filled trek across the Martian landscape and of the comical camaraderie among the crewmen-characters, each of whom disbelieves or makes fun of the protagonist's report.

At first, the nonhuman called Tweel seems to exist only to enliven the narrative by being a sapient "person" to share Jarvis' adventures. By his presence alone, Tweel suggests that we may not be alone in the universe nor even in our solar system; moreover, he gives us the vicarious experience of meeting an alien who is not a bug-eyed-monster. Read naively, the story excites us because its characters are ordinary people of their own era who, owing to advanced mentality and the use of it, are able to travel to Mars. Further, the story presents us with a nonhuman intelligent being even more advanced than its human characters; still reading naively, we share the human explorers' speculation that Tweel's degree of mental evolution may very well be one that they will attain in the fairly near future.

Weinbaum's story may also be read retrospectively. It shows us the human race so advanced that it can travel to other planets while it is still the *H. sapiens* with whom we are too familiar. Jarvis risks not only his own but Tweel's life as well to steal from the barrel people an egg-shaped object that only might be a cure for cancer. Not only does he steal and feel no guilt but his showing the stolen item to his crewmates elicits from them a humorous approval. Actually, "A Martian Odyssey" makes three retrospective thematic statements. The first is that, no matter how intellectually evolved our species may become, it will behave according to a power philosophy (Jarvis was able to steal the object, so he did). The second is that humankind, despite or even because of its advanced evolutionary status, will continue to be anthropocentric (making diagrams in the sand and communicating to Tweel that he is from the third planet, Jarvis basks in his own success and misses entirely Tweel's message that he too is an explorer and not a native of Mars).

The third is more subtle, yet it is clearly a negative judgment about increased mentality as an evolutionary goal for any intelligent life form. When Tweel points "at his middle and then at Arcturus, at his head and then at Spica, at his feet and then at half a dozen stars," it seems that his gestures communicate an important fact. Probably, his species is a hybrid derived from the native life forms that inhabit the solar systems of Arcturus, Spica, and other stars; Tweel's gestures, unintelligible to Jarvis, tell us that he is an experienced interstellar explorer. Moreover, Tweel's behavior in the story reveals his species' very advanced mental evolution, but it also demonstrates that evolution of mind is not necessarily accompanied by greater moral acuity. Tweel does not interfere with Jarvis' theft; in fact, he voluntarily remains with the human explorer-thief to fight off the barrel people. It seems that Tweel's superior mentality merely enables him to explore more planets and to communicate more effectively than humans.

Indeed, if his advanced mentality correlates with any other quality, that quality is a sort of intellectual snobbery. On Mars, amid various kinds of intelligence, Tweel chooses to befriend Jarvis because the human has intellectual *processes* (not necessarily accomplishments) most nearly like his own. The reader examining "A Martian Odyssey" for insight about the evolutionary goal of mentality is left with a discomfiting question: Will evolved human mentality mean merely that a more intelligent humankind can more easily bring harm to species that are different? The answer I imply here is obvious, supported by the record of our treatment of the "lower" life forms that used to share the Earth with us. Although human beings who use their minds to think have for decades agreed that all life on Earth is interdependent and necessary for the maintenance of our fragile ecosystem, not until the 1980s did the United States formally agree to absolute protection of the remaining great whales. Of the true "races" inhabiting our planet, only we, the elephants, and the toothed whales have measurably similar peculiarities of the cerebral cortex, peculiarities which, it has been hypothesized, enable the three of us to "think." A number of science-fiction works have explored the possibilities inherent in this cortical similarity, and two in particular are especially relevant here.

One is Alan Dean Foster's novel, *Cachalot* (1980), which unfortunately suffers from an imperfectly resolved plot as well as (for those who mispronounce French) a title that is a questionable pun. These literary weaknesses do little, however, to diminish the thematic certitude about mentality as an evolutionary goal. From the beginning of the novel we learn that humans had developed a serum that potentiated the cortical activity of toothed whales. In reparation for the genocide perpetrated on the cetaceans for centuries, the humans not only gave the serum to the whales but transported to a pelagic world every whale who wanted to leave Earth. During the temporal setting of the novel, whales (dolphins and porpoises, *orca*s or "killer whales," and the great sperm catadons) can communicate, if they choose, with favored humans by means of a human-made translating device. From the communication between them and one woman cetologist, we learn about their differing uses of mentality.

The smallest toothed whales, the porpoises, use their activated minds to enhance their play, for to them life is simply a prolonged and enjoyable entertainment. The largest, the sperm whales or catadons, use their mentality for thinking as an end in itself; they are ocean-dwelling metaphysicians who resent any interruption—especially by humans—of their philosophizing. The middle-sized killer whales use their minds to compose epics, ballads, lyrics, and other poetical forms they can discuss with the few humans on their world. While they seem to fancy themselves poets, the *orca*s may be the most cunning of cetaceans; one of the sperm whales observed that the apparent "poets" may be only simulating a literary, originally human, interest in order to keep cautious watch on the species that once nearly drove them to extinction.

*Cachalot* is thematically an examination of several kinds of mind. For the porpoises and dolphins, increased mentality is, even if their evolutionary history led them to the use of reason, just another organic refinement that fits them for a more pleasurable life. The great sperm whales embrace their activated mentality as a definite teleology: no longer hampered by the old neurochemical limitations, they literally live to think and, truly sapient, lack all ambition to apply their thinking to anything but themselves. The cunning killer whales are cunning precisely because they *use* their minds; although evolution has selected and enforced their mentality *per se*, they remain in communicative contact with the human characters just in case the humans revert to genocidal behavior. In other words, the *orca*s have evolved for mentality, but the use to which it is put is limited almost exclusively to ensuring their own survival.

Comparing the varieties of mentality in *Cachalot*, one must conclude that increased ability to think *is* an evolutionary end. On Foster's fictional planet, we can observe mental or cortical evolution, but, once we observe the process closely, we find it diverging into four distinct paths. Each of the intelligent mammalian species (including *H. sapiens*), although it is evolving toward increased mental prowess, seems to be headed for a kind of mentality that is unique.

Gordon R. Dickson's "Dolphin's Way" (1964), set on Earth, examines only two intelligent, evolving species. At least one of its basic themes is similar to one in *Cachalot*: we are not the only sapients to have evolved on Earth. Its more fundamental thematic statement, however, is different and more direct. While the sapient species in Foster's novel seem, in terms of mental evolution, different but essentially equal, Dickson's story clearly implies the inferiority of humankind.

"Dolphin's Way" makes use of an old "first contact" plot: an alien arrives on Earth and says, in effect, "Take Me To Your Leader." The alien, who appears to be a beautiful human woman, first encounters a young marine zoologist-ethologist who is genuinely dedicated to his work with wild dolphins. Malcolm Sinclair is intelligent, sensitive to the "person-ness" of the marine animals who voluntarily visit the research station where he works, and, in short, is a thoroughly sympathetic human character. By using so likable a protagonist, Dickson manages to avoid any "we're bad—they're good" connotations that arise from human-dolphin interaction. Sinclair is a credit to our species, realizing as he does that "we've got to go into the sea...to talk to the dolphins in their own mode. We've got to expand to their level of communication, not try to compress them into ours."

Dickson's choice of a hackneyed plot is vindicated by the ending of the story. "Your idea that the ability to communicate with another intelligent race, an alien race, was a test that had to be passed before the superior species of a planet could be contacted by the intelligent races of the galaxy—that was right," the alien says to Sinclair just before entering the dolphin's pool to swim away with them. The test has been passed, and the extra-terrestrial visitor has completed the first part of her mission. When she swims out to sea in the company of two dolphins, the *hubris* of *H. sapiens* is clear, for we finally understand which "the superior species of [our] planet" actually is.

Although few, my examples are representative; they illustrate one of the recurring and important thematic statements embodied in science fiction. We may paraphrase it: Mentality is very probably our evolutionary final cause and, barring a demographic catastrophe, our species will continue to select naturally and socially for increased mentality. As the examples I have used indicate, however, there may be different traits that we simplistically assume to be a single, "mental" quality. A brief exposition, based on what the dictionary (in this case, *The American Heritage Dictionary of the English Language*) tells and does not tell us about the human brain, should make clear what most persons understand when confronted by the word "mentality."

These sketches are based on the illustrations used to clarify the meanings of *cerebral cortex* and *cerebellum*. I have added a third because the dictionary omits it and uses entirely verbal definitions to explain *brainstem* and *midbrain*. The omission and definitions are notable, for the brainstem is more than that which connects the spinal cord to forebrain and cerebrum, and the midbrain is more than the source of the brain's embryonic development. Regarded as one entity—a central core—brainstem and midbrain comprise the oldest and most primitive part of the organ. Together, they are the locus of instinct and "gut feeling," the part that differs very little from corresponding parts of the brains of fairly intelligent animals. More humbling than "Dolphin's Way" is the biological

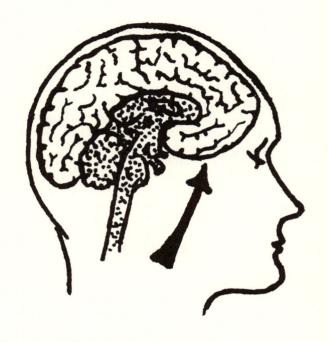

A

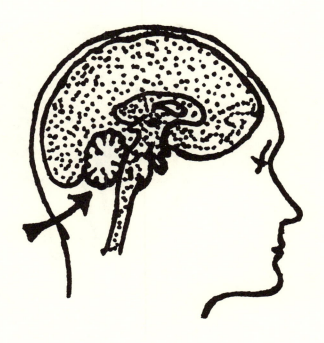

B

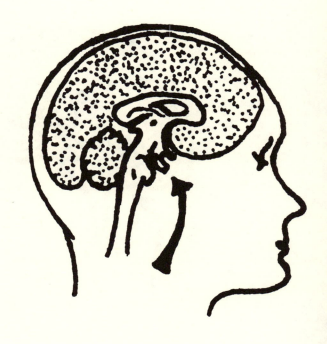

C

truth that a canine brain-core is in most ways the equal of our own.[2] A dog's emotional experience is scarcely less, if it is less, than a human being's; the chief difference is our ability to say things about our emotions.

Figure A emphasizes the cerebral cortex, the convoluted outer surface of the brain in which conscious, volitional, rational thought takes place. The cerebellum (Figure B) is of little relevance to this essay; it is the the part of the brain that controls complex voluntary muscular activity. Figure C shows the brain-core, where much that is not conscious takes place. That the dictionary uses an illustration to help define the cerebral *cortex*, not the cerebrum itself, is significant; so is the omission of any illustration to clarify *brainstem* and *midbrain* and their functions.

A number of inferences can be drawn from this treatment of the human brain by a standard dictionary. First, only those parts of the brain directly related to conscious and volitional activity are deemed relevant to the curiosity of the reading public. Second, because neither brainstem nor midbrain is specifically illustrated, it would seem that we are not interested in, or prefer not to be informed about, the major part of our brain rarely affected by what we call rational thought. Third and finally, the enormous cerebrum (an evolutionary marvel) is deemed less important than its extremely convoluted *thinking* surface.

As I implied earlier, our brain-cores are not, in an evolutionary sense, organic achievements of staggering magnitude; our cerebral cortices are. When we think of the evolution of our mentality, then, we think about the organic part of the brain that enables us to think abstractly and in a logical or rational manner. When we postulate an evolutionary future for our species, we are postulating a physical enlargement of the cerebrum and its cortex or, more likely, some kind of actualization of what, just inside our skulls, is at present in a state of potentiality. Looking into the future by means of science fiction, seeking an evolutionary growth of mentality, we understandably look for an increase in the use of the human cerebral cortex. Nor are we disappointed.

In the same year during which "A Martian Odyssey" appeared (1934), John W. Campbell's "Twilight" was published. An admonitory science-fiction tale, it might have been called "A Temporal Odyssey" and have fulfilled the promise of that title. The story tells of a human being who in A.D. 3059 travels seven million years into the future, is horrified and saddened by what he finds, and hastily attempts to return to his own time. A miscalculation brings him back too far: the time traveler finds himself not in his time but ours, and we are thereby able to learn of his experiences.

By 1934, Campbell had already cast a wary eye on some contemporary technological "advances," and his story thematically questions humankind's ability to remain in control of its technological servitors. His time traveler finds human beings in the far distant future, but they are "little men—bewildered—lost." He sees them "stand about, like misshapen men with huge heads. But their heads contain only brains. They had machines that could think—but someone had turnd them off. . .and no one knew how to start them again. . . .[While they had their thinking machines, they had no need for minds, and] they were turned off, too, and [the pitiful human beings] just haven't thought since then."

The most significant words in this passage reveal the meaning of mentality as most science fiction treats it. The time traveler says "only brains" and implies the absence of active minds; he tells us that the human beings of the future "just haven't thought" and implies no dysfunction beyond the failure to use the cerebral cortex. In "Twilight," then, we recognize cortical activity as the final cause of our species' evolution. Thematically, the story demands that such activity never stop, not even when—or especially when—human mentality can devise machines to perform the proper functions of the mind.

Yet, for all its emphasis on the potentiality of the human mind, science fiction cautions us about the preeminence of mentality as an evolutionary goal. Fredric Brown's "Arena" was repopularized by the *Star Trek* episode in which Jim Kirk refuses to take the life of the leader of humanity's most capable enemy. In the original story (1944), a hopeless battle between humankind and an awesome armada from the deeps of space is interrupted by an "entity." After informing the human protagonist that the impending war would weaken both adversaries irrevocably, so that even the victors could never continue their evolutionary progress, the entity identifies itself:

I am the end of evolution of a race so old the time can not be expressed in words. . . .A race fused into a single entity, eternal—. . .such as your primitive race might become. . . .I—to your limited understanding—am and am not real. My existence is mental and not physical.

"Arena" dramatizes the evolutionary end, not just the process. In its own telepathic "words," an absolute mentality, independent of time, space, and even individual personality as we know it, informs us that evolution for mentality—the path we humans evidently have taken—has been fully achieved by at least one sapient race.

In the context of this essay, Tom Godwin's "Cold Equations" (1954) is a companion piece to "Arena." Although the specific plots, characters, and settings differ and the earlier story seems optimistically naive while the later one embodies a thematic statement so admonitory that it is almost a "message" instead of a theme, the underlying retrospective thematic statements about mentality are very nearly identical.

"The Cold Equations" is a literary exploration of the coldness or indifference of physical laws to the situation of humankind. In Godwin's story, three laws require that a young woman ignorant of them be jettisoned into the cold vacuum of space. The first is that the interstellar cruiser on which she was a passenger can make only the tiniest of alterations in its tight schedule. If alterations were permitted even infrequently, they would "produce a confusion and uncertainty that would wreck the complex interdependence between old Earth and new worlds of the frontier." Should an emergency arise on a planet near the cruiser's route but one at which no stopover is scheduled, the cruiser momentarily drops out of hyperspace and launches an Emergency Dispatch Ship (EDS).

Conduct in those tiny vessels is governed by the second law: "*Any stowaway discovered in an EDS shall be jettisoned immediately following discovery.*" The third law, an immutable physical one, is the reason for the second; the EDS has only the minimum amount of chemical fuel needed to transport it, its pilot, and the authorized cargo from the hyperdrive cruiser to the planetary surface which is its destination. This third law contains two cold equations: "*h amount of fuel will power an EDS with a mass of m safely to its destination,*" and "*h amount of fuel will not power an EDS with a mass of m plus x safely to its destination.*" Unfortunately, the young woman who stows away on the EDS in order to see her brother is merely the *x*. If the pilot is to deliver the emergency supplies, *x* (120 pounds of human being) has to go. After a narrative that elicits our sympathy for the naive young woman and a sense of "It isn't fair!" for the law of physics that determines her fate, she is jettisoned.

These two stories cause us to question the benefit that increased mentality ostensibly brings to human beings. In the first, we are confronted by a being of pure mind who nevertheless destroys an entire sapient race. In the second, we are confronted by an advanced, logically based technology that reduces a human being to an $x$ in a cold equation.

Exploring the value of increased mentality, we find in these stories an unsettling paradox: while reason and logic and other manifestations of the human cerebral cortex are made to reign supreme, these same cortical qualities do not produce solutions that permit the continued existence of either an entire intelligent race or a single innocent young woman. And, still exploring the value of mentality, something within us does not merely ask but demands to know why. Other works of science fiction elicit the same question.

In Jerome Bixby's "It's a *Good* Life" (1953), the mutant Anthony has a strange mentality, horrifying to most readers and to all the other characters in the story. Still, we cannot know of his consciously controlled telekinetic and other abilities without admitting, rationally at least, that his mentality is superior to that of the other, normal human characters. In Damon Knight's "The Country of the Kind" (1955), we find a reasonable culture that refuses to punish persons who commit crimes which originate in some dysfunction for which the "criminal" is not responsible. Yet this form of criminal justice is humane only in the light of reason; in another light—one that allows perception by the non-cerebral parts of the brain—it appears unconscionably cruel.

As we read more science fiction, we begin to notice a prevailing negative judgment of any mentality that is not integrated with instinctual, emotional, and "gut" responses. Asimov's Susan Calvin (*I, Robot*, 1950) is one of the unforgettable characters in science fiction, but she is unforgettable not so much because of her awesome mentality as because of the feminine, human, and emotional aspects of her person that she has suppressed and repressed for the benefit of clear thinking. The sadness that is part of our response to Simak's dogs (*City*, 1952) comes not from a sense of their loneliness on an Earth without humans but from a recognition that most of their difficulties arise from their wholesale adoption of the rational good intentions of their absent human masters.

Although science fiction tells us that we see ourselves evolving toward a mentality that is the product of the cerebral cortex, it also tells us that this sort of mentality is by itself deficient. Marion Zimmer Bradley's novels about Darkover have at their thematic center an urgent directive: if we are as a species to evolve and truly benefit from our evolution, we must as individuals integrate the invaluable heritage and power of our brain-cores with the processes that take place in our cerebral cortices. Anne McCaffrey's best-selling novels about the people and dragons who inhabit Pern contain a similar theme. Central to the well-being of human and dragon in her writing is the process of Impression, which forges a bond of love and communication between dragon and rider. This bond is, for real human beings, an ideal; McCaffrey's verbal art is imitative of human action as it *should* be. Even so, the bonding of her characters is based on fact, on the instinctive occurrence known to biologists as "imprinting." This real phenomenon takes place probably because the brain-core makes it happen; yet among the more intelligent species its effects are intermingled processes in which conscious directives of the cortex play important roles.

Whether or not human evolution is teleological is a moot question, in part because evolution is a process that occurs almost outside human time. Except culturally, *H. sapiens* has not evolved noticeably during the past half-million years, but in the several millions of years before *H. sapiens* appeared on this planet, some hominid did change—or else we could not be.

We are. We affect almost every natural process that takes place on our world. We are very probably affecting our own evolution. If, as science-fiction writers and compilers of dictionaries seem to agree, we are directing our evolution along vectors made possible by the layer of tissue that envelops the largest portion of the human brain, we should be as wary of what we designate mentality as we are wary of what, technologically, our mentality has already brought to pass.

In a science-fiction story not yet written, they—the ones we call Neanderthals, the ones whose cranial capacity a hundred millenia ago was already comparable with ours today—return.[3] This is their home-world, after all, but they find it devoid of human life. There remain artifacts, of course, some greater even than the peculiar wall in eastern Asia, so they infer that the other human life had, for a time at least, flourished and waxed strong. Impelled by curiosity, several of them look for some preserved specimen of the other human beings. When one finds it, he takes the corpse in its container to the biologist among them. After only forty minutes of cranial dissection, she understands, and to her colleagues mindspeaks what has since become a racial epitaph:

"Hypertrophy of the cerebral cortex. How sad."

## Notes

1. This essay contains no formal, scholarly identification of passages quoted because pagination differs according to which text of a story or novel one has

at hand. With two exceptions, the shorter fiction I quote or refer to is reprinted in *The Science Fiction Hall of Fame, Volume 1*, edited by Robert Silverberg (New York: Avon Books, 1970). The exceptions are Ursula K. Le Guin's "The Word for World is Forest," which first appeared in *Again, Dangerous Visions*, edited by Harlan Ellison (Garden City, New York: Doubleday, 1972), and which is currently available as a paperback published by Berkley Publishing Corporation; and Gordon R. Dickson's "Dolphin's Way," which originally was published in *Analog* in 1964 and which is reprinted in *Gordon R. Dickson's SF Best* (New York: Dell Publishing Co., Inc., 1978). The longer fiction I quote or refer to is, or recently has been, in print in paperback editions. It seems appropriate to cite this material here, since a score or more of footnotes which merely identify titles and publishers would be at best distracting in the text.

2.  I use the unscientific but descriptive term "brain-core" to denote those places in our heads where undeniably important, yet for the most part not conscious, activities take place, if in fact physio-neurological phenomena can be located. Were I to use either *midbrain* or *brainstem* exclusively, I would be inaccurate; were I to use both, my sentences would grow cumbersome. Since there is much debate about the physiological location of love, instinct, fear, and other such phenomena, and since accuracy in scientific nomenclature would require that I use *hindbrain*, too, I trust that readers will not misinterpret the generalized label "brain-core." For more painstaking accuracy and for the scientific basis on which my biological exposition depends, I refer readers to the bibliography supplemental to this chapter.

3.  Only the Neanderthals' departure, return, discovery, and "mindspeaking" are proto-fictional. The Neanderthals themselves were real; recent research and deliberation find them to be *H. sapiens*, like ourselves, and unlike us only in the sense that they are an extinct ethnic group. Indeed, if one wants, it is possible to attribute to the Neanderthals a brain statistically larger than our own.

# IV

# Philosophy in *Star Trek* and Problems about Persons

Surely the themes, concerns, and warnings presented by van der Bogert and Arbur in Part III are appropriate for our culture and era. We are reluctantly becoming familiar with "species death" and ecological crisis after crisis. Perhaps equally reluctantly, many of us have begun to recognize the need to reassess ourselves (and/or our species) and our place in what we think of as "our" environment. We are finding it necessary to integrate the several aspects of what seem to be ourselves. Too often we have moved to extremes, emphasizing one aspect to the exclusion of others. Certainly, it would seem, it is time to recognize the affective side of being human.

These concerns relate to the enduring philosophical (and totally practical) question of what it is "to be a *person*": what constitutes "human nature" or "personhood"? What is it to possess a personal identity, self? Human individuality? Human individuality in community? How does one know and relate to the other, that which is not self?

These questions and the answers to some of them permeate the chapters of this volume. However, they have a special relevance for Parts III, IV, and V.

Dorothy Atkins holds that the *Star Trek* phenomenon is derived from what Stanislaw Lem called SF's "genological indefiniteness" and "the profound philosophical concepts" that give *Star Trek* its unity. *Star Trek* offers hope in human abilities and existence that inspires its audiences; human nature is reappraised and found adequate to meet the moral problems and challenges that it confronts.

Human beings, Atkins believes, are basically philosophical. Being curious and more than creatures of instinct, they seek and need ethical guidelines, especially as they face new situations in a changing world. Various segments of *Star Trek* dramatize instances of enduring moral problems in new settings. These present the moral and epistemological problems associated with various attitudes toward innocence and knowledge (as embodied in Kirk, Spock, and Vejur); ontological problems of the self or soul (in the complementary trilogy, Kirk, Spock, and McCoy); problems of immortality, and free will, as well as other problems of fundamental importance to human beings. When the television scripts, films, and other literature are considered as a whole, Atkins feels, a consistent form of a higher humanism that presents humanity or human nature in a balanced perspective emerges. Humans in the literature as a whole come through as "whole beings." Atkins identifies and elaborates seven major premises upon which she holds Roddenberry's "Star Trek philosophy" is constructed. According to Atkins, this new humanism, dramatically struggling with and successfully facing continuing philosophical problems, constitutes the strength, the appeal, and the unity of the *Star Trek* phenomenon.

Richard Double finds the two dominant theories for "being a person" to be Cartesianism and materialism. Working from this premise, he proves that the features essential for being a person are absent from his imaginary planet, which is populated by humanoid life forms. Using "evidence" from accepted scientific brain studies, the tenets of scientific realism, and other "obviously sensible" data sources, Double's procedures seem formally sound, but his conclusion is disturbing, especially when his imaginary planet becomes uncomfortably familiar.

While Double is illustrating the logical technique for holding a negative thesis without falling into logical inconsistency, his argument is appropriate for both philosophic discussions and science fiction studies. Through it, Double warns us about the adequacy of our dominant theories concerning "being a person." Those who build

SF stories, scenarios, scientific discourse, or philosophical discussions on a given theory would do well to assess the theory on the basis of its cost. Does it, for example, exclude aspects of our basic reality, even our personhood? Does the theory lend itself to support, or does it undercut the structure on which it is built? Does the theory account for that which we consider to be real? If the theory does not serve satisfactorily as an explanatory base, does not fill the purpose for which it was adopted, should we not revise the theory or devise a more adequate and appropriate one?

# Star Trek: A Philosophical Interpretation

## DOROTHY ATKINS

Although *Star Trek* was written in separate episodes by such writers as Jerome Bixby, Gene L. Coon, Harlan Ellison, David Gerrold, and Theodore Sturgeon, it has been considered an integrated work, largely because of the editorial control exercised by its creator, Gene Roddenberry. Roddenberry's *Star Trek Guide*, described by Stephen Whitfield, in *The Making of Star Trek*, clearly delineated for writers and directors the major premises of the series. It even included operational procedures for the starship and individual dossiers for the crew. By *Star Trek*'s third year, when Roddenberry as executive producer did not maintain script control, his fundamental premises were so well formulated that everyone associated with *Star Trek* understood what incidents or characteristics would be associated with the series or individual crew members. This unity of theme and characterization can be seen still more clearly in the reruns that are viewed throughout the world and in James Blish's written versions of individual episodes. *Star Trek*'s coherence can be seen in its character relationships and development and its emphasis on the adventure of humanistic and scientific exploration.

Its unchanging fundamental unity probably is the primary reason why fans have vehemently opposed any major revisions in the crew or its mission and why Paramount Studios, recognizing this opposition, worked so hard to reassemble the original crew for the films. *Star Trek*'s fans have promoted the series for years, but ironically enough this popular

This essay was presented at The Midwest Modern Language Asssociation Conference in 1980. I am indebted to Adam Frisch and Tom Remington for their helpful suggestions.

impetus sometimes has worked against the overall creation. Roddenberry's artistic and philosophic statements often are overlooked because they have been written for a popular medium and enjoy popular acclaim. Like Charles Dickens, whose works frequently appeared in weekly or monthly installments, Roddenberry has been seen as a popularizer rather than an innovator.[1]

Star Trek's audience impact has been nothing less than phenomenal, especially among educated, affluent groups.[2] Today, more than a decade after its removal from the NBC schedule, it continues to attract science-fiction fans throughout the world. Novels and fanzines that utilize the Star Trek theme and characters are published and read by an ever-growing and widely divergent group.[3] Star Trek novels now comprise a large and wholly new body of literature; reruns of Star Trek episodes are credited with keeping alive an interest in space exploration during the cutbacks in NASA's program; and Roddenberry himself, in countless talks to college audiences during the 1970s, urged a continued interest in probing the frontiers of space. NASA acknowledged this influence by naming its first space shuttle Enterprise. Star Trek: The Motion Picture, released in 1979, has played to record crowds, received several awards, and has been featured nationally on cable TV. Star Trek II: The Wrath of Khan, released in 1981, was received with widespread cheers.

How can we account for this science-fiction phenomenon? What is Star Trek's appeal to such a wide variety of people in all age ranges and over such a long span of time? Part of its appeal is based in its science-fiction framework, that is, what Stanislaw Lem has called a "genological indefiniteness" that makes science fiction "supposedly not subject to the whole range of the criteria by which literary works are normally judged."[4] It is the fascinating diffuseness of science fiction as a genre that allows us to consider Star Trek as a literary creation and apply to it sociologic, mythic, or philosophic interpretations. The remainder of its appeal, I believe, is due to the profound philosophic concepts that permeate individual Star Trek episodes and unify the separate stories into a harmonious literary creation that depicts a future cosmology in which humans have achieved a deep understanding of themselves and the meaning of human existence. Star Trek's philosophical foundation is comprised of seven basic premises. It presents a future world very like our own in which moral problems are encountered and solved through a philosophy of nonviolent, rational humanism and a reappraisal of the basic nature of human essence.

*Star Trek*, of course, is not alone in presenting a future cosmology and philosophy in the guise of science fiction. The *Star Wars* saga also seems to be working in this vein, especially in its use of "the force," which governs lives and destinies. Indeed, science fiction in general has been described "like much medieval literature. . .not only didactic, but often awed, worshipful, and religious in tone."[5] Theodore Sturgeon also sees science fiction in this light, saying that "both forms of religion—the hierarchal, ritualistic structure, and the infinitely more personal theolepsy, have been a part of science fiction from the beginning." According to Sturgeon it is this aspect of science fiction that most appeals to him:

Religion and science fiction are no strangers to one another, and the willingness of science fiction writers to delve into it, to invent and extrapolate and regroup ideas and concepts in this area as in all other areas of human growth and change, delights me and is the source of my true love for the mad breed.[6]

In creating moral dilemmas that need to be resolved by using a basic philosophy that has been built into the original conception, Roddenberry, then, has been working in a well-established and recognized manner. Perhaps Gerald Heard has best described Roddenberry's methods when he writes that science fiction "does not merely extrapolate inventions. . .it makes real persons and makes them develop psychological maturity under the pressure of unsuspected portentous events." Science-fiction creators like Roddenberry, according to Heard, "take one by one all the rising issues wherein it is clear that within a few years scientific research and applied science must demand new interpretations of the traditional mores," and help us to develop a new ethical philosophy.[7] Roddenberry's established philosophy for *Star Trek* does this in individual episodes of the series as well as in the novel and film versions.

We probably can assume safely that most humans are naturally philosophical. We are interested in the origin and pattern of our lives; we are profoundly curious about the future and worry about the influence of the past; we ponder the possible existence of other sentient beings; and we are concerned that our existences have significance. Moreover, we recognize the need for ethics to guide our lives, simply because we are not merely creatures of instinct; indeed, we recoil from being considered animalistic.

There are seven basic premises in Roddenberry's *Star Trek* philosophy:[8]

first, humans are not flawed because of any actual or metaphorical fall; they are simply an immature species that will evolve through humanistic development. Under this premise, we shall progress not by any natural selection but by learning tolerance and understanding. Kirk's statements that "we've learned not to wage war" or "kill one another" continually reiterate the *Enterprise*'s basic mission to seek knowledge and foster understanding. Roddenberry assumes that our physical evolution is complete—humans in *Star Trek*'s world appear and behave much like present humans. Because of this, Roddenberry can propose philosophical solutions to the problems that beset us now—ignorance, intolerance, war—without positing qualities that we do not now possess. Even Spock, as half-man, half Vulcan, is endowed with characteristics we not only recognize as our own but can actually empathize with.

The second major premise is that we have recognized our technology has the potential to destroy us, and we have survived as the Vulcans have by developing a relatively peaceful, harmonious, unified planet. Roddenberry envisions further wars on earth, wars like the one described in "Space Seed" in which superhumans have been produced through genetic engineering. He also envisions political tensions like those described in his novelized version of *Star Trek: The Motion Picture*, tensions created by the "new humans" on Earth who are critical of Starfleet's aims and values.[9] Yet in Roddenberry's world, humans have survived these wars and tensions and learned that strife is not a satisfactory answer to human problems. Kirk repeatedly insists that humanoid civilizations can survive only in an atmosphere of tolerance and nonviolence. Of course this is highly ironic coming from the captain of a fully armed space cruiser, but that is precisely Roddenberry's point. In this and when he poises the serene Organians between a bellicose Kirk and the Klingons in "Errand of Mercy," he uses situational irony to emphasize the importance of peace. We, and they, finally realize that the peacemakers are not impotent as suspected but profoundly powerful and superior in all ways. The advanced Organians use their powers to promote harmony and justice.

The third premise in *Star Trek*'s philosophy is that different races, religions, and cultures are not to be feared but valued. Consider how important Vulcan IDIC philosophy is to *Star Trek*. This philosophy of infinite diversity in infinite combinations is explained by Spock in "Is There In Truth No Beauty?" and we see Spock endeavoring to live by this concept in a world of humans whom he often does not understand.

Humans in *Star Trek*'s world, however, are not yet adept at following Vulcan IDIC philosophy. Spock repeatedly and patiently shows McCoy and Kirk how the philosophy works, thereby continually reiterating it to the audience. In fact, one of the conventions of the series involves an epilogue in which human and Vulcan differences are harmonized in comradely banter.

Roddenberry's fourth premise is related to his third: no one has the right to interfere in the development of others. This is the reason behind the Prime Directive. If differences are valued and growth through understanding promotes individual maturity in knowledge and tolerance, then moral improvement is taking place all over the galaxy. Rarely is the Prime Directive violated, and only after some argument among the ship's officers.

All of this could pertain to humans even if they never left Earth, but Roddenberry holds a fifth premise: humans belong in space. When a crewman in "The Corbomite Maneuver" wonders what he is doing there, we are brought to understand that contact with the alien unknown is necessary and can be enjoyable. Roddenberry's sixth major premise is based on this belief—space is our final frontier. We hear this in the voice-over to the introduction to each episode, and in Kirk's answer to Sulu's request for direction at the end of *Star Trek: The Motion Picture*. When Sulu asks, "Which direction Captain?" and Kirk answers, "Out there, thataway," the audience cheers. No doubt this basic premise appeals strongly to humans today. Roddenberry seems to believe that space exploration will benefit Earth as European exploration of the New World did in the fifteenth and sixteenth centuries. Roddenberry, however, insists that his future explorers will not repeat the mistakes of earlier adventurers and therefore establishes the Prime Directive. Roddenberry further believes that humankind will be improved by space exploration. While the voyages of the *Enterprise* benefit the federation, it is humanity, even on the starship, that is improved. For example, the Horta, an alien rocklike creature, is not destroyed once it is understood; the Gorn, a huge lizardlike alien, is not killed because Kirk and his watching crew understand the bestiality of combat. Even Kirk repeatedly tries to accept Spock's more philosophical views on combat.

Roddenberry's seventh and final philosophical premise is his most important: humans will survive. In episode after episode Roddenberry glorifies humanism. Human tolerance, intuition, and insistence on harmony constantly are shown to be superior to the qualities of aliens and machines. It is, in Roddenberry's philosophy, our noble qualities of goodness, decency, and integrity that assure our endurance. While *Star Trek* does provide scoundrels like Harry Mudd and enemies like the Klingons for its audiences, the majority of episodes show humans encountering alien forces or machines and triumphing through compassion and understanding rather than fear and force. *Star Trek: The Motion Picture* is the culmination of this idea. The most advanced technology in the universe without the human element can only go so far before it asks, "Is this all there is?" The cosmic union Decker achieves with Vejur through the Ilya probe signals the triumph of humanism in the cosmos. That is why the audience cheers when Kirk tells Sulu, "Out there, thataway." The human adventure is indeed just beginning. Roddenberry's insistence on the superiority of humanism appears in all the episodes. The *Enterprise*'s enemies consistently succumb to the dominance of human qualities. In "The Savage Curtain," or "Day of the Dove," for example, whenever good is challenged with evil, the evil is vanquished through simple human emotions that can be shared with others. Perhaps the most remarkable instance of this universality of shared human qualities is shown in "Balance of Terror," when, at the end of a carefully waged strategic battle, the Romulan commander tells Kirk, "In another reality I could have called you friend." The concepts that grow out of these basic philosophic premises can be found in Roddenberry's original *Star Trek Guide*. They support the entire literary and philosophic framework of Roddenberry's creation, and they force us to consider it as an integrated whole.

Roddenberry's world is two centuries into our future. Earth's conflicts have been solved, there are few wars, little racial intolerance, and most medical and technological problems have been solved. In *The Making of Star Trek*, Whitfield tells us that if NBC had not objected, the *Enterprise* crew would have been half female with a nonwhite captain, a woman as second-in-command, and several aliens like Spock.[10] Roddenberry thus postulates a future Earth on which equality and tolerance are predominant. All humanoids found in the galaxy are believed to have equally significant opportunities for improvement. By order of the Prime Directive, no culture is interfered with, except in unusual circumstances.

Why does Roddenberry postulate all this? In the past five centuries exploitation and despoilation have usually followed exploration. In *Star*

*Trek* Roddenberry gives us a galaxy to explore, millions of class-M planets from which to absorb a myriad of ideas, foods, rituals, arts, and sciences, but because of the Prime Directive no exploitation or despoilation. Indeed, the entire series involves seeking out new life and new civilizations and *not* exploiting them.

In two of the first three televised episodes, "Charlie X" from a story by Roddenberry, and "Where No Man Has Gone Before," Roddenberry conveys the idea that humans themselves can become alien to their own species, if they misunderstand and exploit special attributes. Charlie X and Gary Mitchell have unusual psionic powers that they do not understand and misuse. While the idea that power tends to corrupt is familiar to us, Roddenberry extrapolates this idea to show that the alienness thus produced is the real source of potential evil, not the power itself. Although, during her planned five-year mission, the *Enterprise* will encounter other beings with varying attributes and powers, this does not mean that those with more power will conquer the others. In Roddenberry's philosophy, misused power will be negated largely through its bearer's own actions. *Star Trek* thus emphasizes the truth that evil forces are not vanquished by a similar show of force, but rather destroy themselves. In the end the essential human qualities of compassion, tolerance, and integrity will triumph.

From the beginning of his series, then, Roddenberry formulated basic ethical concerns for his plots. "Plato's Stepchildren," shown near the end of the series, also considers the problem of the misuse of extrasensory power. Alexander the dwarf is cruelly enslaved by the step-Platonians, not because his size makes him different, but because they have extraordinary telekenesis. When the *Enterprise* crew acquires similar power, Kirk does not destroy the step-Platonians as Alexander urges but teaches them the cruelty of their ways and removes Alexander from the corrupt world. In "Return to Tomorrow," another episode dealing with the misunderstanding and misuse of special powers, Sargon and Thalassa experience the excitement of corporeal senses when they borrow the bodies of Kirk and Dr. Ann Mulhall. Because they understand the danger of such borrowing, however, they use their incredible powers to exist eternally as disembodied essences. "The Lights of Zetar" learn a similar ethical principle when they attempt to usurp the body of Lieutenant Mira Romaine to support their own existence. In these and other episodes Roddenberry reiterates his beliefs about human responses to the possession of tremendous power. In his future cosmology basic ethical principles dictate that no one individual should destroy another, however different, but rather learn to live in reasonable harmony.

In those *Star Trek* episodes dealing with the problem of war Roddenberry confronted the most basic ethical issues of human life. During the second season of the series, two episodes written by Roddenberry, "A Private Little War," and "The Omega Glory," comment eloquently on the futility of war. In "The Savage Curtain," also written by Roddenberry, the Excalibans pit the forces of good against evil in order to judge the nature and value of each. They are confused when good and evil both use forceful methods, but they "perceive the difference" when Kirk points out that he has fought for the lives of his crew while evil has fought for selfish gain.

Roddenberry obviously used the *Star Trek* format to speak out on what he considered to be significant moral problems not just of the moment, but for all time. In "A Taste of Armageddon," Kirk ends the computer war between Eminiar VII and Vendikar, and Roddenberry implies that for generals and the high command war may be nothing more than a complex game. He suggests that when they too bleed and die, they may find ways to create peace. In "Day of the Dove," when the Klingons and the *Enterprise* crew are trapped in eternal warfare with crude weapons by an entity that feeds on violent emotions, we contemplate the existence of an entity within ourselves that causes us to hate, a force that takes control of us and forces us to violence and evil unless, as the episode suggests, we learn to laugh at ourselves and drive the entity away. This theme is continued in "The Squire of Gothos," when Squire Trelane, General, Retired, lover of eighteenth-century humans because they are predatory, respecter of the warrior tradition of the English, the French, and Napoleon, is shown to be in actuality only a small child. As he stamps his foot and objects to the suspension of his cruel treatment of the *Enterprise* crew because, as he says, "I was winning, I was winning," we are forced to laugh at our absurd predilection for war.

But a question remains for us: can we control our impulses to wage war and win at any cost? Through the character of Spock who adheres to Surak's rational, nonviolent Vulcan philosophy, Roddenberry seems to say, "Yes, of course." One episode, also written by Roddenberry, makes this quite clear. In "Bread and Circuses," the *Enterprise* crew encounters a civilization based on that of ancient Rome but possessing technological advances that allow those in power to televise and commercialize their gladiator contests. This immoral culture is opposed by a group of "sun worshippers" whose religion confuses the crew until Uhura explains that they are not worshipping the sun but the son of God. Roddenberry thus implies that the seeds of imperial Rome can continue into the future but that a basic, nonviolent Christian ethos—with which Kirk, Spock, and McCoy have sympathized during the episode—is an effective counterforce.

While Roddenberry suggests that a return to basic Christian principles and the adoption of a Vulcanlike rational philosophy will help to deter moral disintegration, he is uncertain of the desirability of paradise. Certain episodes entirely reject the idea of paradise while others emphasize its benefits for humans. "The Way to Eden," for example, leads to an acid-soaked garden where the hippie Adam dies from his first bite of an apple. In "This Side of Paradise" the Sandoval colony is affected by spores that provide health, peace, and love. Spock greatly enjoys their effects, but Kirk believes, "a man stagnates if he has no ambition," and he argues that "maybe we don't belong in paradise, maybe we're meant to struggle." If Kirk is to be taken seriously, and he usually is, Roddenberry is suggesting through him that an Edenic paradise during life is not necessarily good. In still another paradise episode, "The Apple," the *Enterprise* crew rescues the people of Vaal from their god who keeps them in a garden where there is no death, no disease, and no growth. Spock insists that the Prime Directive should be obeyed, but Kirk and McCoy argue that the people are not living but stagnating, that it is not a viable culture, and the Prime Directive, therefore, does not apply. Spock is not convinced, however, especially when violence is introduced, and he reminds Kirk and McCoy of the story of Eden. Although McCoy jokes about Spock's satanic appearance to restore harmony at the end of the episode, Spock's words remind us of the allusion. He is not convinced that Kirk is right.

Spock, in contrast to Kirk, seems to find paradise desirable. In "This Side of Paradise" Spock himself has savored the joys of innocence at the Sandoval colony. Although he agrees with Kirk that the *Enterprise* crew cannot stay in the colony, the episode ends with his sad statement that there, for the first time in his life, he had been happy. If Spock is to be taken seriously, and he also usually is, Roddenberry is suggesting through him that ambitious striving for knowledge may smother one's capacity to experience the intrinsic value of simple emotions. Through the character of Spock Roddenberry is able to repeat this point in his novel of

*Star Trek: The Motion Picture.* Spock, like Vejur, has sought ultimate knowledge in rational logic only to arrive at the final query: "Is this all that I am. . .Is there not more?" After his devastating mindmeld with Vejur, Spock expresses to Kirk the value of "simple feeling," and Vejur through its final transcendence with Decker apparently achieves that capacity that Vaal's people presumably have lost when their Eden changes. Balance is the key: Vejur has lost touch with humans during its cosmic journey, and Vaal's people have never developed the human desire for knowledge. Kirk, too, is given the opportunity to experience the balancing effect of paradise in "The Paradise Syndrome." In this episode he finds the joys of innocence when his memory lapse frees him from his striving as a starship captain. He returns from Miramanee and her Edenic world as Spock had from Sandoval—sadly. The conflicting tensions produced in the paradise episodes cause us to wonder about the direction of our struggles for discovery. Kirk, Spock, and Vejur in their divided attitudes toward innocence and knowledge dramatize a basic moral and epistemological problem that has been pondered by philosophers since the early Greeks.

Perhaps the most intriguing aspect of Roddenberry's *Star Trek* philosophy involves the ontological problem of the self, or soul. For many people, the central focus of *Star Trek* is the triune nature of the chief officers, Kirk, Spock, and McCoy. In their interaction and interdependence, it is possible to consider them as one entity, as the unified aspects of the self or soul. Kirk, the decision maker, represents will and intuition; Spock, supplier of logic and information, represents reason; and McCoy, provider of healing and compassion, represents emotion. These divisions of the self, or soul, have been widely recognized in the Western world. Philosophers and psychologists continue to ponder the divisions of the human essence, and Roddenberry's *Star Trek* format pursues this philosophic problem. In nearly every episode the tensions between Spock and McCoy as reason and emotion are mediated by Kirk as will.

To further complicate and make fascinating the use of the aspects of the self or soul, Roddenberry also posits the threefold conflict in one character, Spock. We as viewers can see various aspects of the self warring in three individuals and in a single individual. The conflict can thus be verbalized and communicated when experienced by the top officers, yet internalized and felt when it is manifest in Spock. It is Roddenberry's recognition of the conflict between emotion, reason, and will that rescues the series from becoming a mindless adventure of surface conflict. Roddenberry's formula places the major tension of the action within the human self, or soul, which accounts for some of the enormous popularity of Spock in whom the conflict is most strained. As part Vulcan, part human, Spock's reason and emotion are in constant battle. His will remains on the side of reason but not always. In "The Naked Time," "This Side of Paradise," and "Amok Time," his struggles between reason and emotion become more pronounced. Will and clear judgment ultimately prevail, but the pain and drama of the episodes indicate how great the tension is.

Roddenberry could not have developed this fascinating device of the conflict of the self, or soul, for entertainment purposes alone—the show's "cerebral" nature led to its cancellation. Rather, he seems to have wanted to use television drama as a vehicle for expressing the profound internal conflicts suffered by humans. Through the resolved tensions in each episode, Roddenberry seems to suggest that there is hope for those humans who constantly battle within and among themselves for understanding and survival in a frequently alien universe. If Kirk, Spock, and McCoy, so individual and widely different, can interact and can maintain humanistic values in their galactic voyages, we too can strive successfully to maintain them on Earth. When we see Spock internally harmonizing emotion, reason, and will, then we feel that we as individuals may also learn how to achieve this essential psychic balance.

Several key episodes dealing with the basic ontological concept of the self, or soul, force us to confront serious moral issues. In "The Enemy Within," through a transporter malfunction Kirk experiences a doubling, which produces a good Kirk, fearless and compassionate but without the drive for leadership, and an evil Kirk, afraid and violent but with the ruthless ambition of a starship captain. In this dramatization of the philosophical problem of human nature, it is Spock who explains to the good Kirk that he must take the ruthless, violent Kirk back within himself in order to restore his true essence. Again the series conveys the idea that evil does not need to be destroyed but understood and controlled. In "The Alternative Factor" and "Mirror, Mirror" the *Enterprise* crew encounters parallel universes that echo the divisions between good and evil in the human realm. Again the alternate images representing a darker side to existence are not destroyed but understood and tolerated so that cosmic balance can be maintained.

Even the *Enterprise*'s transporter sometimes operates as a moral device, prompting us to question problems of personality definition or integration. McCoy continually objects to having his atoms scattered about the universe and wonders whether his atoms have been reassembled into new patterns similar on the surface but with internal changes in his basic essence. This is so much a part of his characterization that it is continued in *Star Trek: The Motion Picture*. He mutters about stepping into the transporter and complains about engineers who always want to change things. Given Roddenberry's basic philosophy, this is not surprising. Philosophers have argued McCoy's grumblings, and we have experienced the legal ramifications of this same problem when accused criminals claim, "I'm a different person now."

Roddenberry presents an equally difficult moral problem in his story, "Turnabout Intruder," which questions what happens to the self, or soul, when external bodies are changed. Dr. Janet Lester discovers a device that allows her to switch bodies with Kirk and become captain of the *Enterprise*. Ultimately she is forced to realize that an external change will not alter her essence, but until she does the crew goes through many painful deliberations in their attempt to judge the nature of each body's true essence. In an episode entitled "What Are Little Girls Made Of?" we are forced to ponder the existence of the soul if it is transferred to an android body. Dr. Korby creates a robot to house his self, or soul, after a terrible accident destroys his natural body. While Kirk, after his rescue, tells Spock, "Dr. Korby was never here," he has earlier urged the Korby android to "prove" that he is the Roger Korby that Christine Chapel knew and loved. The Korby android is torn between his two natures; he kisses his fellow android in a fond farewell but at the same time presses the phaser button to obliterate the androids that threaten the humans. Have his actions proved what his reasoning could not? Does Roger Korby's soul actually exist in the final moments? Christine's tears and Kirk's compassion certainly indicate that it has. A similar situation appears in the episode, "The Ultimate Computer." Dr. Richard Daystrom programs M-5 with his own brain engrams and thus creates a machine with a human personality and conscience. Roddenberry obviously is fascinated with the implications of this concept because he returns to it in *Star Trek: The Motion Picture*. M-5's dangerous adjustments to human essence are stopped when Daystrom's brain engrams respond to his humanistic arguments, but it remains unclear how Vejur will evolve. In a culture such as ours in which it is possible to transplant organs, chemically alter cells, implant mechanical devices in the human body, and clone antibodies and other human cells, the problem of where the self or soul resides and how it operates is especially troublesome.

"Return to Tomorrow" ponders a related problem, the possibility of disembodied entities and ultimate immortality for the self or soul in a noncorporeal mode. It is this form of existence that Sargon and Thalassa choose after discovering that existing in borrowed human bodies tempts them to enjoy overwhelming human desires and powers. "The Gamesters of Triskelion," "The Lights of Zetar," the Kelvins in "By Any Other Name," and the Medusan in "Is There In Truth No Beauty?" are similar disembodied essences that borrow human bodies for a time and demonstrate how conflicts between the external body and the inner self can lead to great suffering. The Medusan, housed temporarily in Spock's body, voices a profound philosophic awareness of each human's essential isolation as he delights in the sensuous joys of the body yet exclaims, "But oh, how lonely you are! How can you stand it?" The loneliness of human existence is further explored in "Requiem for Methuselah." Flint's gift of physical immortality alienates him from other humans.

Flint's very existence asks still another question: is the essence of genius—Flint is da Vinci, Napoleon, Mozart, "a hundred others"—transmitted through human agents or developed through time? By contrast "Wolf in the Fold" dramatizes the effects of a destructive essence transmitted through time and space into Jack the Ripper, Rejak, and others until imprisoned in the *Enterprise* and ejected into deep space. Roddenberry's attitude toward these opposing essences may be seen in the way they are presented. While the essence of genius remains with one human, Flint, through countless identities, the destructive essence moves from one body to another, suggesting that the positive, creative force is compatible with human nature while the evil force is tolerated only temporarily by any humanoid body. While it is true that these various episodes were written by different writers, the *Star Trek* format established in Roddenberry's *Star Trek Guide* assured that Roddenberry's basic principles would be maintained.

The disembodied entities and essences inhabiting the *Star Trek* world posit the possibility of an existence similar to the one described by the seventeenth-century philosopher Spinoza in which life is viewed *sub species aeternitatus*, "under the aspect of eternity": timeless, eternal and unchanging. And, in fact, Spinoza is mentioned in an early episode entitled "Where No Man Has Gone Before." Certainly his ethical system closely resembles that of Roddenberry's character, Surak the Vulcan, who explains his philosophy in "The Savage Curtain." Roddenberry's Surak, like Spinoza, advocates a nonviolent, rational philosophy based on understanding and control of the emotions that hold one in "human bondage."[11] Spock, advocating Surak's philosophy, thus voices Spinoza's rational doctrines when he attempts to persuade Kirk of their validity. Spinoza's eternal perspective, his insistence upon an existence *sub species aeternitatus*, is basic to *Star Trek*. Indeed, all science fiction does this. By giving us a window in the future through which we may contemplate fundamental human fears and desires, science fiction gives us more than the opportunity to comment on moral problems in another setting. It gives us the more subtle and therefore more compelling opportunity to discover a true "final frontier" in which we may discover essential truths about our existence. Space as the final frontier may free us physically and intellectually, but Roddenberry's *Star Trek* format emphasizes that the philosophic freedom suggested by Spinoza is fundamental to human continuance.

The continuity of a humanistic ethos is important to remember when we consider another philosophic problem that *Star Trek* raises: the problem of free will when humans are able to create life. In "Requiem for Methuselah" Rayna, the android woman created by Flint, learns to love, to "choose," and to feel the fatal anguish of free will. Flint believes that he "owns" Rayna because he has created her, but Kirk insists that she should be allowed free choice. The moral problem that fascinates us when presented in a *Star Trek* episode must trouble us considerably when scientists today are creating new life forms and arguing legally about the ownership of these creations. The episodes dealing with "The Doomsday Machine," Nomad, "The Changling,"and M-5 with its human brain engrams, force us to consider, as Gerald Heard says, "issues wherein it is clear that within a few years scientific research and applied science must demand new interpretations of the traditional mores."[12] All of the episodes dealing with disembodied entities, machines, or life forms that have acquired consciousness and reasoning powers urge us to consider the nature of human rationality and essence. The thought-provoking issues raised by *Star Trek* apparently bothered NBC, as Whitfield explains in *The Making of Star Trek*, but they seem to form the basis for its continued appeal to countless humans who perceive the difficulty of maintaining human values in a technologically advanced culture.

Roddenberry continually returns to these issues of basic human nature. Again and again he focuses on the significance of basic human emotions clearly understood and controlled. It is, in fact, Spock and Vejur, the embodiments of great knowledge and rational logic, who acknowledge the absolute importance of humanistic belief in Rodden-berry's *Star Trek: The Motion Picture*. The philosophic and artistic credo expressed in this work is similar to that expressed in "Who Mourns For Adonais?" This episode is a confrontation between the ancient Greek beliefs that formed the basis of Western humanism (Apollo) and the scientific future (the men of the *Enterprise*). When Kirk persuades Lieu-tenant Palomas to reject Apollo's love because, as he states, "accept him and you condemn all of us to slavery," he appears to spurn the classic, pastoral past. He insists that humans must enter the scientific and tech-nologically advanced world of *Star Trek*, even though he agrees with McCoy that it wouldn't have hurt to "gather a few laurel leaves." But Kirk's advice, it should be noted, is weighted ironically with ancient humanistic wisdom. In a foreshadowing of Spock's emotional sick bay scene in *Star Trek: The Motion Picture*, when Spock clasps Kirk's hand to indicate that his and Vejur's answer lies in "this, simple feeling," Kirk clasps Lieutenant Palomas' hand and explains his philosophy: "give me your hand. . .feel human flesh against human flesh. . .remember who you are. . .a bit of flesh and blood in the cosmos. . .the only thing that's truly yours is the rest of humanity. . .that's where your duty lies."

## Notes

1. *Star Trek*'s unity of idea can be seen in such publications as David Gerrold, *The World of Star Trek* (New York: Ballantine, 1973), and Karin Blair, *Meaning in Star Trek* (New York: Warner Books, Inc., 1977).

2. For an analysis of science-fiction fans in general, see Albert I. Berger, "Science Fiction Fans in Socio-Economic Perspective: Factors in the Social Con-sciousness of a Genre," *Science-Fiction Studies* 4, pt. 3 (November 1977): 232-46. Berger explains that in England and America a high percentage of science-fiction fans have some college education and good incomes.

3. Novels and fanzines are too numerous to chronicle here; however, two sources are especially rewarding: Susan Sackett, *Letters to Star Trek* (New York: Ballantine, 1977), and Jacqueline Lectenberg; Sondra Marshak; and Joan Win-ston, *Star Trek Lives: Personal Notes and Anecdotes* (New York: Ballantine, 1975). Gerry Turnbull's *A Star Trek Catalog* (New York: Grosset & Dunlap, 1979) lists Star Trek clubs throughout the world and gives information on the Star Trek Welcommittee. Allan Asherman's *Star Trek Compendium* (New York: Simon & Schuster, 1981) is organized on the lines of the *Star Trek Concordance* by Bjo

Trimble (New York: Ballantine, 1976). Both of these are helpful in securing information about *Star Trek*.

4. Stanislaw Lem, "On the Structural Analysis of Science Fiction," *Science-Fiction Studies* 1, pt. 1 (Spring 1973): 26-33.

5. Joanna Russ, "Towards an Aesthetic of Science Fiction," *Science-Fiction Studies* 2, no. 6, pt. 2 (July 1975): 112-19. Russ was picking up on Darko Suvin's remark, made at the 1968 meeting of the Modern Language Association, that science fiction is "quasi-medieval."

6. Theodore Sturgeon, "Science Fiction, Morals, and Religion," in *Science Fiction, Today and Tomorrow*, ed. Reginald Bretnor (New York: Harper and Row, 1974), pp. 103, 112.

7. Gerald Heard, "Science Fiction, Morals, and Religion," in *Modern Science Fiction: Its Meaning and Its Future*, ed. Reginald Bretnor (Chicago: Advent Publishers, Inc., 1979), pp. 249, 258.

8. I am indebted to Robert F. Anderson with whom I've had many long conversations about *Star Trek*, for the delineation of the philosophical premises outlined below.

9. Gene Roddenberry, *Star Trek: The Motion Picture A Novel* (New York: Pocket Books, Inc., 1979), p. 40.

10. Roddenberry is not alone in having plans for science fiction thwarted by television or motion picture executives. See, for example, Richard Hodgens, "The Short Tragical History of the Science Fiction Film" in *The Other Side of Realism* ed. Thomas D. Clareson (Ohio: Bowling Green University Press, 1971), pp. 248-62; and Don Fabun, "Science Fiction in Motion Pictures, Radio and Television" in *Modern Science Fiction: Its Meaning and Its Future*, ed. Reginald Bretnor, pp. 43-70.

11. Spinoza, "Of Human Bondage," *Ethic*, Bk. 4, trans. William Hale White, 3d ed. rev. by Amelia H. Stirling (London: Duckworth, 1889).

12. Gerald Heard, "Science Fiction, Morals, and Religion," in *Modern Science Fiction: Its Meaning and Its Future*, ed. Reginald Bretnor (Chicago: Advent Publishers, Inc., 1979), p. 249.

# 8

## There Are No Persons

### RICHARD DOUBLE

Sometimes stating one's position on philosophical issues involves no appearance of paradox. Saying that one believes that God exists or that one does not believe that God exists seems equally "logical." One may even say that one believes value judgments are true or are not true. For other problems, however, defenders of the negative position must be more circumspect. The sceptic should not say that he *knows* that scepticism is true, nor should the solipsist say that *others* ought to accept solipsism.

One who proclaims that there is no freedom of will continues to act as if there is—in his own case at least. This apparent need to act *as if* one is free has been taken by some to be an adequate defense of freedom of will. This is incorrect, of course. If determinism of all human behavior is true and if this implies that no human actions are free, then this holds *a fortiori* for the actions of the critic of freedom while he is devising philosophical arguments against it. Hard determinism (as it is known) is expansive enough to encompass the necessity of the individual hard determinist to act as if freedom existed.

The philosopher who asserts that there are no persons faces problems similar to these. He should not *say* "I believe that there are no persons" since that sentence will be taken to entail the existence of at least one person, himself, and, thus, refute the statement. And as with freedom of the will, one who devises a strategy to show that there are no persons will be taken to have refuted that view since what else but a person could have devised a strategy or proposed an argument? This is also incorrect. If there are no persons, then *a fortiori* there is no such thing as someone's devising a strategy or proposing an argument, although there may be a rapid-fire succession of thoughts that create the illusion that a strategy has been devised or an argument proposed. It is easy to beg the question against a negative answer to certain philosophical problems, but one should be careful not to jump to pseudo-refutations.

On a planet much like Earth, hurtling somewhere through our galaxy, there exist humanoid forms that resemble human beings. Upon our inspection, the humanoids give every indication of being persons. Out of the soil of their planet they have constructed various artifacts like those found on Earth—buildings and bridges, computers and cyclotrons. To our ears the humanoids seem to praise their children and lovers and criticize their political leaders and football coaches. Yet communication and civilization notwithstanding, there are no persons here.

How can this be? Why are the humanoids not persons? If I place in front of us a being that looks like a person, feels like a person, sounds like a person, thinks like a person, and acts like a person, can I deny that it is a person? You don't program a computer or run a civilization with chopped liver, you know. An explanation of why the humanoids are not persons necessarily will be a fantastic one, but maybe not so fantastic.

Our explanation has three parts. The first will clarify what it is to be a person. The second and third together will show that the humanoids do not answer to the requisite specifications.

What sort of being would a thing have to be in order to count as a person? This question has been debated since the beginning of Earthling philosophy, and over the years there have evolved two major schools of philosophers, the Cartesian and the Materialist. Cartesians, so named after René Descartes, the French philosopher and creator of analytical geometry in the seventeenth century, believe that persons are immaterial minds ("souls") to which their physical bodies are somehow connected.[1] In this view, a person, strictly speaking, is his nonphysical mind wherein all his mental states occur, although his body, including the brain, causally interacts with the mind. Cartesians, who are sometimes called "dualists" for obvious reasons, typically hold with Plato that these nonspatial, nonphysical centers of consciousness are indestructable, thus providing both unified personal identity throughout time despite changes to the body and immortality after the body perishes.[2] The Cartesians think that each of us can intuitively prove the distinctness of mind and brain by scrutinizing our own consciousness and realizing how different it is from matter.

The Materialists, who are typically more observation oriented, put little stock in such intuition. Materialists build a theory of persons in the same way they would build a theory of physics, biology, or engineering—and with similar results. They hold that persons are their physical bodies (including the brain, of course) in the way that lightning flashes are discharges of electricity in the atmosphere or genes are molecules of nucleic acid.[3] In this view, persons are held to be continuous with the rest of the physical world as the most complex and subtle physical organisms on the phylogenetic scale. For the Materialist, the identity of a person over time is relative, no greater than the unity of any other living physical thing whose matter is constantly changing.[4]

The dispute between Cartesians and Materialists shows no sign of abating, and it would be hazardous even to guess which position is more popular among contemporary Earthling philosophers (not that it would prove anything, anyway).[5] For our purposes, we shall avoid choosing sides in this debate by providing a characterization of persons that both Cartesians and Materialists could accept. At the same time we may borrow from each theory in order to arrive at the most fundamental idea of what a person is.

The most obvious lesson that the Cartesians and Materialists have taught us is that persons are agents who possess rich, unified mental lives. A person does things, exists (whether absolutely or relatively) through time, and is the sort of thing that may be subject to praise and blame, rights and duties. A person thinks, believes, desires, wills, affirms, denies, dreams, sees colors, wishes, wonders, has emotion, feels sensation, and experiences self-consciousness.[6] A person is *someone*, a *self*, in philosophical parlance, a *substance* that retains its own identity while it changes its "accidental attributes." A person, in short, is a substance, whether structurally it turns out to be a nonphysical mind (with the Cartesians) or the physical body (with the Materialists).

Our reasoning that persons are agents and agents in turn are substances is aimed specifically at rejecting any view of persons as simply welters of events or processes. This does not prejudge the ultimate physicality or nonphysicality of the substances. It does emphasize that only substantial beings could *do* all the things that persons do—streams of physical or nonphysical events will not fill the bill. For example, the eighteenth-century Scottish philosopher David Hume held that the human mind is merely a stream of conscious events with no agent who has the conscious events.[7] By our lights, if Hume is correct, then there is no such thing as the human mind.

The task before us now is to explain why the humanoids do not answer to either the Cartesian or Materialist conception of persons.

We begin by showing why the humanoids are not persons in the sense of nonphysical Cartesian substances. Let us consider some remarkable medical research done on planet Earth. It has been discovered that sometimes epileptic seizures in humans can be reduced in severity by performing a brain bisection (commissurotomy) in which the connective tissue that permits the transmission of electrical charges between the two hemispheres of the cerebrum is severed.[8] The commissurotomy inhibits both the spread of the epileptic disorder and the communication of information across hemispheres. Although the mental abilities of the patients who were operated upon were largely unimpaired by the operations, careful testing disclosed some interesting exceptions.

If a small physical object like a key was placed in the patient's right hand, which he held behind his back, he could say what the object was. But if the object was placed in his left hand, also out of his visual field, he could not. If the fingers of one of his two hands placed behind his back was positioned in a certain way (for example, the number three), he could not duplicate that pose with his other hand. If a word was flashed on the left side of a screen so quickly that it was seen only as part of his left visual field (which is received by the right hemisphere), the patient would deny having seen the word. At the same time, however, if given a pencil in his left hand, which was kept out of sight, the patient would scrawl the word that was flashed to the right hemisphere. If a patient was given a different physical object in each hand while blindfolded and then, with the blindfold removed and the objects mixed with others in a pile before him, was asked to retrieve what was in his hands, each hand would search separately, rejecting the item that the other hand held while looking for the object it held. Finally, there seemed to be conflicting motivations within patients; one hand seemed to be trying to countermand the activity of the other.[9]

There seems to be mounting neurological evidence that mental activity in humans is not only lateralized but also localized. Artificial stimulation of the brain is now so sophisticated that brain scientists know what part to probe to make the patient experience certain colors. Radioactive glucose injected into the arteries of manic-depressives and tracked by x-rays discloses that the frontal lobes of their brains gobble a larger amount of blood sugar than the brains of non-manic-depressives.[10] There have been experiments in which impulses from one sensory modality have been switched over to receptors of another modality so that, for example, sounds may be "seen" or visual input may be "heard."

It is possible to argue in the face of this increasing evidence of lateralization and localization that there remains a unifying center of consciousness somehow underlying human mental activity.[11] This position, however, becomes increasingly implausible in light of the empirical data. Can we really say that there is one single consciousness involved, given the bizarre behavior shown by brain-bisected patients? If we do not maintain this, shall we say that there are two unified consciousnesses inside the human being (each associated with its own hemisphere) communicating and cooperating before bisection but now quarreling?[12] If we reject this alternative, then shall we say that somehow severing the connective tissue between the hemispheres of the brain creates two unified centers of consciousness where only one had existed earlier? None of these alternatives seems optimal. A better solution is to surrender the prescientific notion of unified centers of consciousness, as we have had to surrender such other prescientific notions as up/down and sunrise/sunset. What we have on this view is a plethora of mental activity associated with various sorts of brain functioning without any underlying unified center of consciousness that has the mental activity. Instead, some mental activity is brought about by this part of the brain, some is brought about by that part, all with no more unity than that which is provided by the brain's three pounds of protoplasm.[13]

By applying the above Earthling neurological evidence to our aforementioned humanoids, it follows that if the humanoids are persons, Cartesian or Materialistic substances, then they must be Materialistic substances. The Cartesian concept of persons as nonphysical substances requires that they possess unified centers of consciousness, and we have shown that the only unity of human (or humanoid) consciousness is the unity of the body. Perhaps it now can be shown that humanoid bodies cannot provide the required substantiality.

The Earthlings who support the philosophical theory known as Scientific Realism are the most recent heirs of a philosophical tradition, dating back to the Greek Atomists, that attempts to reduce the world around us to a combination of mere appearance and reality.[14] According to the Scientific Realist, there are no buildings, bridges, computers, cyclotrons, or, what is most important for us, humanoid bodies on the planet of the humanoids. We have *talked* as if there were with good reason, for if we were to confront what is real our species-wide sensory apparatus would give rise to that appearance. For the Scientific Realist, however, this appearance is illusion; our senses systematically cause us to believe that there are colored, shaped, textured, solid, enduring, macroscopic physical objects where there are none.

If the appearances that we would experience if we were on that planet are illusion, then what is reality? Scientific Realists disagree over whether or not reality throughout the universe should be conceived as subatomic particles, force fields, warped space-time, or some other esoteric entity, much as the ancient Greeks disagreed over whether or not reality was water, fire, air, or "the apeiron"—the indefinite.[15] Often Scientific Realists say, "Let the physicists figure *that* out." Scientific Realists do agree, however, that reality on the humanoids' planet is nothing like the good old-fashioned physical objects of common sense that we believe in on Earth.[16]

Why do Scientific Realists believe in such a strange picture of physical reality? Isn't it more sensible to hold that there exist both macroscopic physical objects and the bizarre entities of microphysics, so that the latter are simply the "building blocks" of the former?

For the Scientific Realist the answer does not lie simply in the disparity in "size." Although it is true that trillions of atoms are necessary to compose anything visible to the eye, this fact could be accommodated by imagining the microentities as little slivers of matter stacked tightly together. The problem is that reality at the level of specification that physics discloses is categorically different from common sense's conception of everyday physical objects. Atoms, for instance, are not simply little pieces of macroscopic physical objects. Atoms are mostly emptiness with strange things flying around them at breathtaking speeds, compelled by electrical charges. As the physicist/philosopher A. Eddington wrote, the combined bulk of the atoms that make-up my commonsense table amounts to less than one-billionth of the table's bulk.[17] The two levels of reality are so different that any explanation that allows us to avoid saying that the subatomic world miraculously coexists with macroscopic physical objects deserves consideration.

Happily, there is a familiar line of reasoning that is not only elegant and plausible in its own right but also permits us to avoid saying that the microworld and macroworld share a specious coexistence in the same space-time.[18] Consider the following case. You are lost in a desert without water and have begun to hallucinate. You look to the east and see an oasis, resplendent with pools of blue water and palm trees. You look to the west and experience a *qualitatively indistinguishable* mirage—that is, from where you stand the mirage and oasis appear identical. In the case of the mirage, you do not see a physical thing, since the mirage, *ex hypothesi*, results solely from your dehydrated condition. But for all that, you have not seen *nothing*—you are experiencing mental activity of a certain qualitative character. In philosophical parlance, you have mirage *sense-data*.

Now consider the oasis to the east. Since seeing the oasis is qualitatively indistinguishable to you from mirage sense-data, here, too, you have sense-data presented to you. The difference is simply that in seeing the oasis, your oasis sense-data are caused by the oasis, while your qualitatively indistinguishable mirage sense-data owe their existence to causes within your body.

When, in the case of veridical perception, your sense-data are caused by the oasis, is it necessary to ascribe to the oasis all the properties that your sense-data have, such as color, shape, texture, solidity, permanence? No. In fact, many philosophers of science maintain that one has not explained the phenomena at one level until they have been reduced to phenomena at another level that possess fundamentally different properties. Moreover, it is redundant to say that, for example, both your sense-datum and trees are green. How could you ever verify this ambitious claim, since an inspection of trees yields more green sense-data but does not disclose the tree itself? What we have here is a situation that calls for theory construction rather than naive reliance on prephilosophical common sense.

The Scientific Realist thinks that his theory complements the sense-data theory. The sense-data of oases (and, by parity of reasoning, visual and nonvisual sense-data of all other physical objects) are not caused by the macroscopic trees and pools of water of common sense but rather by bizarre collocations of the theoretical entities of physics, which are the real things that exist independently of experience. The color, shape, texture, solidity, permanence, and other commonsense properties of the physical world are only properties of our sense-data and hence do not exist independently of the perceivers. The Scientific Realist has pulled the commonsense properties out of the publicly observable world, relocated them within the private sense-data of observers, and left the world itself a truly bizarre place.

We are now in a position to say why there are no persons on the humanoids' planet. According to lateralization and localization evidence there is no unity of mental states, which is required by the Cartesian notion of a person as a unified, nonphysical center of consciousness. Instead, mental states are associated with brain activity in a decentralized way. If a person exists, that person must be the physical body (or brain) with which the mental activity is associated. But, according to Scientific Realism, there are no macroscopic bodies (or brains) existing on the humanoids' planet that could count as persons in the Materialistic sense characterized earlier. Thus, there are no persons on that planet.

All that exist on that planet are (1) strange scientific entities described by physicists, which give rise to the false belief that there are macroscopic commonsense physical objects, and (2) mental states that lawfully result from the interaction of various scientific entities. Owing to the laws of physics as they apply on that planet, these mental states occur in an orderly succession, thus giving the appearance of *agents* or *persons* who have them. In fact, the nature of some of the mental states, such as "I think, therefore, I am,"[19] "Thoughts can exist only if there are thinkers," and "Only persons can deny that there are persons," have so much initial cogency that it is difficult to realize there are really no persons who have the thoughts. But there are not any on that planet. That planet is Earth.[20]

## Notes

1. R. Descartes, "Meditations on First Philosophy," in *The Philosophical World of Descartes*, trans. E. Haldane and G. Ross (New York: Cambridge University Press, 1972). See especially Meditations II and VI.

2. Plato, "Phaedo," in *Plato: The Collected Dialogues*, ed. E. Hamilton and H. Cairns (Princeton: Princeton University Press, 1969), pp. 61-63 (78c-80d).

3. The seminal work in the rebirth of contemporary interest in Materialism is J. Smart, "Sensations and Brain Processes," in *Materialism and the Mind-Body Problem*, ed. D. Rosenthal (Englewood Cliffs, N.J.: Prentice-Hall, Inc., 1971), pp. 53-66.

4. See W. Halverson, *A Concise Introduction to Philosophy* (New York: Random House, 1976), chap. 31, especially pp. 223-24.

5. Perhaps the most influential recent defense of the Cartesian view is found in S. Kripke, "Naming and Necessity," in *Semantics of Natural Language*, ed. G. Harman and D. Davidson (Dortrecht: Reidel, 1972), pp. 253-353. Powerful arguments for Materialism are provided by D. Armstrong, *A Materialist Theory of the Mind* (New York: Humanities Press, 1968); J. Cornman, *Materialism and Sensations* (New Haven: Yale University Press, 1971); R. Rorty, *Philosophy and the*

*Mirror of Nature* (Princeton: Princeton University Press, 1979); and E. Wilson, *The Mental as Physical* (London: Routledge and Kegan Paul, 1979).

6. This sort of characterization is provided by Descartes in Meditation II, *The Philosophical World of Descartes*, p. 153.

7. D. Hume, *A Treatise of Human Nature* (London: Oxford University Press, 1968), Bk. I, pt. IV, section 6, pp. 251-63.

8. Los Angeles neurosurgeons Joseph E. Bogan and Philip J. Vogel are credited with developing this technique on humans.

9. These "split brain" experiments are largely due to neurophysiologist R. Sperry, who has published both technical and lay accounts such as "Hemisphere Deconnection and Unity in Conscious Awareness," *American Psychologist* 23 (1968): 723-33, and "The Great Cerebral Commissure," *Scientific American* 210 (1964): 42-52. A popular account of the experiments can be found in C. Sagan, *The Dragons of Eden* (New York: Ballantine Books, 1977), chap. 7.

10. D. Landis, "A Scan for Mental Illness," *Discover*, October 1980, pp. 26-28.

11. This is maintained by J. Margolis, "Puccetti on Brains, Minds, and Persons," *Philosophy of Science* 42, no. 3, (1975): 275-79 and C. Cheng, "On Puccetti's Two Persons View of Man," *The Southern Journal of Philosophy* 16 (1978): 605-16.

12. This conclusion is drawn by M. Gazzaniga, *The Bisected Brain* (New York: Appleton-Century-Crofts, 1970) and "One Brain-Two Minds?" *American Scientist* 60 (1972): 311-17, and R. Puccetti, "Brain Bisection and Personal Identity," *British Journal for the Philosophy of Science* 24 (1973): 339-55.

13. T. Nagel argues in favor of this position in "Brain Bisection and the Unity of Consciousness," *Synthese* 22 (1971): 396-413, reprinted in *The Philosophy of Mind*, ed. J Glover (New York: Oxford University Press, 1976), pp. 111-25.

14. The Greek Atomists are discussed in J. Robinson, *An Introduction to Early Greek Philosophy* (New York: Houghton Mifflin, 1968), chaps. 10 and 11.

15. See ibid. for a lucid account of these fathers of Western philosophy, Thales, Heraclitus, Anaximenes, and Anaximander, respectively.

16. Besides the Greek Atomists, other philosophical forerunners of Scientific Realism are the seventeenth-century scientists Galileo and Newton and philosophers Descartes and Locke who distinguish between the "primary" and "secondary qualities" of physical objects. Influential contemporary accounts of Scientific Realism include J. Smart, *Philosophy and Scientific Realism* (New York: Humanities Press, 1971), and W. Sellars, *Science, Perception and Reality* (New York: Humanities Press, 1968), especially "Philosophy and the Scientific Image of Man." A simplified account is found in W. Halverson, *A Concise Introduction to Philosophy*, chap. 13.

17. A. Eddington, *The Nature of the Physical World* (Ann Arbor: The University of Michigan Press, 1963), p. xii.

18. "Sense-data" theories were quite big in the middle years of the twentieth century in Britain and the United States. The following example owes to those given by one of the foremost exponents of sense-data, A. J. Ayer, *The Foundations of Empirical Knowledge* (New York: Macmillan, 1969).

19. R. Descartes, "The Principles of Philosophy," in *The Philosophical World of Descartes*, p. 221 (Principle VII, Part I).

20. I am grateful to Gregory A. Ross for helpful comments on an earlier draft of this paper.

# V

# Alien Perspectives:
# The Other and the Self

In our search for personal identity and in our attempt
to understand ourselves, we may seek information and
assurance from within (the Cartesian "center of consciousness which continues through time") or we may
seek information and assurance from outside ourselves.
We try to learn about ourselves through what others say
to us or through what others tell us by their actions.

"The other," however, whether another human being
or a nonhuman being or entity, is not us, is not identical
with us but rather is different. How can we know this
other, this not-self, that is outside us and that, in being
"other" is alien to us? If the difference, the otherness, is
total, we seem to be at an epistemological dead end, for
to be able to communicate or to engage successfully in
any of the cognitive or affective processes presupposes
the existence of some basis of commonality or similarity,
some basic likeness.

Ted Krulik presents and assesses a sequence of alien
responses to the very human question, "What do you
think of us?" The responses come from alien beings who
are "bounded by metal," that is, they are various forms of
robots. This type of perspective is a real possibility, Krulik points out, because of the rapidly developing industrial robotry in our era.

Starting with the basic differences between biological
humans and nonbiological robots, Krulik, citing stories by
Asimov, Knight, and Phillips, explores and elaborates the

different viewpoints that robots present as they attempt to deal with the various problems arising from the "confrontation of the psyche-in-metal with human beings."

The differences are pronounced and the exposition of these confrontations does "tell us" something about ourselves. Krulik poses and answers the question: If human beings reach out to the unknown in a search for themselves, what would or does the robot seek, and what is its reason for being? In spite of the differences, Krulik hopes for a point of meeting and compatibility between humans and robots.

Paul Rice approaches this problem from a different angle. He identifies and assesses the various literary devices and techniques available to the science fiction writer who attempts to characterize an alien self, a being that is outside the normal experiential fund of the reader and writer. Metaphor, selected and used properly, according to Rice, is the science ficiton writer's most effective means of "saying the alien self." Good writing enables the well-chosen metaphor to bridge the created alien world, which has not been experienced, with the world of the reader's experience. What Rice discusses is precisely what Krulik finds in the stories he cites. We must understand or must be able to understand the alien "self" in order to understand the message that that alien self gives about us.

# Bounded by Metal

*TED KRULIK*

## The Robot as Alien

At the heart of science-fiction literature is the human desire to find ourselves. Everything humans have done has been a seeking of the self, and it is the reason for our yearning to reach outward, to other, possibly inhabited worlds. We want some other form of life to speak to us about us. We would like to find a "Tobermory," Saki's house cat who tells his masters exactly what he thinks of them. We want to meet the alien so we may say, "Here we are. What do you think of us?"

While asking this question of an intelligent, communicative life form outside of the earth probably will not occur during our lifetime, human beings do interact with another form of intelligence on earth—the robot mind. Although for the present robots can only parrot what is fed into their computer processors, the robotic industry holds out the hope of intercommunication with a mind that, with the sophistication of a rapidly developing technology, may soon fashion an answer to the question, "What do you think of us?"

At a recent conference devoted to the robot in fact and fiction, author Andrew Beer explained the goals of the modern robot industry. For example, Quasar Industries, one of several companies developing robots, is attempting to give to robots a personality and a rapport with people not previously considered in the development of computer technology.

Although Klatu, a robot present at the conference, was an entertainment robot, used for promotional purposes, it could learn to give weights and distinguish priorities. Programmed for a wide range of verbal responses, the robot had been used to talk to a boy hospitalized in a catatonic state, and the boy had responded to him. Thus, the modern communicating robot already has found simple, rudimentary uses. But, as Mr. Beer made clear, Klatu "follows a set of instructions without having a consciousness," so it is still within the purlieu of science fiction to explore the implications of coexistence with robots that possess a consciousness.[1]

## To See the Robot Mind

Human beings are creatures of biology, and they are reminded of their biology everyday. They need to eat, to excrete wastes, to have sex, and to sleep. They are resigned to their biological needs, tying themselves to overly large shelters that include outsized sleeping facilities, over-stocked eating facilities, and facilities used exclusively for the excretion and disposal of both organic and inorganic wastes.

His biological dependence upon his environment causes the human being to look upon the robot with a kind of envy. The robot is alien to us because it is not limited by biological needs; it has no dependence on an environment external to its own regulatory functions. It can survive in extremes of heat and cold; it can exist with no air at all. It has what all humans want: virtual indestructability.

This essay intends to look at the alienness of the robot in fiction, and in so doing learn something of the humanness of human beings. In speaking of the robot mind, I mean any conscious intelligence in fiction that is encased within an artificial, metallic body. Three stories, "The Bicentennial Man" by Isaac Asimov, "Masks" by Damon Knight, and "Lost Memory" by Peter Phillips, present diverse viewpoints of the metal-bounded psyche. The stories by Knight and Phillips are classic short tales that are not part of any larger series. "The Bicentennial Man" is Asimov's latest robot story. Although it begins with Asimov's Three Laws of Robotics and makes mention of Susan Calvin, a continuing character in his robot collections, it is not connected to any of his earlier stories and is unlike them in its length and chronological scope.[2] These three works are unique in their individual approaches to the problems created by the confrontation of the psyche-in-metal with human beings.

In "The Bicentennial Man," Andrew Martin is a robot servant whose intrinsic creativity leads him to seek, quite literally, more and more humanity. Over a period of 200 years, Andrew sheds his metal shell and earns the title of the novelette before surgery-induced death overtakes him.

The protagonist in Damon Knight's "Masks" is the total opposite of

Asimov's Andrew Martin. The brain of the protagonist, an ordinary man whose body was destroyed in some unexplained accident, is placed in a self-sufficient robot body. The humans who care for him misinterpret the attitude he expresses in their presence: what they see as self-hatred, is in reality, the reader comes to realize, a revulsion for the soft, liquid forms of life around him.

The "intelligent manufactures" in "Lost Memory" are robotic, but not humanoid, beings whose self-contained society is invaded by a spaceship. The plot revolves around the lack of understanding these robotic beings have of any other form of living organism. A seriously wounded human in the spacecraft cannot convince them that living forms other than themselves exist. The story turns on their differing meanings of life and causes of death.

## The Human Condition

In order to rationalize Andrew's desire to become a human being, Asimov, in "The Bicentennial Man," carefully developed family ties and a cultural background for his characters.

Episodic sections that show the changing scenery revolving around the existence of Andrew Martin are at the heart of Asimov's method. Family members grow older, businesses develop, acquaintances and life-styles change while Andrew remains unaged and unmoved, although robot technology improves his metal shell. With each new episode, as people age and die, we are reminded of the mortality of man. As readers, we feel Andrew's sadness, particularly in his memories of "Little Miss," a name that remains unchanged even when she becomes a mother and a grandmother. We are struck by a sense of time passing, and we are aware of Andrew's need to hold onto his memories; we feel his sense of loss. Although we can recognize man's age-old dream to live forever in the story, we are forced to wonder if it would be worth the kinds of loss that Andrew feels.

As a biochemist, Asimov must view man's place in the universe as coexistent with his biological needs. If so, then the humanlike Andrew, enclosed in an immortal form, feels like a lost soul. He needs a human biology to exist in concert with his view of his place in the universe, which has been formed by his association with a human family and has given him his reason for existence. For him, the universe consists of such familial relationships.

His relationship with the family is used to reveal his need to become human. Paul, the grandson of "Little Miss," who is himself reaching old age, discusses Andrew's financial future. Knowing that he is the last of the human Martins, Paul shows genuine concern for the robot Andrew. Immediately after we are told that Andrew "could not get used to the deaths of the Martins," we are given Andrew's feelings about his physicial form.[3] Asked by Paul about his latest project, Andrew replies:

> "I am designing a system for allowing androids—myself—to gain energy from the combustion of hydrocarbons, rather than from atomic cells."
> Paul raised his eyebrows. "So that they will breathe and eat?"
> "Yes."
> "How long have you been pushing in that direction?"
> "For a long time now, but I think I have designed an adequate combustion chamber for catalyzed controlled breakdown."
> "But why, Andrew? The atomic cell is surely infinitely better."
> "In some ways, perhaps, but the atomic cell is inhuman."[4]

At this point, we understand Andrew's intention, and we are in sympathy with it, for in Asimov's view human biology is not a limitation but a necessary and life-affirming part of living.

The protagonist in "Masks" has no such emotional ties to human beings. In spite of the caring of a team of medical personnel and the proximity of an old friend with an artificial limb, the metal-bounded man feels no closeness to his human kin. Quite the contrary. Jim, as the protagonist, feels real enmity for life. For him, living, breathing beings are horrors that cause a recurring nightmare:

> slithery kidneys burst gray lungs blood and hair ropes of guts covered with yellow fat oozing and sliding and oh god the stink like the breath of an outmouth. . . .
> His heel slid and he was falling could not stop himself falling into slimy bulging softness higher than his chin, higher and he could not move paralyzed and he tried to scream tried to scream tried to scream. . . .[5]

Rather than viewing human biology as a life-affirming experience, Damon Knight takes us into a mind that is alien to the soft wetness of humanity. As Mr. Knight explains in his notations to the story:

> You are made of plastic and metal, running clean and cool. The others, the flesh people, are bags of decaying meat; they have pimples, their skin is shiny

with grease, there's food stuck between their teeth, they're crawling with microbes, scaly with dandruff, they ooze and they stink.[6]

Imperfect man is revealed to us in a frightening way. His imperfections are not simply a cause for distaste but of total aversion. Jim, in metal guise, wishes to push away from life in much the same way that some of us would wish to push ourselves away from a large and hideous waterbug.

While the characters in both Asimov's and Knight's stories make comparisons between biological human and automatous entity, Peter Phillips's "Lost Memory" concerns itself with characters who have no basis for that comparison. For the "intelligent manufactures," there is no life that grows of itself. Life is a manufacture that has a consciousness, death is the fusion of mechanical parts, and oxygen is the great destroyer, causing a plague called rust. The problem in the story is not theirs but one of a living organism, a man, who must try to communicate his nature to the manufactures. Biology becomes the unknown factor, and its processes, including oxidation, are antithetical to everything known to these beings. The human being becomes the alien; for these robot minds, no such thing can exist.

## Morality and the Robot Mind

The safeguards given to a robot, that is, behavior that human society would deem acceptable, depend on its programming. Its sense of morality is controlled by the planning of human beings. As Andrew Beer indicated at the Robotic Futures Conference, it is possible to systematize human traits. We can impress such human values as honesty on the robot brain, if the specific actions and behaviors desired can be broken down and programmed.[7]

In "The Bicentennial Man," we see a gradual loss of honesty in Andrew Martin. Asimov seems to be using that loss to illustrate the increasing humanness of Andrew. It is as if the coming to humanity is a corruptive process.

Of course, all of Asimov's robots have been given the safeguard of his Three Laws of Robotics, but these laws can be circumvented without being broken. Although Asimov established in an earlier short story that a robot may lie if the reason is to prevent a human being from mental or emotional harm, it would be uncharacteristic of an Asimovian robot, especially if the intent of the lie is to cause mental or emotional anguish.[8]

However, Andrew's sense of humanity has been established early in the story, and his "coming of age" is gradual, almost painful to him.

When Andrew wants to arrange a meeting with the head of U.S. Robots, he depends on the grandson of "Little Miss" to lie for him by threatening to take legal action for further robot rights. As Paul Martin remarks to Andrew, "Ah, you can't lie, but you can urge me to tell a lie, is that it? You're getting more human all the time, Andrew."[9] When Paul and Andrew see the head of U.S. Robots, Paul takes the initiative in making threats that coerce the head into transferring Andrew's positronic brain into an android body. In a seeming attempt to make Andrew an accessory, Paul asks for his approval. Andrew internalizes:

It amounted to the approval of lying, of blackmail, of the badgering and humiliation of a human being. But not physical harm, he told himself, not physical harm.

He managed at last to come out with a rather faint "Yes."[10]

These two instances are a part of his apprenticeship in becoming a manipulative, corrupt being. Left to his own devices after Paul's death, Andrew speaks to the director of research at U.S. Robots. No longer dependent on humans to lie, deceive, and threaten for him, Andrew "wheels-and-deals" to arrange major surgery to convert his body to an organic source of energy. Internally, Andrew rationalizes his actions:

Andrew felt scarcely any First Law inhibition to the stern conditions he was setting a human being. He was learning to reason that what seemed like cruelty might, in the long run, be kindness.[11]

In the Asimovian world in which "The Bicentennial Man" takes place, morality in the robot mind turns upon the necessity for coexistence with humans. Morality for Andrew Martin becomes a wrestling with the question of self-interest as opposed to an act in deference to the wishes of man. In his world, Andrew is breaking new ground, and the question that arises is: To what extent should humans allow robots their rights as sentient beings? In Andrew's world both humans and robots must accept the responsibility for setting moral standards, and if the definitions guiding those standards no longer hold, both are responsible for their expansion.

American society places a high premium on human life, but the morality involved in the taking of a life is a relative concept. In a war, for example, it is acceptable to kill another person who is defined as your national enemy. In China in the last century, allowing the sick, the elderly, and the poor to die was considered correct behavior, and it was thought improper to avoid succumbing to death. The rightness and wrongness of causing loss of life has always been determined by the rules of men. Those rules may be quite different in different places.

This kind of relative morality concerning life appears in "Lost Memory." Although the robotic beings kill the human with every action they take, they are not destroying life as they know it. The reader may feel the same horror and hatred toward the manufactures as the wounded human, but as the author makes clear, the robots are simply doing what is right for the saving of their own kind. While showing a complete ignorance of any life that grows, the manufactures reveal the fears and concerns that are part of their lives:

> . . .strength going. Can't get into my zoot. . .done for if they bust through lock, done for if they don't. . .must tell them I need oxygen. . . ."
>
> "He's in bad shape, desirous of extinction," I remarked to Chur-chur, who was adjusting his arc-cutter. "He wants to poison himself with oxidation now."
>
> I shuddered at the thought of that vile, corrosive gas he had mentioned, which causes that almost unmentionable condition we all fear—rust.[12]

It was Philip K. Dick who wrote of his fears of a machine intelligence and the implications of giving the machine independent mobility:

> —the machine, lacking empathy, watching as mere spectator, [is] the same horror which I know haunts Harlan Ellison. It is perhaps more frightening than the killer himself. . .this figure which sees but gives no assistance, offers no hand.[13]

This is precisely the man's view of the intelligent manufactures in "Lost Memory." If it had been possible for him to do so, the man would have liked to have stepped out of his spaceship, stood before these unfeeling machines, and said, "See? Here we are. We're quite different from you. We are life."

The sardonic irony that runs through Phillips's story, however, does not allow for the robot's discovery of a different form of life. The charred remains of the dead astronaut are, to the machines, a complex "kind of insulating material," and they are left with the puzzle of why such a material could be found in only one small area of the ship.[14]

By having the narrator of the story a robotic machine, Peter Phillips offers an intriguingly alien point-of-view. The reader is torn between the plight of the only human in the story and a comprehension of the machines' feelings and thoughts. The robots think only in terms of the large manufacture, the ship. They are incapable of accepting the idea of a small, soft growing thing within their comrade. When the human speaks to them of his brain, they posit it to be a computer brain at the top of the spacecraft; when the man cries out in pain as they burn him with their tools, they assume that their fellow machine's skin currents have been reactivated. Sympathetically, like a doctor's bedside manner with an ailing patient, one robot pats the spaceship and speaks soothingly to it, while the man screams inside.

The intelligent manufactures talk and act like humans. They are enchanting characters and chillingly unwavering in their preconceptions. In the last few lines of "Lost Memory," Phillips hits home with an image that makes the machine frighteningly human:

> There is something I wish I could forget. I can't explain why it should upset me so much. But I always stop the tape before it reaches the point where the voice of the stranger rises in pitch, going higher and higher until it cuts out.
>
> There's a quality about that noise that makes me tremble and think of rust.[15]

## The Joys of Nonlife

A being in metal, by virtue of its nature, is in adversity to life. If a robot's arm or leg, or even torso is removed, the robot still exists. In "The Bicentennial Man," Asimov shows that the positronic brain itself can be the owner of the body entire, that is, the robot "lives" as long as its mind exists intact.[16]

Jim, the main character in "Masks," faces a problem that puts him at war with himself. His brain is not metallic and indestructable; a simple "cerebrospinal infection" can kill him, and his mind can suffer the consequences of fatigue, which a robot brain does not.[17] The director of the project explains to a government investigator that Jim's mind needs sleep even in a mechanized body so he will not hallucinate or become psychotic. In order to keep him in touch with the world he had inhabited as a human being for forty-three years, Jim is given programmed dream suggestions, a somatic input in areas of sex, exercise, and sports. But the doctor's expectations of maintaining a sense of corporal reality in Jim are not successful. Jim takes comfort in his mechanized body:

> Inside, he was running clean and cool; he could feel the faint reassuring hum of pumps, click of valves and relays. They had given him that: cleaned out all the offal, replaced it with machinery that did not bleed, ooze or suppurate.[18]

As his human caretakers are unaware of his separation from living beings, Jim works out a way of living a life away from contact with the living forms that revolt him. His solution, which he confides to Babcock, the project director, is to be placed in the sterile environment of a spaceship, the brain of its command module. Babcock leaves him with the faint hope that his plan may be accomplished. Jim's murder of a dog because of his feelings of revulsion foreshadows what could happen if he is forced to remain in the proximity of human beings.

Given a robot with a consciousness and a will of his own, can humankind expect an enemy who will turn against the human race? Asimov called this the "Frankenstein complex," and his robot stories were written to dispel this fear. The safeguards Asimov gives his robots are deeply engrained and remarkably consistent, considering the variety of problems that develop in his stories with the Three Laws of Robotics. Andrew in "The Bicentennial Man," for example, adheres to the Three Laws in spite of a situation that is potentially dangerous to him:

> The two were backing away slightly, looking uneasy.
> George said sharply, "Andrew, I am in danger and about to come to harm from these young men. Move toward them!"
> Andrew did so, and the two young men did not wait. They ran fleetly. . . .Andrew said, "I couldn't have hurt them, George. I could see they were not attacking you."
> "I didn't order you to attack them; I only told you to move toward them. Their own fears did the rest."[19]

There are enough exploitative people in "The Bicentennial Man" to support Asimov's concern for the rights of robots once they possess enough independent thought to cooperate and work with man.

Andrew is a special robot. Unlike any other in existence in "The Bicentennial Man," Andrew has an innate creativity that has found its way inexplicably into his positronic circuits. He can feel enjoyment in carving figures, as he explains to his master, "It makes the circuits of my brain somehow flow more easily. I have heard you use the word 'enjoy' and the way you use it fits the way I feel."[20]

But Patricia Warrick believes that a robot with creativity lies in the realm of impossibility:

Granted that a machine can think logically, does not the human brain have another kind of capacity—creative intelligence and intuition—which the machine can never be made to duplicate? Since we have no agreement about what intelligence is and have little understanding of how the human brain works, it is not possible at this point to make any kind of meaningful prediction about whether it can ever be reproduced mechanically.[21]

Many computer programmers and robotics technicians, however, disagree with Warrick. Intelligence in the computer mind is observable: the computer is capable of accumulating vast amounts of information, assimilating them, and presenting a workable output that may vary slightly according to the characteristics of the computer. Perhaps, when it is possible to break the wide variations in human traits into individual actions and to program them into a robot, a kind of creative ability and enjoyment may be inscribed onto the mind of the mechanical being.

In Asimov's work, through the robot Andrew and through the humans that Andrew must contend with, we see the way in which mankind manipulates and exploits others. In "Lost Memory," we catch glimpses of another human foible—prejudice. As soon as the wounded man realizes he is speaking to mechanized beings, he assumes that they must have human masters tending them: "I am a friend of your master, your maker. You must fetch him to me at once."[22] He refers to the manufactures as "sentient slaves" made to serve man. If this man has a character flaw that gives reason for his dire circumstances, it lies in his belief that man is superior to the machine. It might even be possible to rationalize that the astronaut's death is necessary to point out the invalidity of his prejudice.

What can man learn from a mechanized Tobermory? Perhaps only that both man and machine are governed by a natural law. In "Lost Memory," the machines' concept of their maker, a cubical-shaped form of primal metal (a computer) that had deliberately omitted all knowledge of man, may be not very different from the religious dogma that guides humankind to its maker. We model our machines after ourselves, and one capable of independent thought may not look to us as its creator but rather to some unknown force in nature that rules over human beings as well as mechanized beings.

If humankind reaches out to the unknown in a search for itself, what does the robot seek? What is his reason for being?

Using the stories discussed in this essay, we can postulate that a robot civilization would search for something other than sentient beings.

The "sterile rock and metal" of the robots' planet in "Lost Memory" would be most suitable for a self-contained robot society, for it exists without the contamination of living organisms or the destructive forces of an atmosphere of gases.[23] Although one of the robotic machines in this story has attempted space travel, their interest in going into space would not be the same as ours. They have no need to discover other forms of life. Like man, such a voyage of discovery would be undertaken out of curiosity, with the hope of learning more of their creator and seeking an exchange of information with other intelligent manufactures. The robot society would undertake such an enterprise for the purpose of accumulating knowledge only—that is the "be-all and end-all" of their existence. It seems quite possible that Jim in "Masks" might embark on that sort of exploration in order to find the sterile environment he seeks but nothing else. Man's need to expand his horizons by traveling to the stars may be analogous to the robot's need to assimilate knowledge— and find satisfaction in the knowing.

Science fiction may prepare us for our first encounters with robots capable of independent thinking. Even though such beings may have a different orientation toward life than we do, we must hope that the metal-bound psyche and the human intellect will find a common ground and will prove to be compatible.

## Notes

1. Andrew Beer, "Robots with Human Traits" (Paper delivered at the Robotics Futures Conference, Long Island University, Brooklyn Campus, April 26, 1980).

2. Isaac Asimov, *I, Robot* (New York: Signet Books, 1964), and *The Rest of the Robots* (New York: Pyramid Books, 1966).

3. Isaac Asimov, "The Bicentennial Man," *The Best Science Fiction of the Year #6*, ed. Terry Carr (New York: Holt, Rinehart and Winston, 1977), p. 364.

4. Asimov, "Bicentennial Man," pp. 364-65.

5. Damon Knight, "An Annotated 'Masks,' " *Those Who Can: A Science Fiction Reader*, ed. Robin Scott Wilson (New York: New American Library, 1973), p. 231.

6. Knight, "Masks," p. 228.

7. Andrew Beer, "Robots with Human Traits."

8. Isaac Asimov, "Liar!" *I, Robot*, pp. 82-99.

9. Asimov, "Bicentennial Man," p. 357.

10. Ibid., pp. 361-62.

11. Ibid., p. 367.

12. Peter Phillips, "Lost Memory," *Themes in Science Fiction*, ed. Leo P. Kelley (New York: McGraw-Hill, 1972), p. 350.

13. Philip K. Dick, "Man, Android and Machine," *Science Fiction at Large*, ed. Peter Nicholls (New York: Harper & Row, 1976), p. 218.

14. Phillips, "Lost Memory," p. 352.

15. Ibid., p. 353.

16. Asimov, "Bicentennial Man," p. 360.

17. Knight, "Masks," p. 217.

18. Ibid., p. 227.

19. Asimov, "Bicentennial Man," p. 351.

20. Ibid., p. 337.

21. Patricia Warrick, "Images of the Man-Machine Intelligence Relationship in Science Fiction," *Many Futures, Many Worlds: Theme and Form in Science Fiction*, ed. Thomas D. Clareson (Ohio: Kent State University Press, 1977), p. 210.

22. Phillips, "Lost Memory," p. 347.

23. Ibid., p. 349.

# 10

# Metaphor as a Way of Saying the Self in Science Fiction

*PAUL RICE*

In order to provide examples of the various considerations mentioned in this chapter, I could have referred to various well-known science fiction works, but I felt that the ends of illumination and continuity would be better served by taking all the examples from one work. Obviously, the only work that could perfectly fit my purposes would be one of my own making, hence the following piece, complete with problems.

*As Darkon, the Topian ship commander, shot the last of his torpedoes into the upland quadrant of the Fotian outpost, the Fotians stampeded from their domelike structure. Phillips, the Earth commander, found himself alone in the station's war room as Marvo, the Fotian war priest, entered with two Fotian lieutenants who took up stations at the great flashing console in the rear of the room.*

*Marvo, an imposing creature with light blue saurian skin, was in all ways leonine, with a bushy mane that waved rhythmically as he moved catlike into the room.*

*"Vodi shez cao mato," he roared in a thunderous voice to the two who stared intently at the faces of various gauges and dials.*

*Immediately the lieutenants pulled levers on the console and the droning noises that filled the space began to wind down.*

*"Yes Phillips," said Marvo. "This must be very like the fate of your heroic Trojans those many Earth years ago." He had read the Earth man's thoughts. "I can only say that great waves of* lateez *are rolling through me at this very moment." Visible through the skylight the alien sun was a slice of blue vegetable in the sky.*

*"What's* lateez?" *asked Phillips.*

*"Lateez is an emotion we Fotians feel when our moons set, an urgent but not unpleasing finality, for we know that endings are but beginnings. It is similar to the sweet/sad feeling*

*you Earth people have when one of your children grows up and leaves home, a sense of loss and of possibility at the same time." Marvo was still probing the Earth commander's consciousness.*

*"Is there a god who can save you?" asked the Earth man.*

*"Zotar is the quiet crystal at the heart of the huge blue sun. But that is something that you Earthlings cannot understand," said Marvo, and as he spoke he raised to his chest an instrument that looked like a small shovel. There was a crackling sound and Marvo slumped to the floor.*

*Phillips ran from the structure, entered his craft, and took off. As he did so, an unearthly glow began to emanate from beyond the Fotian horizon. He thought to himself, "It's beginning."*

Readers of science fiction, when encountering a nonhuman, an alien in the context of the narrative, should understand the problems inherent in writing the dialogue of a nonhuman self. The sayer, which is to say the author, is, of course, always a human with human cognition and human experience, yet he must say an alien self and make that self appear in some significant way other than human. In the most effective science fiction, authors rely heavily on metaphor to create an alien being from bits and pieces of earthly reality. The author must use the familiar, yet move past the familiar into a convincingly real and unfamiliar alien self. Metaphor (from the Greek *metapherein*, to carry across), has long been a *casus belli* in discussions of the language of science and the matters of precise knowledge generally. Metaphors have been said to be the basis of all knowledge on the one hand, and on the other, to be nonexistent. Any useful discussion of metaphor in science fiction lies between these extremes.

For the purposes of this essay, metaphor may be defined as a comparison between two things, actions, or ideas that are essentially not alike. In addition, the metaphoric comparison creates a certain "tension" in the reader because of the violation of expectations, caused by a deviation from familiar patterns that may be linguistic (grammar, diction, and so forth) or may extend to the phenomenal bases for metaphor into actions and things and even into violations of customary relationships. The comparison is always between a literal term (often called the tenor) and a figurative term (the vehicle). Either, both, or none of the terms may be expressed. And whatever the forms they may take, all metaphors may be expressed ultimately as "x is like y." For example, in the statement, *"the Fotians stampeded from their domelike structure,"* the literal term "Fotians" is expressed but the figurative term is not. The word "stampede," because of its associations with cattle, creates, when a *to be* verb form (were) is added, a metaphor, "the Fotians were like cattle." Each such comparison is a hypothesis formulated by the writer that invites but does not demand the cooperation of the reader or auditor and is often used as a means of "teaching," particularly when the tenor is something not perceptible to the senses. The scientist who speaks of the planetary theory of the atom invites his student to imagine the atom is *like* the solar system because electrons are *like* planets orbiting the nucleus of the atom as real planets orbit the sun. As Jack Kaminsky has noted, "Once a subject matter has been converted into sentences,. . .derivations become possible that would not be possible under other conditions."[1]

Discussing certain aspects of atomic structure in sentential form provides the starting place for a discussion of how the atom is really built. Similarly, a writer of imaginative literature finds, in metaphor, a means of converting a hypothesis into a sentence, "x is like y," which invites its readers to derive meaning from it, to compare it with the readers' experiences, and to elaborate upon the comparison or drop it as meaningless.

While metaphor also does heavy aesthetic duty in writing, what is important to this discussion is the use of metaphors to permit readers to construct, from their own experiences, a self for a fictional character. To discover the problems peculiar to the writing of a nonhuman self, it is useful to consider how an author creates a human character, beginning with the external aspects of that character and moving inward.

Any fictional character is the sum of the author's choices within several rhetorical modes. All of these modes may employ metaphor to carry across the literal level of the language used into a sense of a unique and readily identifiable character or self.

The author may describe the character in such a way that the reader is able to draw inferences about the character's "mind" from the description of his "body." A character may be described as "muscular, with a great amount of yellow hair," which gives the reader literal clues to the appearance of the character, or a character may be described as *"leonine, with a bushy mane,"* which forces the reader to deal with the character connotatively, thus permitting him or her to speculate on the hypothesis that there is something lionlike about the inner being.

Various narrative techniques help the author to construct a self for a character. The author may do the talking or may permit a character to speak, either as a part of dialogue or as interior monologue, spoken by the "mind" of the character. Limited narration forces the reader to deal with the surface actions of the character, and these can be telling. A character who torpedoes a planet may be assumed by the reader to be different from a character who spends money providing food for the survivors of that bombing. Even in limited narration, however, the author may force the reader inside the character by employing metaphor (and hence a certain authorial intrusion) in the choice of character action. A character walking "catlike" into a room may not have the same self as a character who simply walks through the room.

The omniscient narrative technique provides direct access to the internality of the character, especially when a character thinks on the page and the narrator comments upon the character's thoughts. In this technique it is possible for the author, a narrator apart from the author, and a character apart from them both to use metaphors, all of which may contribute to the construction of the "character" of a character. In fact all of the metaphors used may be reinforced by the understanding gained from the content of any dialogue, which may also contain metaphor, written into the mouths of any of the various *dramatis personae*. This creates the marvelous complexity through which metaphor, by its step-by-step accounting for individual "things" in the context of fiction, provides a "mediating bridge between discrete systems."[2] That is, *this* thing compared to *this* thing equals more than the combined individual properties of the two.

To appreciate fully the importance of metaphor in science fiction, it is necessary not only to understand the importance of metaphor in the creation of self in fiction generally but also to understand the levels of metaphorical suggestiveness with which a reader must deal. Comparisons may be nearly pure expressiveness and may then move from this level to various levels of suggestiveness.[3] "Frozen," or dead metaphors as they are sometimes called, are more expressive than suggestive. What was once the original metaphorical comparison, "*faces of various gauges*," has now become the only available term for the readable portion of a gauge, even though it is still impossible to avoid some slight connotative ripple with the word "faces." When, however, an author mentions a "*thunderous voice*," and makes the "x is like y" statement, "the sound of the voice is like the sound of thunder," the reader is not likely to dismiss past experience with thunder when mentally recreating the voice.

Moving through various levels of increasing subjectivity, it is even possible to create metaphors that have no relationship in the experience of the reader. *"The alien sun was a slice of blue vegetable in the sky"* expresses almost nothing if realistic criteria are used, although it may be more suggestive to some readers of a highly intuitive bent. In all cases, what is used to test the hypothesis of the metaphor is the common experience of the maker of the metaphor and the auditor of the metaphor. And this leads to some interesting questions concerning the creation of workable alien selves in science fiction.

The sum of the choices of a science-fiction author may differ little from those of an author of general fiction, but the author of general fiction must create human characters from human language, while the author of science fiction must create nonhuman characters from human language. The extraterrestrial selves a reader constructs come from the reader's experience, which cannot have overlapped with the experience of the alien, except in ways resembling life as the reader has experienced it. Whatever moves the earthbound reader into the sphere of the alien character's self must lie in the suggestive power of language, for language that is merely expressive must of necessity remain at home.

The reader's understanding of the self of a nonhuman character, then, is accomplished largely through the suggestive qualities of metaphor. The alien being, in some manner or the other, to some degree or the other, must be like aspects of quantities and qualities known to the humans engaged in reader/writer relationships.

Readers expect the author to violate expectation in creating both the external and the internal self of the alien. No one wants to read about an alien who looks and thinks like a human. The verbal account of the alien's appearance is most often an expressive catalogue of body parts and shapes familiar and terrestrial but incongruously juxtaposed. The description may move toward suggestiveness through metaphor when the narrator speaks of *"saurian skin"* or the like. Since metaphor is characterized by a violation of reader expectation, it is an exceptionally appropriate form/content commensuration. From here, matters become more complicated.

Since it is possible to have four selves at different levels in a piece of fiction (the reader, the writer, the narrator, and the nonnarrator character), it might be wise to assume for a moment that there is one writer talking to one reader. All else is elaborative context for an idea or set of ideas the author wishes to impart to the reader for any number of reasons, including didactic impulse and financial gain. The reader may, if he or she wishes, attempt to unravel this elaboration, and is, or may be, prompted to do so for reasons including a love of complexity and a desire to fill idle hours. To initiate this communication, the author creates a narrator, either participatory, detached, or implied, and charges him or her with the responsibility of telling the story and saying the characters, both human and nonhuman, as well as all the other details making up the fiction, thereby assisting the author in communication with the reader. At the very least, a writer tells the reader what the facts of the story are on a literal level. If all goes well, the reader is told much more that the writer has put on the page. While the reader and the writer are human, those in the middle need not be, but they must deal in human terms in a number of important ways.

First, any narrators/characters who happen to be alien must speak the language of the reader. They may also speak the nonhuman language of any other alien characters in the story; they may even do so in front of the reader, but the reader must be provided with an explanation of the interchange or be left to infer the meaning in the absence of translation. If the narrator is human, however, omniscient narration is in a bit of trouble because it is limited to the extent of the sparse common experience of the two creatures and therefore ceases to be omniscient. The omniscient human narrator in science fiction is limited to those ways of alien knowing that are like human ways of knowing; he can state only that other means of knowing exist, not what "insights" can be derived from them. The alien narrator/character is forced to resort to metaphor to suggest alternative, nonhuman selves and ways of knowing. This limitation has forced science-fiction writers to create a sizable repertoire of literary conventions that serve as the bases for the inculcation of human experience in the alien consciousness and thus allow the alien to speak in human terms about a nonhuman and often extraterrestrial existence. Human characters in a story (Phillips, for example) often serve merely as proxies for the reader, that is to say, as devices for information release. They save the author a means for his aliens to translate alien reality into human terms. The alien releases information first to the human character who responds in a manner characteristically human, thus providing the reader with a concrete and verbally accessible version of things.

Among the many devices for transmitting human experience to an alien in science-fiction stories, these are the most common:

1. Direct access to the contents of the human mind through telepathy

2. An eons-long longitudinal study of life on earth conducted by aliens
3. A biological/cultural half-human, half-alien being capable of knowing in both modes
4. Alien access to records of activity on earth
5. Alien knowledge of earth from past contacts with expeditionary forces from earth

These, and there are others, give the author (or the narrator, or the characters) credibility when expressing various "x is like y" relationships in which x is the unknown quantity/quality from alien discourse and y is the known vehicle of comparison.

There are, of course, breakdowns in the suggestive use of metaphor in saying a self. In these instances in science fiction the author is obviously straining against the limits imposed upon saying. The most familiar of these instances occurs when an alien character attempts to explain to a character of another kind, often human, some aspect of alien life and/or emotion as the alien knows it. The alien may say "Lateez *is an emotion we Fotians feel when our moons set. It is similar to the sweet/sad feeling you have when one of your children grows up and leaves home.*" But implicit in this statement is the understanding that the alien knows more about Earth culture than the Earthling knows about Fotia. The dramatic situation now demands that the author supply some account of the means by which the Fotian acquired his knowledge of Earth and child-rearing patterns.

Authors sometimes attempt to deal with the circumscription of human understanding of alien selves by moving away from the "x is like y" comparisons that are non-metaphorical and purely expressive ("*he carried an instrument that looked like a small shovel*"), toward comparisons that are almost pure suggestion. Comparisons of this type are familiar to those who have had experience with Zen koans, which attempt to make a break with rational (and comfortable) language patterns, in other words, to "kill" logic by creating analogies in which the x term often relates to some aspect of the religion and the y term is some apparently nonsensical vehicle. "What is the Daiba Sect?" "The Daiba Sect is filling a silver bowl with snow." This is not meaningful in any Western sense because the comparison has little or no expressive value, moving past literalness into suggestiveness, and having no ground in the hearer's experience. Common in science fiction is the description of some alien being in terms like, "*Zotar is the quiet crystal at the heart of the huge blue sun.*" Human readers are acquainted with "quiet" and with "crystal" and may be aware that some suns are blue, but whatever they may infer of Zotar from this description has no basis in experience beyond a knowledge of the parts. Even so, some meaning relating to Zotar's "nature" may be suggested by the comparison and may be constructed from the juxtaposition of Zotar and the connotative schemata that readers carry to the various elements in the comparison. Zen notwithstanding, it is successful writing, the most skillful creation of alien characters, that permits readers to derive meaningful, if nonverbal constructs from the metaphors presented. "Easy" and not very successful writing constructs "mystical-seeming" metaphors that compare x to any y that presents itself merely for the sake of doing so. It is more difficult to create comparisons that have complex and meaningful resonance in the readers' experience.

Equally unsuccessful are clumsy alien attempts to explain to human readers that a concept exists that humans *cannot* grasp. In this situation a human character is often told by an alien that "z" is a concept *"you Earthlings cannot understand."* This simple statement of the existence of human-unknowable things is an easy convention by which aliens are shown to be different from, and often superior to, humans. Still clumsier are statements like, *"an unearthly glow began to emanate from beyond the Fotian horizon,"* which, if one wishes to reduce matters to a familiar pattern, produces, "The light was like the light of which no example exists on Earth." Statements such as these simply tell the readers what a more careful writing of the scene could show.

It is the mark of a successful metaphor (in terms of how well it serves to elucidate) to become embedded in the language and used as a synonym for the thing itself. The imponderable black holes of contemporary astronomy are *like* black holes in some respects and in some respects *are* black. But "black hole," which began as a metaphor, has become the name by which we call this postulated phenomenon. The well-known danger of this process is that the auditors of metaphor are often guilty of "confusing an instrument of knowing with what is known."[4] Thus it is remotely possible that a naive attender could think it possible to pour water into a black hole until it is full.

Metaphor transformed to myth has been and is still responsible for numerous examples of humankind's inhumanity toward itself. For example, the Hawk Clan may declare war on the Rabbit Clan because the hawk is the natural enemy of the rabbit. But few examples of myth derived from metaphor have entered conventional wisdom through science fiction, although the increased acceptance of futurist/science-fiction literature enhances the possibility that this will occur. One obvious exception is the Big Brother of George Orwell's *1984*. Certainly there is no better example of the need for authors to understand the power that a well-constructed metaphor has over humankind. While those who accepted the Big Brother myth were the fictional inhabitants of Orwell's world and not the inhabitants of our contemporary society, it only takes one person to make one metaphor that may have far-reaching effects on contemporary thought.

While it is the responsibility of writers of good science fiction to construct their fiction carefully for their potential readers, it is the responsibility of readers to bring to the work as broad an experiential spectrum as possible and, at the very least, the vocabulary and decoding skills needed to deal with the language at slightly more than a literal level. Then and only then can the two ultimate "conversationalists," the writer and the reader, apart from any intervening created beings, have an exchange resulting in the transfer of ideas to the reader, especially ideas of the complexity posited by the author's metaphoric hypothesis of what an alien self might be. It may be, too, that the best readers to hear an alien self being said are those with the fewest preconceptions of how things *should* be; readers guided by a sense of possibility, not probability, readers who know a fair amount about what is not known and those who have a fair understanding of the kind of communication that can take place without words and even beyond words. As Thomas Cottle and Stephen Klineberg have noted, "Without the ability. . .to imagine events that have no concrete reality, there can be no creativity in general nor any possibility of creating the images of future goals that inform present experiences."[5] It may be that through the suggestion of selves not human we are glimpsing human possibility. It has been said by Robert Scholes "that fabulation. . .is fiction that offers us a world clearly and radically discontinuous from the one we know, yet returns to confront that known world in some cognitive way."[6] Since there is no fiction without character, it is reasonable to say that the author's most important job is the creation of character. If any character is not human, then the best device for saying the nonhuman self is metaphor, for it is the device that best permits us a bridge spanning the distance between the Earth of our experience and the alien worlds of our imagination.

## Notes

1. Jack Kaminsky, *Language and Ontology* (Carbondale: Southern Illinois University Press, 1969), p. 107.

2. Felicity Haynes, "Metaphoric Understanding," *Journal of Aesthetic Education* 12 (April 1978): 113.

3. Earl R. MacCormac, *Metaphor and Myth in Science and Religion* (Durham: Duke University Press, 1976), pp. 83-91.

4. Walker Percy, "Metaphor as Mistake," in *The Message in the Bottle* (New York: Farrar, Straus and Giroux, 1975), p. 72.

5. Thomas J. Cottle and Stephen L. Klineberg, *The Present of Things Future* (New York: The Free Press, 1974), p. 31.

6. Robert Scholes, "The Roots of Science Fiction" in *Science Fiction: A Collection of Critical Essays*, ed. Mark Rose (Englewood Cliffs, N.J.: Prentice-Hall, 1976), p. 47.

# VI

# Communication: Turmoil and Impact Messages

Social scientists, philosophers, and science fiction writers have been fascinated and troubled by tendencies within our culture toward the unqualified worship of technology and the unrestrained effort to increase the technological complexity of our world. Noting current influences of these tendencies upon society, they portray the possible consequences for human values, civilization, community, and communication if these tendencies continue unabated. In this process, and with the "if this goes on" assumption, they elaborate answers to such questions as: If human beings are fundamentally "social creatures," who "belong" in community, what happens to them when that community breaks down? What happens to the individual's need for a sense of belonging and psychic and personal assurance of worth, when the community has disintegrated and there are no longer others to respond "in community" to those needs, when there are no longer others who *can* respond in this way? What happens to the individual who is alone—isolated, due to technological complexity—when, in the histories of most human cultures, separation, isolation, and exclusion from the group have been used as forms of punishment?

Pursuing the "if this goes on" theme, they also explore answers, or possible answers, to other questions: What happens to the basis of communication, when the community breaks up and the "shared realities" (metaphysical, physical and/or symbolic), as well as shared meanings and rules upon which the possibility of communication depends also dissolve under the impact of an unrestrained technological advance? Left alone, isolated from others, psychically isolated, without common rules and meanings, the individual certainly seems to be without "an ordered system of ideas or concepts" by means of which she/he can interpret the world and the self. Must the individual, then, as some have suggested, remain in a private world, where meanings are totally arbitrary and without order, consistency, or reason? What significance would language have in such a world?

Some social critics and some science fiction writers believe an uncontrolled, passionate love affair with technology may lead to such a state as is implied by the questions posed above. Given this belief, how could a science fiction writer—who must use words, spaces, and punctuation marks—present such a theme effectively?

Adam Frisch examines works by Joanna Russ, Philip K. Dick, and Samuel R. Delany in which the effects of technology on the abilities of human beings to communicate with one another are considered. These are literary portrayals of the difficulties these authors feel technology has created for normal, effective communication. The fragmentation involved in the authors' technique mirrors the fragmentation of meaning that is thought to exist "in the world."

Frisch explores the claims that an objective reality has dissolved, that voice alone is not sufficient for meaning, and that memory blurs and private hallucinations that occur when there is internal dialogue hardly qualify as conditions for communication. Through these authors' works and supplemental interpretations, Frisch examines the possibilities of metalogic operating when logic goes bankrupt in an illogical world.

Joanna P. Cobb argues that Harlan Ellison has written a paradigm of the "new form" called for by Robert Scholes. In Ellison's story, the abstract language of the computer is set in sharp contrast to the concrete sensory experience of its captive humans and the reader. The choice and use of vivid word descriptions, which "bombard the senses of the reader," successfully transmit the message to the feeling, or "viscera," as well as to the intellect of the reader. Through his story, Cobb claims, Ellison embodies the structuralist imagination in which the author not only informs the reader but also makes him/her feel the consequences of actions taken or not yet taken. In this case the author transforms the medium into the message itself. In his unconventional use of language and style, Ellison uses language itself as an instrument of torture.

# Language Fragmentation in Recent Science-Fiction Novels

*ADAM J. FRISCH*

In recent years some science-fiction writers have turned their attentions to the effect technology has had on the abilities of human beings to communicate clearly with each other. Most of these examinations end pessimistically; the main characters of the novels are so destroyed mentally that they can only babble by story's end. Novels written between 1975 and 1980, such as Joanna Russ's *We Who Are About To. . .*, Phillip K. Dick's *A Scanner Darkly,* and Samuel Delany's *Triton,* have proven so depressing and so stylistically complex that it has been charged that serious science fiction can no longer be entertaining. But if these works demand more from their readers, they offer in return significant observations on the reasons for the growing confusion in our twentieth-century modes of discourse. In the end, they may even suggest a few ways in which modern man can begin to untangle some of his language perplexities.

Lying at the core of Joanna Russ's *We Who Are About To. . .* is an examination of language and meaning. The protagonist of the novel is the last surviving member of a small group of travelers accidentally marooned on an isolated planet somewhere outside our galaxy. During the first half of the novel, Russ's unnamed narrator becomes more and more disenchanted with her fellow travelers, the young athlete Alan, the upper-class Grahams, the "smiling professor" John Ude, and several others. When her companions refuse to allow her to leave the group, the narrator kills each of them, some deliberately, some impulsively. In the second half of the novel the narrator, alone and slowly starving to death, recalls various friends and religious and political activities from her past until she can no longer separate memory from hallucination. The final fragment, which ends with the narrator holding a suicide capsule in her bony hand and stating, "well, it's time," is followed by the silence of a blank page.

Although stranded outside the galaxy of ordinary human discourse, all of the novel's characters, with the exception of the narrator, insist on retaining their traditional speech and behavioral patterns, even when those patterns are no longer functional. John Ude, the smiling professor, conducts all group meetings as if he were on a university committee:

> Mister-not-Professor Ude said, "I call this meeting to order."
> Oh. Oh my. Important.
> "You're chairman?" I said. "Well! Who made you chairman?"[1]

As long as her companions are not threatening in their social games, the narrator tries to show them the meaninglessness of statements that are based on conceptions rendered irrelevant by their situation. When the "capitalistic" Mrs. Graham calls her a "Communist," the narrator responds:

> I'd prefer it if you called me what we call ourselves: Nobodies—I'm Nobody, who are you? Are you Nobody, too? How nice. Which is no bar to being a Communist. Which I was.[2]

But the narrator's companions are incapable of change because they are incapable of listening. They have been nurtured in a culture that is almost devoid of the ability to discriminate sounds. The narrator finds their music mere noise that "goes deedle deedle deedle deedle deedle deedle deedle deedle for half an hour and then it goes doodle just once, and you could die with excitement."[3] Thus, when the males in the group, in an assumption of atavistic roles, decide the women must bear children immediately to insure "survival," she feels threatened and attempts to flee. It is when those attempts are thwarted that she turns and fights.

Throughout the novel, the narrator is desperate to communicate. When her fellow survivors cannot or will not listen, she turns to her imagined future listener, the reader:

> "Speaking" comes from a different place than "breathing." You must understand this. Those marks, "-", indicate speech. Communication. You must listen.

You must understand that the patriarchy is coming back, has returned (in fact) in two days. By no design.[4]

Although the narrator at first attributes her desire to communicate to the return of "the patriarchy" (that is, to the group's rapid reversion to male dominance), her repetition of the phrase "I must" suggests that the need for communication may arise from each individual's perception of death's inevitability. "I must speak" becomes "I must die." We, as the audience, are to learn from the narrator's plight not only the danger of our primitive, instinctive behavioral roles but also the fundamental necessity of social discourse.

Having killed the last of her companions, the narrator turns inward for companionship, and the second half of Russ's novel examines the gradual deterioration of her internal monologue. "Every mind is its own galaxy," the narrator tells us, and when outward criteria for meaningful discourse fail her, she turns to an intuitional standard:[5]

So ideas stick. Meanings stick. Anything you can force inside your head and keep it there. Also emotion. Which shouldn't last but it does. My God, it lasts and lasts. Wish it didn't.[6]

At first, even though she understands the radical limitations of her self-imposed isolation, Russ's narrator enjoys the freedom to remember and reflect without interruption:

Everything's being sublimed into voice, sacrificed for voice; my voice will live on years and years after I die, thus proving that the rest of me was faintly comic at best, perhaps impossible, just an organic backup for conversation. Marvelous, marvelous conversation! The end of life.[7]

But even this "end" (in the sense of an ideal) breaks down as the narrator's physical end approaches. As the narrator herself notes, "voice" alone, no matter how refined, is not sufficient for meaning. Sound, pure sound, demands some sort of noetical response on the part of the listener.

Even music, beautiful music, hearing, that won't last unless you translate it into ideas, put it into your head, recreate it, drum it in.[8]

Soon the combined effects of isolation and starvation blur the boundaries between memory and hallucination, causing the narrator to lapse into long periods of confusion and silence, which Russ indicates with white space and dots:

> She's been walking around dead for years.
>
> •         •         •
>
> Evening. Dawn. Morning? Can't tell.
>
> •        .        •         •
>
> I started to say something.
>
> •         •         •
> •         •         •
> •         •         •
>
> Oh yes. It's hotter.[9]

Strains from Handel begin to penetrate the syntax of her internal monologue. As the story nears its end, the narrator's recorded remarks break into numerous associative title lists and strings of admonitory verb fragments:

> What I could have
> Should have
> Couldn't
> Should have thought really
> Really! Arrogant, solitary, secretly cruel, I am.
> I am.[10]

If the narrator's ideal is the "sublime, refined music of conversation," then her story shows the futility of that ideal. In this sense, *We Who Are About To. . .* closely parallels Beckett's absurdist drama, *Krapp's Last Tape*. Both narrators attempt to penetrate that peculiar memory-experience-anticipation intermix that we term self-consciousness by confronting recorded fragments of themselves. Both find their attempts to fix identity in language frustrated by approaching death. Like another of Beckett's title characters, Russ's narrator, despite her most dedicated efforts, ultimately must remain even to herself: "the unnameable."

Like Joanna Russ, Philip K. Dick often explores the limits of discourse in his works. Unlike Russ, however, he seldom announces his intention. Perhaps his late novel, *A Scanner Darkly*, most closely focuses on this topic, for it details the gradual, drug-related breakdown in communication between the left and right hemispheres of the protagonist's brain.

The protagonist in *Scanner* has two names from the start: publicly, he is Robert Arctor, an easygoing street person and occasional drug pusher; privately he is a government narcotics agent known only as "Fred." While on duty Arctor, as Fred, protects his identity by wearing a scramble suit, a tonal and chromatic aberration device that distorts his appearance beyond recognition. Among his "friends," however, Arctor must consume more and more of the identity-destroying drug, Substance D, in order to avoid suspicion. Eventually, this toxic agent ruptures his corpus callosum beyond repair, and he seeks help at a neural-aphasia rehabilitation clinic, where he takes on yet another identity, the childlike "Bruce." The novel ends with Arctor a retarded field laborer, barely able to think in complete sentences and harvesting the very drug that has destroyed him.

Where Russ's narrator confronts a homogenized "deedle deedle" culture whose behavioral models for actions and languages tend toward the neurotic, Robert Arctor faces a society whose ultimate goal is for the same hamburger to be bought and sold 50 million times, and for there to be only one telephone number for everyone (including information), one medicine for all ills, and one law for all crimes.[11] Even in his early law-and-order speech to the Anaheim Lions Club, Fred finds the "pre-prepared texts" of his culture meaningless.

"Each day," Fred, Robert Arctor, whatever, said, "this disease takes its toll of us. By the end of each passing day. . . ." They didn't notice any difference, he noticed, even though he had dropped the prepared speech and was wandering on, by himself, without help from the PR boys back at the Orange County Civic Center. What difference anyhow? he thought.[12]

If Arctor has little faith in the establishment's "line," he has even less trust in his own instincts. His occupation forces him to lie to companions, thus encouraging his paranoid interpretation of their remarks to him:

But in this dark world where he now dwelt, ugly things and surprising things and once in a long while a tiny wonderous thing spilled out at him constantly; he could count on nothing.[13]

Arctor's built-in suspicions allow his roommate, Barris, who already suspects his government connections, to manipulate him. Barris spends much of the novel feeding Arctor long, contradictory hypotheses about the "enemy's" identity, even suggesting he himself is the foe, acting "under post-hypnotic suggestion, with an amnesia block so I wouldn't remember."[14] With every alternative possible, with everyone part of someone else's game, speculative thought soon becomes useless. In the novel's ultimate irony Arctor himself is being "used" by the two friends he never suspected as government agents, Donna and Mike, to penetrate the rehabilitation clinic's Substance D operations.

Arctor's mistrust of intuitional criteria is justified, for throughout the book his ability to communicate even internally is gradually destroyed by the deterioration of his corpus callosum, the fundamental "communications channel" between the associative, intuitional right hemisphere of the brain and the more rational, more linguistic left side. Arctor experiences this breakdown as an identity split between his friendly Bob Arctor personality and the super-ego, "Fred" identity.

Is Fred actually the same as Bob? Does anybody know? I would know, if anyone did, because I'm the only person in the world that knows that Fred is Bob Arctor. But, he thought, who am I? Which of them is me?[15]

As the destruction continues, Arctor finds himself thinking as if another person or mind were thinking: "But different from the way you would think. Even foreign words that you don't know."[16]

Facing paranoia and schizophrenia, Arctor desperately tries to hold onto the notion of an objective, recordable reality somewhere beneath all the masks, hallucinations, and identity games. Should this perceptional anchor fail, he realizes he is doomed.

Murk outside; murk inside. I hope, for everyone's sake, the scanners do better. Because, he thought, if the scanner sees only darkly, the way I myself do, then we are cursed, cursed again and like we have been continually, and we'll wind up dead this way, knowing very little and getting that little fragment wrong too.[17]

And it does fail. At one point, as Fred, Arctor watches a scanner videotape of himself under the influence of Substance D sleeping with a girl named Connie, but imagining that he is actually in bed with his girl friend, Donna Hawthorne. All eight scanner holograms show Fred an image "still half Connie; already half Donna."[18] The scanner is now also registering Arctor's hallucination. Dick simply may be pointing out that Arctor's mental deterioration is affecting his "Fred" side, or he may believe that there is no such thing as a recordable reality. For the individual the result in either case is similar: when he looks for objective truth he finds only "his own face reflected back up at him, reversed—pulled through infinity."[19] After the scanner incident, Arctor's world quickly collapses, until soon: "He heard nothing now. And forgot the meaning of the words, and finally, the words themselves."[20] Arctor's tautological pun near the end of the novel, "I am an eye," becomes finally the only kind of knowledge he can communicate.

Our last view of Arctor, now called Bruce, shows him repeating instructions like a child learning language through mimicry. Although personally destroyed, Arctor still manages at the end of the novel to hide one sprig of the farm's Substance D plant in his shoe, "a present for my friends." Dick may be suggesting that Arctor's loss will be redeemed at least partially by the government's capture of one drug supplier, but this is scant solace for the individual whose voice, without and within, has been silenced by social isolation, self-doubt, and death:

"Substance D. Which is for Dumbness and Despair and Desertion [and] finally Death. Slow Death."[21]

As Dick himself observes in his "Author's Note" at the end of the book: "This has been a novel about some people who were punished entirely too much for what they did."[22]

While the novels of Russ and Dick illustrate the destruction of external and internal criteria for language, Samuel Delany's *Triton* attempts to identify the causes of that destruction. Delany believes that modern technology has created a gap between individual perception and mass behavior, and he attempts to erect a "metalogical" bridge across that gap. "Some Informal Remarks toward the Modular Calculus," the novel is a self-conscious examination of the way language works. The book's epigraph is a quotation from Mary Douglas's *Natural Symbols*: "The body itself is a highly restricted medium of expression. . . .To be useful, the structural analysis of symbols has somehow to be related to a hypothesis about role structure."[23] As Sam, one of the books principal characters, points out, "The episteme is *always* the secondary hero of the s-f novel."[24]

*Triton* depicts a future in which technology has populated even the outer moons of the solar system. The story follows Bron Helstrom from the beginning of his love for a "microdramatist" known as "the Spike," through his trip to Earth and a subsequent short but deadly war between the satellites and planets to an eventual sex-change operation that Bron hopes will make him a more appealing person. The two long, highly analytical appendices that follow the story proper contain the foundations of the metalogical systems of the fictitious philosopher, Ashima Slade.

Delany's novel is in essence a chronicle of failures in communication. It begins with the breakdown of a government "ego booster" booth, which eats Bron's identification card until its power is shut off. As Bron roams through the unlicensed sector of Tethys (more confusion: Tethys is the name of one of Saturn's moons as well as the capital city of the Neptune moon on which Bron lives), he encounters the ninety-seven syllable mantra of the Poor Children of the Avestal Light and Changing Secret Name: "mimimomomizolalilamiolomuelamironoriminos. . . ." Political posters on his left proclaim, "Know Your Place in Society," on his right, "Triton with the Satellite Alliance." Suddenly Bron becomes an audience of one for the newest of the Spike's (whose name is Gene Trimbell) microdramas, a short play that Bron doesn't even realize is a play until the actors begin to applaud him at its conclusion.

Time and again Delany bombards Bron with the changing names and new labels of a twenty-second century culture that is frantic to catalogue each new product of its own burgeoning technology. When threatened, this culture turns these labels into weapons, as Ashima Slade, the novel's philosopher, explains:

Our society in the Satellites extends to its Earth and Mars emigrants, at the same time it extends instruction on how to conform, the materials with which to destroy themselves, both psychologically and physically—all under the same label: Freedom. To the extent they will not conform to our ways, there is a subtle swing: the materials of instruction are pulled further away and the materials of destruction are pushed correspondingly closer. Since the ways of instruction and the ways of destruction are *not* the same, but only and secretly tied by language, we have simply, here, overdetermined yet another way for the rest of us to remain oblivious to other peoples' pain.[25]

This kind of language tactic, however, is always self-defeating, for it undermines the world of meaningful discourse that it was designed to protect. What is true for the emigrant becomes true for the citizen, a fact that Bron (who is both citizen and emigrant) discovers as the novel progresses. Already saddled with a "traditionally masculine" propensity

toward inflated language, Bron approaches the unintelligible as he trots
forth complicated mathematical formulas and parenthetical qualifica-
tions within parenthetical remarks to impress friends and attract
acquaintances:

> Bron set the cup down and fingered up the thick pack. He unwrapped the
> blue silk cloth from around it. Along the napkin's edge, gold threads embroidered:

$$\sum_{n=-\infty}^{\infty} \frac{1}{\pi} \log_2 \frac{\left|\int_{-A}^{A} M(\Theta)\exp(j\frac{\pi n\Theta}{A})\,d\Theta\right|^2 + \left|\int_{-A}^{A} N(\Theta)\exp(j\frac{\sin\Theta}{A})\,d\Theta\right|^3 + A_M^N}{A_M - \prod_{r=\pm n}^{N} \frac{1}{\Theta}\log_\pi \left|\int_{-A}^{A} N(k\frac{\cos\Theta}{A})\,d\Theta\right|^3 - \prod_{r=A}^{\infty} \frac{1}{\pi}\log_\phi \left|\int_{r}^{\bullet} M(j\frac{\pi n\Theta}{\pi})\,d\Theta\right|^5}$$

—the rather difficult modulus by which the even more difficult scoring system
(Lawrence had not taught him that yet; he knew only that $\Theta$ was a measurement
of strategic angles of attack [over different sorts of terrain N, M, and A] and
that small ones netted more points than large ones) proceeded.[26]

Such grotesque parodies of clear communication dot the streams-of-
consciousness of both Bron and his society, until both perceptual systems
are overwhelmed with technical detail. The final breakdown of communication is mirrored by the satellite-planet war that decimates the
Earth and Mars, where Bron first formed his sexual identity. It is further
symbolized by the destruction of Lawrence's tiny war figurines, the van-
dalism of the art sculpture at Bron's place of work, and by Bron's own
"dissolution" of the male side of his personality.

Out of this technological nightmare of complexity arises metalogic, a
complicated mathematical model of abstractions designed "to—well, explain how what-there-is manages to accomplish what-it-does."[27] Several
explanations of metalogic are offered during the course of the novel
and its appendices. Bron's sex-change counselor suggests the following
definition:

> The point is, with life enclosed between two vast parentheses of nonbeing and
> straited on either side by inevitable suffering, there is no *logical* reason ever to
> try to improve any situation. There are, however, many reasons of other types
> for making as many improvements as you reasonably can. Any reasoning process,
> as it deviates from strict, deductive logic, is a metalogical one.[28]

Ashima Slade's Harbin-Y lectures, on the other hand, offer complex attempts to chart the entire language process. He analyzes in detail man's labeling format, with examples such as how a child might come to call a fire engine a "Red Squealer" because of a "morphological path-of-least-resistance," while pointing out that subsequent generations may construct perfectly "logical" explanations for this label that would be historically inaccurate.[29]

At the heart of all these definitions of metalogic lies the notion of a language "calculus." Delany believes that linguistic units, rather than "adding up" bit by bit to a cumulative meaning, tend to generate when combined new parts/context dynamics. Slade is killed before he can complete his work on a "modular calculus" that will accurately describe the language process, but Bron's story offers a visible manifestation of the theory at work. The "traditionally male" role structures Bron has inherited from his Mars-Earth past as a male prostitute spawn exaggerated language postures whenever he seeks to communicate with such friends as Lawrence, Sam, Miriamne or the Spike herself. As Russ's narrator and Dick's Robert Arctor also discover, however, there are few ways for the individual to overcome such built-in discourse limitations. Bron is offered an option that the former characters were not. He can change "contexts," that is, he can become a female. Multiple points of view are vital, as Delany points out at the beginning of his first appendix: "Everything in a science-fiction novel should be mentioned at least twice (in at least two different contexts)."[30] While Bron's sex-change operation does not bring about a sudden, total shift in his/her perceptual base, at least Bron begins to question the pretensions and lies that seem to have underlined most of his statements. Unsure at last about the nightmare that has been his life, Bron, Delany hints, is finally ready for a new dawn, even though the Spike still rejects him.

While it may be nice that a sex-change operation has helped Bron overcome certain intellectual and linguistic handicaps, such an outcome hardly inspires any hope for more effective human communication in the near future. If Russ, Dick, and Delany seem pessimistic about technology's effects on human language, their characters' stories at least illustrate the process of citing "essential instances of admonitory or pedagogical negatives," which Kenneth Burke has labeled the "Dramatistic Approach" to language.[31] Observing that "the essential distinction between the verbal and the nonverbal is in fact that language adds the peculiar possibility of the Negative," Burke notes that the best literary works are often most valuable when somehow "infused with the spirit of the thou-shalt-not":

> However "positive" a style, or moral injunction, may contrive to be in its wording, behind it always lurks the Basic Negative, the Great, Tragic, Feudlike *Lex Talionis,* itself a universal principle of Justice, and one without which the art of an Aeschylus would be meaningless. . . .Such reduction by no means imposes impoverishment or distortion upon the analysis of human motives.[32]

Hallucination, paradox, fragmentary streams-of-consciousness, the disintegration of thought patterns, all these elements mark the novels of Russ, Dick, and Delany. But perhaps these authors illustrate not so much the inherent absurdity in all human language as the probable linguistic dead-ends. If our protective garments of traditional logic and language patterns have been stripped away, leaving us naked and raving upon the technological heath of the twentieth century, then like King Lear we may need to learn that only the Fool can speak clearly. Perhaps Russ's narrator, Robert Arctor, and Bron Helstrom are trying to teach us through their stories how to become that Fool.

## Notes

1. Joanna Russ, *We Who Are About To. . .* (New York: Dell Publishing Co., 1977), p. 54.
2. Ibid., p. 33.
3. Ibid., p. 52.
4. Ibid., p. 34.
5. Ibid., p. 124.
6. Ibid., p. 141.
7. Ibid., p. 127.
8. Ibid., p. 138.
9. Ibid., pp. 134-35.
10. Ibid., p. 154.
11. Philip K. Dick, *A Scanner Darkly* (New York: Ballantine, 1977), pp. 28-29.
12. Ibid., p. 24.
13. Ibid., p. 66.
14. Ibid., p. 72.
15. Ibid., p. 101.
16. Ibid., p. 118.
17. Ibid., p. 193.
18. Ibid., p. 181.
19. Ibid., p. 220.

20. Ibid., p. 261.

21. Ibid., p. 26.

22. Ibid., p. 289.

23. Samuel R. Delany, *Triton* (New York: Bantam Books, 1976).

24. Ibid., p. 333.

25. Ibid., pp. 357-58.

26. Ibid., pp. 26-27. For another example, see p. 63.

27. Ibid., p. 60.

28. Ibid., p. 268.

29. Ibid., pp. 335-36.

30. Ibid., p. 333. True to his own advice, Delany repeats this observation at the end of the first appendix, within the new context: "with the possible exception of science fiction" (p. 341).

31. Kenneth Burke, *Language as Symbolic Action* (Berkeley: University of California Press, 1966), pp. 420-22 ff.

32. Ibid., p. 453.

# 12

# Medium and Message in Ellison's "I Have No Mouth, and I Must Scream"

*JOANN P. COBB*

Harlan Ellison's "I Have No Mouth, and I Must Scream" is a nightmare vision of a future world at the mercy of an insane computer, motivated only by hatred and revenge.[1] The communication of these emotions creates a compelling, if disgusting, story and illustrates Ellison's talent for combining traditional narrative techniques with modern rhetorical devices to produce science fiction that in its exaggeration of the probable future of computer technology demonstrates the evils of contemporary attitudes toward knowing, understanding, and communicating. Ellison contrasts the abstract language of the computer with the concrete, sensory experience of the humans and illustrates the surrender of human purpose and value that is inherent in contemporary attitudes toward technological progress.

"I Have No Mouth, and I Must Scream" asserts that time poorly spent by humans who are unaware of their purpose and the consequences of their attitudes will result in the destruction of the species. Implicit in the narrator's retrospective lament, that because humans did not understand what they were doing they brought on catastrophe, is the assertion that contemporary society is incapable of coping with the so-called age of science. Through his story, Ellison illustrates the dangers inherent in what Archibald MacLeish has called "the age of abstraction":

Abstractions have a limiting, a dehumanizing, a dehydrating effect on the relation to things of the man who must live with them. The result is that we are more and more left, in our scientific society, without the means of knowledge of ourselves as we truly are or of our experience as it actually is. . . .We begin with one abstraction (something we think of as ourselves) and a mess of other abstractions (standing for the world) and we arrange and rearrange the counters, but who we are and what we are doing we simply do not know—above all what we are doing. With the inevitable consequence that we do not know either what our purpose is or our end.[2]

Using computer language, Ellison pushes the abstract to its ultimate lunacy and in the process produces science fiction that is both McLuhanesque and structuralist.

In his celebrated and controversial speculations about communication, McLuhan discusses the effects of "hot" and "cool" media in which the degree of "heat" inversely regulates participatory response. Thus a "hot" medium like print, which "extends one single sense in 'high definition,' " is low in participation and completion by the audience.[3] To increase audience participation, the medium must be "cooled," forcing the reader, in the case of a literary work, to become more involved in the completion of the communication. Ellison "cools" his medium with a typographical format that is new in the sense that it represents the voice of the computer. But while it intrigues and involves the reader, it does not of itself increase participation or understanding until the context of irrationality communicates "nightmare."

In communicating that message, Ellison exhibits the "structuralist imagination" described by Robert Scholes, who has asserted that it is "futuristic" in its ability to inform the human race of the consequences of actions not yet taken. Scholes also insists that the structural imagination "must not merely inform, it must make us feel the consequences of those actions, feel them in our hearts and viscera." Ironically, Scholes all but ignores Ellison's contribution, yet "I Have No Mouth, and I Must Scream" serves well as an example of that "change in the system of literature" or "new form" that must arise, according to Scholes, "if man is to continue."[4]

Ellison's technique for assaulting his readers in their "hearts and viscera" involves transforming the medium into the message itself, a message that hatred, duplicity, and horror will result from machine supremacy over human values. The master computer, AM, transmits hate and revenge to the trapped humans, and in turn, the first-person narrator transmits that same message to the reader. As AM manipulates his helpless victims, the narrator victimizes his reader, arousing frustration, disgust, and outrage. Although the literary techniques that provoke the desired response are not new, they are used by Ellison in a radically new manner.[5]

Typographical format, shocking imagery, and an unreliable narrator function in concert to force the reader to complete the communication loop in its visceral horror.

AM is composed of a chain of computer banks that are described as "chittering as thought ran through the machine" (p. 8). Although the master computer is capable of inserting thoughts directly into the minds of its five live victims, it also presumably communicates through the computer tapes that are inserted at irregular intervals throughout the story. The "voice" of the computer, which is expressed in a highly organized but meaningless series of dots, is the ultimate "cool" medium. The reader has no key to the coded message, which is never translated, yet he desperately needs to understand it. Ironically, modern communication theory suggests that just such a situation offers the greatest learning opportunity to the reader:

In a highly organized (read "conventional") situation the information transmittable is minute. . . . The less freedom of choice, the higher is the reader's certainty that he "got" the message. And the less he learns.[6]

Forced into selecting a message from an infinity of possibilities, the reader of Ellison's story "learns" frustration, fear of the unknown and probably sinister intentions of AM, and the immediate experience of the lunacy of the computer's world.

The narrator, Ted, is the only guide through this nightmare, and it is never known whether or not he understands the computer message. His unreliability as a communicator is established in the insertion of the computer tapes without comment. Ellison's narrator is a modern version of fictional communicators who use "language" not to enlighten but to confuse. Thus, he is the literary descendant of such madmen as Sterne's Tristram Shandy and the Hack writer of Swift's *Tale of a Tub*. But the eighteenth-century narrators are admittedly disorganized, while Ellison's narrator represents sanity in an otherwise lunatic world. The Hack writer's rows of asterisks to represent a hiatus in the manuscript arouse frustration in the reader but not the fear projected by the impenetrable message of the computer. The reader's outrage is directed toward Swift's narrator, while Ellison's narrator transfers that emotion to the computer.

Contributing to the fear generated by the code is an occasional, more explicit message. AM expresses his attitudes "in a pillar of stainless steel and neon letters" inserted into Ted's mind:

HATE. LET ME TELL
YOU HOW MUCH I'VE
COME TO HATE YOU
SINCE I BEGAN TO
LIVE. THERE ARE
3 8 7. 4 4 MILLION
MILES OF PRINTED
CIRCUITS IN WAFER
THIN LAYERS THAT
FILL MY COMPLEX.
IF THE WORD HATE
WAS ENGRAVED ON
EACH NANOANGSTROM
OF THOSE HUNDREDS
OF MILLION MILES
IT WOULD NOT EQUAL
ONE ONE-BILLIONTH
OF THE HATE I FEEL
FOR HUMANS AT THIS
MICRO-INSTANT FOR
YOU. HATE. HATE. [Pp. 12-13]

But the neon letters communicate little more than the computer tapes. The total message is the one-word sentence: "Hate." This isolated abstraction becomes no more intelligible with AM's attempt to describe how much hate is in the computer. AM's ancestors had been designed to make war, programmed to hate, and now the computer's total consciousness is absorbed in hate.

Ellison projects an aggressive human nature that "hates" its own kind to the ultimate abstraction: all-consuming, unreasoning, extant hate. But the abstraction is meaningless except in the concrete consequences it engenders, which Ellison recounts in grisly detail. AM's hate for the humans who gave him sentience without purpose has resulted in the extermination of all but five whom he keeps alive for "everlasting punishment." The computer tortures these five physically and spiritually, and the pain is transferred to the reader.

The torment endured by the trapped remains of the human race impinges on the nerve fibers of the reader with almost unbearable intensity. While it is impossible to approach the sensory impact of the entire story, a few examples can serve to illustrate the quality and effect of the imagery. AM's victims are always hungry, and the always unfulfilled promise of nourishment is part of the torture. The movement of the plot is a journey to the ice caves where they find canned goods but no can opener. AM provides just enough sustenance to keep his prey alive. When the computer sends down "manna," however, it tastes "like boiled boar urine" (p. 5).

The auditory torture is variously described as "the shriek of babies being ground beneath blue-hot rollers," and "the lunatic laugh of a fat woman." Compounding the pain is the stench of matted wet fur, charred wood, dusty velvet, rotting orchids, sour milk, sulphur, rancid butter, oil slick, chalk dust, and human scalps. The visual images engender both disgust and pity. Benny (formerly a brilliant, handsome, gay college professor) has been transformed into a mad apelike creature with "an organ fit for a horse" (p. 10). His punishment for attempted escape is visual: "His eyes were two soft, moist pools of pus-like jelly" (p. 7). Madness and hunger finally drive Benny to cannibalism:

Benny was eating Gorrister's face. Gorrister on his side, thrashing snow, Benny wrapped around him with powerful monkey legs crushing Gorrister's waist, his hand locked around Gorrister's head like a nutcracker, and his mouth ripping at the tender skin of Gorrister's cheek. . . .Benny's head pulled back sharply, as something gave all at once, and a bleeding raw-white dripping of flesh hung from his teeth. [P. 17]

Here all the horror of loss of humanity is seen. Elsewhere the pain is felt: "AM said it with the sliding cold horror of a razor blade slicing my eyeball" (p. 13), and "the pain shivered through my flesh like tinfoil on a tooth" (p. 7).

Ellison's attack on the total sensory vulnerability of the reader approaches overkill, but its impact is unforgettable.[7] Only a totally insensitive reader could escape a "visceral" reaction to the torture, and thus Ellison transfers to the reader the physical pain that is the consequence of computer takeover. The physical consequences are accompanied by intellectual consequences as well. AM rages at his entrapment: "We had allowed him to think, but to do nothing with it. . . .He could not wander, he could not wonder, he could not belong. He could merely be" (p. 13). His revenge takes the form of entrapment of his victims, for although they know existentially that they are hopeless victims of inhuman rage, they retain human expectations. AM permits these expectations in order to frustrate them. The narrator, in turn, exploits the reader's expectations for exactly the same purpose.

In telling the story of the last five humans, Ted elicits the sympathy of the reader, even though his unreliability is established in the title of "his" story. The reader who expects resolution of that paradox experiences only disappointment and further frustration. The story opens with a graphic description of the body of Gorrister hanging upside down from the ceiling, drained of blood through "a precise incision made from ear to ear under the lantern jaw." But the next paragraph begins: "When Gorrister joined our group and looked up at himself, it was already too late for us to realize that once again AM had duped us, had had his fun." This beginning, which has been called "inexplicable" except in terms of an "Exodus motif,"[8] is structurally significant as the initial establishment of the basic relationship: computer/narrator; narrator/reader. As AM dupes his victims, the narrator dupes the reader.

Even so, the reader continues to empathize with Ted, through his nonchalant revelation that the small group has been "in the computer" for 109 years, through his attitude toward the "black bitch" who services each of the men but enjoys only Benny, through his self-pitying assertion that the others hate him because he is "the youngest, and the one AM had affected least of all" (p. 9). While the others are grotesques physically and spiritually, Ted appears to the reader as normal and even heroic in his "rescue" of his companions from the computer. In his inverted sacrifice (everything in the story is transformed by inversion), Ted offers his death so that the others may die. He succeeds in killing the others, but AM will prevent eternally his suicide, as the ominous computer message that follows the death of Ted's last companion seems to assert.

This seventh and last computer tape insertion, however, is exactly the same as all the others. The unintelligible series of dots remains untranslated, but by this point the reader has been "programmed" to understand the message of maniacal rage and awesome consequences.

Although the reader has learned to accept the powerful hatred of the computer and should have learned to distrust even the narrator, nothing prepares him/her for the final shock. With only his mind left intact, Ted describes his physical appearance as it is reflected in the metal surfaces:

I am a great soft jelly thing. Smoothly rounded, with no mouth, with pulsing white holes filled by fog where my eyes used to be. Rubbery appendages that were once my arms; bulks rounding down into legless humps of soft slippery matter. I leave a moist trail when I move. [P. 19]

The final trap is sprung: no mouth, no eyes, no fingers, no typewriter. The reader knows the hopelessness of attempting to make sense of something that is beyond the power of human rationalization. While Ted may comfort himself with the knowledge that his friends are safe, there is no comfort for his victims.

The reader is left with a sense of outrage. But the outrage is directed at AM, the surrogate god whose sole reason for being is the torture of the human race, now crystallized in the reader's friend Ted. It is a tribute to the literary power of the story that no amount of pedantic patience can redirect reader outrage to Ellison or his unreliable narrator. Ellison's masterful presentation so captures the reader that any explanation of the narrative trickery is superfluous. Irrational treachery is the message, and the "medium" functions to communicate it and provoke the desired response. The reader becomes the victim of mechanical madness and gratuitous torture.

Language itself becomes an instrument of torture as the sinister computer tape messages are reinforced by the narrator's disruption of syntactical expectations. Ellison's one-word sentences both express the painful situation of the narrator and permit the narrator to torture the reader. The evocation of his hunger requires the narrator to remember when he has last eaten and what: "Three days it had been since we'd last eaten. Worms. Thick, ropey." The one-word "sentence" is a shocker, followed by a double aftershock that forces the reader to feel the revulsion that a more conventional sentence structure would not elicit.

The single concrete noun "worms" forces the reader to supply both syntactic and imaginative content and, in the process, creates a prolonged confrontation with a concept the reader would prefer to abandon. Escape is frustrated, however, by the two-word sentence that follows, thus doubling the length and impact, while forcing attention back to the noun. The force of this experience of the individual concrete thing is further enhanced by the contrast to the single-word abstraction spit forth by the computer: hate. Humans do not live, it is implied, in the abstract world of computer technology, but in the physical experience of worms for dinner. Hate becomes meaningful only in the experience of its consequences. And the ultimate consequence for Ted is psychological as well as physical.

Still reeling from the shock of Ted's physical description of himself, the reader must now face Ted's description of his psychological state at the end of the story. With almost unbearable intensity, Ted's spiritual isolation is emphasized by syntax and typography:

Alone. Here. Living under the land, under the sea, in the belly of AM, whom we created because our time was badly spent and we must have known unconsciously that he could do it better. [P. 19]

Once again the single-word sentence functions to intensify meaning. The word is both typographically and semantically alone. Ted is the only human left alive, although he describes himself as "a thing that could never have been known as human, a thing whose shape is so alien a travesty, that humanity becomes more obscene for the vague resemblance" (p. 19). Hate has become a concrete shape, a travesty of humanity—its source not AM, but Ted: "Blotches of diseased, evil gray come and go on my surface, as though light is being beamed from within" (p. 19).

If the reader's identification with the unreliable narrator is complete, the message is clear. We externalize our hate, remove ourselves from its horror through creative technology, and eventually destroy all that is human in ourselves.

Thus, Ellison, in his unforgettably moving story, provokes in the reader a felt realization of the harrowing consequences of the surrender of human purpose and freedom. Ellison's visceral warning that human creativity must be spent wisely and the consequences calculated carefully is ample proof that the modern literary imagination is equal to the task Scholes demands of it.

## Notes

1. In *Alone Against Tomorrow* (New York: Macmillan, 1970), pp. 3-19. References to this edition of "I Have No Mouth, and I Must Scream" are cited parenthetically in the text.

2. Archibald MacLeish, "Why Do We Teach Poetry?" *Atlantic Monthly* 197 (March 1956): 51.

3. Marshall McLuhan, *Understanding Media: The Extensions of Man* (New York: McGraw-Hill, 1964), p. 22.

4. Robert Scholes, *Structuralism in Literature* (New Haven: Yale Press, 1974), p. 200. Although Scholes omits comment on Ellison here and in *Structural Fabulation* (Notre Dame: University Press, 1975), "I Have No Mouth, and I Must Scream" is mentioned briefly in *Science Fiction* by Scholes and Eric S. Rabkin (Oxford: University Press, 1977), pp. 131-32.

5. Ellison's technique is reminiscent of Jonathan Swift's satiric entrapment of the reader through similar devices. A detailed explication of Swift's practice can be found in Joann P. Cobb, "Jonathan Swift and Epistemology: A Study of Swift's Satire on Ways of Knowing" (Ann Arbor: University Microfilms, 1975).

6. Edward M. Jennings, ed., *Science and Literature: New Lenses for Criticism* (Garden City, N.Y.: Doubleday Anchor Books, 1970), p. 14.

7. Students not notable for careful reading recall Ellison's imagery with striking accuracy and consistency.

8. Charles J. Brady, "The Computer as a Symbol of God: Ellison's Macabre Exodus," *Journal of General Education* 28 (1976): 60.

# VII

# Feminist Science Fiction and Medical Morals

It is not only technology that poses real or possible dangers for human values and human culture. Social critics, philosophers, science fiction writers, and others, have often characterized Western culture in general, and American culture in particular, as pragmatic and utilitarian. Perverted for or through popularization, these forms can be expressed as, "It's good if it works," and "We ought to do whatever 'makes' the greatest happiness for the greatest number." While the accuracy of this characterization may be questioned, there are a number of arguments for technological, social, and/or political programs that sound remarkably similar to these.

Surely it does not call for genius-level thinking to recognize that simply because some "thing," policy, or practice works, it is unqualifiedly good. Similarly, what we "should" do is often supported by a "greatest happiness" data fund that is derived from questionably representative "opinion surveys" or "competent experts" whose expertise is in an area of specialization not directly relevant to the action which their "expertise" is supposed to support decisively. Such stilted, although highly convincing, greatest happiness appeals may win the argument while ignoring significant numbers of individuals who are far from happy and equally far from treatment that recognizes their worth and dignity as human beings.

Within a society, culture, or subculture certain dominant attitudes or thought patterns, often simply unconscious assumptions, tend to influence and justify the practices and "norms" within that group. Until we become aware of their existence and until we have some identifiable frame of reference, it is difficult to assess critically these underlying assumptions.

Anne Hudson Jones claims that the special techniques and the nonrealistic novel form of science fiction enable us to detect and assess certain dominant attitudes within our culture. Tying together a novel by Marge Piercy and several actual cases, she explores the sexist, racist, and paternalistic ethos of medical practice which she feels is a microcosm of American culture at large.

In the alternate future societies that Piercy presents, the reader is able to identify and evaluate assumptions that are too close to recognize otherwise. As Jones points out, Piercy's heroine is able to act as an individual, thus achieving an individual solution, yet, in and through her special awareness, her action acquires a political dimension.

Although Jones recognizes that there are those within the medical profession who want changes in medical practice and attitudes, she warns that fully ethical treatment of human beings will not be possible as long as our society and culture remain "both sexist and racist, for the ethos of the medical profession is reinforced by the cultural ethos."

David White focuses on the special and popular arguments used to counter the adoption of innovations. It is possible to cite reasons both for and against an innovation but how can one reach a decision that may have significant moral consequences when seeming opponents, using what White calls "the slippery slope strategy," reach a logical stalemate?

Medical science fiction, with its special techniques (termed "narrative necessity") may give invaluable assistance in making good, considered decisions. White examines a number of cases and SF stories, arguing that the persuasive elaboration of such "thought experiments" may well render guidelines and an enlightened train of reasoning that will be decisive in issues dealing with either attitudinal or technological medical innovations.

# 13

# Feminist Science Fiction and Medical Ethics: Marge Piercy's *Woman on the Edge of Time*

*ANNE HUDSON JONES*

## Introduction

Few works of feminist science fiction are more than a decade old. Before that time most science fiction was written and read by men, and most postulated a future in which almost anything except traditional sex roles might have changed. Feminist science fiction developed out of the women's movement, and the reasons for its popularity are easy to understand. Even liberated women who write mainstream fiction are greatly limited in what they can present by the reality of the sexist society in which they live.

Both Joanna Russ and Marilyn Hacker have discussed the problems facing women writers. In her essay "What Can a Heroine Do? Or Why Women Can't Write,"[1] Russ claims that women writers are hampered by living in a male culture whose myths allow female protagonists to appear only in a Love Story, in which they are primarily concerned about their relationships—or lack thereof—with male lovers or husbands. Russ mentions a new pattern that has emerged in the last few years—female authors writing about heroines. who go mad—and she goes on to suggest that science fiction is a genre that may offer relief to women writers. Hacker points out in her essay "Science Fiction and Feminism: The Work of Joanna Russ" that "the endings of feminist or proto-feminist novels [are often] unsatisfactory," usually portraying defeat or "very ambiguous reconciliation" for the female protagonist.[2] The problem, according to Hacker, is that "the mainstream . . . novel, as a form, demands the individual solution, or, failing that, the individual defeat. The feminist novel is . . . difficult to envision for that reason: the solution is, by definition, *not* individual."[3] Both Russ's and Hacker's essays are important conceptual background for my discussion of Marge Piercy's *Woman on the Edge of Time*, a work of feminist science fiction that presents a feminist utopia. Piercy's female protagonist, incarcerated in a mental institution, ends in individual defeat, but she does so in a way that bespeaks both an individual and a political solution, a way made possible only by the science-fiction, or nonrealistic, form of the novel.

Inherent in Piercy's novel is an assumption that Phyllis Chesler's study, *Women and Madness*, makes explicit: sex-role stereotypes cause much of what is called mental illness in women, and much of what is diagnosed and treated as mental illness in women (or all too often diagnosed and *not* treated, but used as grounds for institutional confinement) is simply the inability to adapt to a sexist culture.[4] As long as these women are treated by psychiatrists who themselves accept and act out the sexist culture, they have little hope of achieving complete selfhood or even, in many cases, of living outside mental institutions. Within Piercy's novel, the medical world serves as a microcosm of American culture at large, with white (Anglo) men at the top of the hierarchy, having literal power of life and death, as well as death-within-life, over others, especially women and third-world peoples.

The civil rights movement, the women's movement, and what might be called the patients' rights movement have helped focus attention on the plight of women patients in general and of minority women patients and women mental patients in particular. With the increase of interest in medical ethics in the past two decades, issues such as abortion, medical paternalism, truth-telling, and informed consent have been much debated. On some issues, for example the right of patients to give informed consent before undergoing medical treatment or before becoming subjects in research experiments, there is reasonably widespread agreement among professionals. Yet even when such an ethical standard is recognized, reinforced by federal regulation and law, and widely followed, it does not always produce ethical medical practice. The ethos of the medical community is powerful, so powerful that when ethos contradicts ethics, ethos prevails.[5] As long as that ethos includes the sexist and racist attitudes of the larger society, female and nonwhite male patients will be treated differently (less ethically) than white male patients. It is my thesis—and, I maintain, that of Piercy's novel—that establishing, teaching, and even following standards of medical ethics will not be sufficient to produce a truly ethical medical practice until our society is both nonsexist and nonracist.

Middle-class readers, men *and* women, may have difficulty identifying with the protagonist of Piercy's novel. Consuelo (Connie) Ramos is a Mexican-American welfare mother who has both a police record and a psychiatric record. She has been convicted of aiding a pickpocket and of child abuse, and from the very first page of the novel readers are aware that she may be hallucinating. That Connie Ramos is not easy for readers to identify with is important, for those in the novel who have power over Connie do not identify with or understand her either. It is easier for them to treat her as if she is mentally ill than it is to assume the burden of understanding how her plight is part of the politics of her culture. To the extent that readers share the world view of the white and privileged characters in the novel, their predilection will be the greater to accept Connie as a mentally disturbed and unreliable narrator.

Even so, narrating the story from Connie's point of view would certainly increase readers' understanding of why Connie became a pickpocket's accomplice and why she abused her daughter. But understanding only Connie's individual history would not produce the insight into the larger culture that readers must have to understand the political—and individual—solution Piercy poses at the end of the novel. That insight depends upon the presentation of an alternative society that forces readers to question the basic assumptions of their own society, which is much like Connie's. To present that society, Piercy uses the science-fiction device of time travel, from Mattapoisett, Massachusetts, in the year 2137, to New York in 1976. By having Luciente, a person from that future society, travel to Connie's society and Connie travel to that future nonsexist society, Piercy offers readers an external judgment of Connie's society as well as a look at a future alternative. Piercy further enriches the novel by providing a second alternative future, a sick and sexist one, that helps Connie realize her responsibility to choose between such futures and then to act to help make possible the future she chooses.

## New York, 1976

The present time of the novel is that of Connie's second incarceration as a mental patient. The circumstances leading to her commitment help establish the context of Connie's world. Connie's niece Dolly, bloodied from a beating by her pimp, who wants her to have an illegal abortion even though she insists that she is carrying his child, knocks frantically at Connie's door. The pimp, Geraldo, arrives only a few minutes later, accompanied by a "doctor" and by Slick, one of Geraldo's bruisers. As Geraldo tries to hold Dolly down so that the doctor can perform the abortion, Connie picks up a bottle and smashes it into Geraldo's nose. Slick then knocks Connie out. On the way to Bellevue, Geraldo and Slick beat and kick Connie again and again. At the hospital, Connie is put in restraint and given a massive dose of "hospital tranks"[6]—Thorazine or Prolixin. Dolly corroborates Geraldo's claim that Connie has attacked them both. The doctor speaks exclusively to Geraldo—"Man to man, pimp and doctor discussed [Connie's] condition" (p. 19)—and asks Connie only her name and the date. Neither doctor, nurse, nor attendants listen to Connie's story, examine her, or treat her for her physical injuries.

Days later Connie discovers she has been committed once more to Rockover State Mental Hospital even though she has not talked to the doctor since she first arrived at Bellevue. Her brother Luis has, however: "Luis had signed her in. A bargain had been struck. Some truce had been negotiated between the two men over the bodies of their women" (p. 31). The nurse explains to Connie that *Lewis* (my italics) signed her in: "So you won't hurt yourself or anyone else. You've been a bad girl again, Mrs. Ramos" (p. 30).

Already the pattern is clear: the male doctor listens only to other men, be they relatives of the patient or be they pimps, and takes their word as truth, rather than listen to his female patient. The women—Dolly and the nurse—treat Connie no better than the men do. When Connie asks Dolly how she can still care for Geraldo after he has beaten her and is forcing her to have an abortion, Dolly answers: "He is my man. . . . What can I do?" (p. 24). Dolly values having a man above all else. To have her man, she sacrifices her own dignity, her unborn child, and Connie, who loves her enough to fight for her. Connie understands and shares that value system. She has abused her own daughter Angelina, whom she loves desperately, because she hates herself and she sees in Angelina a young version of herself. The nurse is simply playing her role in the male-dominated medical hierarchy, where grown women are "girls" and patients are treated as bad children.

Connie's expectations about her second commitment to Rockover State are markedly different from those she had the first time:

The first time she'd been committed, when she belived [sic] herself truly sick, she had expected treatment. A kindly gray doctor, a sort of Marcus Welby of the mind, would sit behind a desk asking her questions in a learned but soothing voice, explaining to her exactly how she had gone wrong. She would weep and understand. Confessional. Priests that healed. But all the doctor asked in the five minutes granted her had been the name of the President, the date, why she thought she was there. [P. 340]

This time she does not expect treatment. She has learned from her previous stay in the hospital how to cope with the medical professionals around her. She knows, for example, that she must not make her own diagnosis of anything, even a burn or broken rib, because "the authority of the physician is underminded [sic] if the patient presumes to make a diagnostic statement" (p. 19). This she has learned from a doctor who was instructing a resident, "teaching him not to listen to patients" (p. 19). Thus, she has learned how to couch her requests and complaints in a language that the staff will hear. For example, she can say, "I hurt so much" and beg for a doctor to look at her. When asked, "Where do you *believe* you feel pain?" (my italics), she can then reply, "In my side" (p. 27), or she can say, "I think something's wrong inside me" (p. 27). But she cannot say that she thinks she has a broken rib without eliciting hostility from the attendants and nurses.

Connie has also learned that any behavior, such as walking up and down the ward for exercise, will be recorded as a symptom: patient paces ward. She has even learned how to play Ms. Model Patient: "Taking a shrewd and wary interest, volunteering for every task defined as women's work, cleaning, sweeping, helping with the other patients, picking up clothes, fetching and carrying for the nurses"(p. 339). Connie plays this role during her first commitment to gain favors from the staff and finally release; during her second commitment, to gain opportunities for escape.

These examples help show the paternalism, sexism, and lack of respect for patients, especially women patients, that pervade Bellevue and Rockover State Mental Hospital. But Connie's experience has shown her they are not limited to Bellevue and Rockover State. When she was twenty, Connie had an illegal abortion and had to go to Metropolitan Hospital because she was bleeding: "Unnecessarily they had done a complete hysterectomy because the residents wanted practice" (p. 45). Connie vividly remembers life on the women's ward:

She was lying in bed with the doctor going rounds and cracking jokes for the amusement of his residents over the bodies of the women patients, mostly black and Puerto Rican, whom some female troubles had cast up on this hard white beach, this glaring sterile reef. They were handed releases to sign, carefully vague so that the residents could get practice in the operations they needed. In the bed next to her was a nineteen-year-old black woman on welfare who had been admitted for an abortion in the fourteenth week and been given a hysterectomy instead of a saline abortion. The woman had gone into withdrawal shock, which made her a quiet patient. Nobody bothered about her as she stared at the ceiling. The women with syphilis were treated to obscene jokes. All the doctors ever said to any complaint was, "We're giving you some medicine that will take care of that." They did pelvics and rectals seven or eight times in a row on interesting cases, so all the doctors and residents could get a look, all the time explaining nothing. "You're a very sick little girl," the doctor said to a forty-year-old woman whose intestines they had accidentally perforated in removing an embedded IUD. [Pp. 159-60]

In this context, the legal (and ethical) requirement for informed consent is meaningless. The external form is observed and the letter of the law obeyed, but consent is neither free nor informed. The physicians' paternalistic attitudes keep them from explaining to the "girls" they treat what is, or is not, wrong. And vaguely-worded releases cover procedures not spelled out anyway.

The issue of informed consent comes up several times in the novel. Claud, the blind, black pickpocket whom Connie loved, has died as a result of participating in a medical experiment while he was in prison. In return for a little money and the hope of a shortened sentence, he volunteered to be infected with hepatitis. Connie's claim that the State of New York has murdered him is entered into her medical history as more evidence for her diagnosis as a paranoid schizophrenic. But her statement is not unreasonable. How can a prisoner "volunteer?" Prison is a coercive setting, and the incentives of money and possible early release are too great for most prisoners to refuse.

For readers who object that Claud's situation is fictional and therefore not to be taken seriously (despite our society's history of medical research on prisoners), there is Connie's allusion to the factual Willowbrook incident to consider. In that case, retarded children were deliberately exposed to hepatitis. Although the children's parents were asked to give their consent, details indicate a coercive situation. In 1964, Willowbrook, a New York State facility for the mentally retarded, was so overcrowded that it was closed to new admissions, except to "the hepatitis research unit if [parents] cared to consider volunteering their child for that."[7]

The issue of informed consent comes up again in the novel when Connie tells Luciente about an experiment carried out on a group of Mexican-American women who sought birth-control pills. The physician they saw gave some of them birth-control pills and the rest of them placebos but allowed all of them to believe they were taking birth-control pills. Not surprisingly, many of the women taking placebos got pregnant. This actually happened in San Antonio in 1971.[8] Connie goes on to say that her sister was one of the women given the placebo pills. Although fiction, the story of Connie's sister offers a plausible context and consequence for the women who were the subjects of that research:

> "Like my sister Inez, she lives in New Mexico. Her husband drinks, she has seven kids. After the sixth, she went to the clinic for the pill. You know—No, you can't! It's so hard for a woman like her—a real Catholic, not lapsed like me, under his thumb too and him filling her with babies one right after the other— so hard for her to say, Basta ya! And go for the pill. See, she thought she went to a doctor. But he had his scientist cap on and he was experimenting. She thought it was good she got the pill free. But they gave her a sugar pill instead. This doctor, he didn't say what he was doing. So she got heavy again with the seventh child. It was born with something wrong. She's tired and worn out with making babies. You know you have too many and the babies aren't so strong anymore. They're dear to you but a little something wrong. So this one, Richard, he was born dim in the head. Now they have all that worry and money troubles. They're supposed to give him pills and send him to a special school, but it costs. All because Inez thought she had a doctor, but she got a scientist." [Pp. 274-75]

The mixture of fact and fiction in the novel makes it easy to believe in the possibility of what happens to Connie when she is chosen as a subject for a research experiment. She and several other mental patients are to have electrodes with microminiaturized radios implanted directly into their brains, allowing the doctors to monitor and control their emotional reactions. Informed consent again becomes an issue. Connie is told that her brother has already given his consent and therefore the researchers do not need hers. She is, after all, a mental patient. But they *want* her consent, and they seek it by pointing out to her where she will end up if she refuses: "on the violent ward, L-6. With comments on [her] record about how uncooperative [she] proved to be" (p. 216). Because her brother has consented for her, she will be subjected to the experiment whether or not she consents, yet her consent is sought to make her participation seem voluntary. She consents at last only because she is afraid of what they will do to her if she does not.

## Mattapoisett, 2137

The future time of the novel and the alternative society of Mattapoisett provide readers with another way of evaluating Connie. Neither Luciente nor any of the other people of Mattapoisett believe Connie is mentally ill. They consider Connie's society sick; they call it the Age of Greed and Waste. That Connie is labeled insane and held against her will by those who have power in her society saddens but does not surprise Luciente and her fellow villagers, who do what they can to help Connie and try to enlist her help in ensuring their own future. But their evaluation of Connie goes beyond just certifying her sane. Luciente is able to communicate with Connie because Connie has an unusual mind; she is what the Mattapoisett villagers call a "catcher," someone exceptionally receptive to the thoughts of others. In Mattapoisett, being a "catcher" is highly valued. Connie, of no apparent value to her own society, is of great value to a different society. In fact, of the people in Connie's society whom Luciente and her people have been able to visit telepathically, most are female and prisoners or mental patients. Ironically, those who have the special mental gifts required to communicate with Mattapoisett are usually the outcasts of New York in 1976.

There is a great contrast in the way madness is conceived of and treated in Connie's society and Luciente's. In Mattapoisett, it is taken for granted that people go mad when they need to. Luciente explains:

"Our madhouses are places where people retreat when they want to go down into themselves—to collapse, carry on, see visions, hear voices of prophecy, bang on the walls, relive infancy—getting in touch with the buried self and the inner mind. We all lose parts of ourselves. We all make choices that go bad. . . . How can another person decide that it is time for me to disintegrate, to reintegrate myself?"[P. 66]

In Mattapoisett, there is nothing shameful about spending time in a madhouse.

The practice of medicine in Mattapoisett is also different from that in the New York of 1976. Physicians are called healers, and the most prominent among them are two beautiful women, Diana and Erzulia.

Diana, a white woman named for the goddess of the moon, is the most important of a group of women healers who dress in knee-length white tunics, the only vestige of the traditional physician, and wear as decoration a crescent moon. Diana specializes in healing madness. Erzulia, a tall, strong black woman, combines voodoo practices and more traditional medicine. Connie has trouble believing Erzulia is a healer because she cannot imagine Erzulia as "a doctor in a white coat in a big hospital" (p. 159), but Luciente assures her that Erzulia "teaches people to heal themselves. Does surgery. Manipulating, pain easing, bone knitting. Erzulia's skilled! Person has trained hundreds of healers and pioneered new methods of bone knitting and pain easing. There's a way of setting pelvic fractures in the aged named after per" (p. 159).

The relationship between healer and patient in Mattapoisett is correspondingly different. More "co-op" curing, in which "the healer helps the person firm [sic] better habits of minding, better eating or carriage of the spine" (p. 276), is practiced. The assumption is that people can learn to heal themselves and should be helped to do so, not practiced upon. When Connie asks how and on whom drugs are tested, Luciente answers that computers are used for biological modeling, but most drugs are discarded before the testing stage. If drugs are tested on humans, they are tested on volunteers, Luciente says. When Connie expresses her skepticism about "volunteers," Luciente responds that there is no coercion within the society to make people volunteer. No one lacks for any necessity, and no incentive is offered other than prestige or time off. If there are not enough volunteers for a project, the project is put aside.

The kind of medicine practiced in Mattapoisett is possible only because of the nonsexist, nonracist, nonauthoritarian structure of the society. The nonsexist nature of the society is first seen in the language Luciente uses. The generic masculine pronouns "he," "his," and "him" have been replaced by the nonsexist "person" and "per." This linguistic change may seem small, but it reflects and symbolizes radical changes. Women have given up their one great power, giving birth, in exchange for "no more power for anyone" (p. 105). For women to become equal, men humanized, and society nonsexist, basic biology had to be changed. Nuclear bonding and dyadic pairing had to be broken. By producing babies in laboratories, the society has managed to break the "bond between genes and culture" (p. 104). Thus, the society is inherently nonracist. With these changes, the society has developed a nonpatriarchal/nonmatriarchal and nonauthoritarian structure. The autonomy of each person is respected and enhanced by society in general and by medical practice in particular. Healing in Mattapoisett is innately ethical.

## New York, 2137

During the course of the novel Connie becomes skilled at time traveling and can go to Mattapoisett almost anytime she wants. For a fleeting moment once while traveling there, she sees a strange assemblage of women with enameled legs, posing in one-legged positions like storks, and men in silver uniforms. She does not actually visit this second future until she has had the dialytrode implanted in her brain. In the New York of 2137, Connie finds herself with a woman called Gildina 547-921-45-822-KBJ, "a cartoon of femininity" (p. 288). Gildina has been cosmetically altered for sex use. She has a tiny waist and huge breasts and buttocks. She can barely walk, but since she is never allowed to leave her room, it doesn't matter. Gildina, gilded as her name implies, is the quintessential playmate kept as a pet.

Even more important than the grotesqueness of Gildina, who is only a slight exaggeration of Connie's niece Dolly, is that of the man who keeps her. Named Cash, he has a superneurotransmitter in his brain that can turn him into an instant Assassin whenever the "multi" that owns him desires. Cash is the future result of the kind of experiment in which Connie is involved. The structure of this society is also recognizable as an extension of Connie's society, but the hierarchical stratification is more rigid: the "richies" control and can live as long as 200 years because they can afford "medicos" and organ transplants; the "duds" live like animals and serve as walking organ banks for the rich; those in the middle, like Gildina, never see doctors but go to medimated clinics and medimats.

Although this future is radically different from Mattapoisett, it is as much an extrapolation from Connie's New York of 1976 as is Mattapoisett. Neither future—New York 2137 or Mattapoisett 2137—is assured; both are possible. The real future of Connie's society depends upon actions taken by people in the present, in Connie's time.

## Solution, 1976

Seeing the alternative to Mattapoisett mobilizes Connie. She finally understands what the villagers have been trying to teach her, that their future is not assured and she must help to bring about Mattapoisett.

There is very little she can do for herself or for them, but Bee, her Mattapoisett lover, gives her tactical advice: "There's always a thing you can deny an oppressor, if only your allegiance. Your belief. Your co-oping. Often even with vastly unequal power, you can find or force an opening to fight back. In your time many without power found ways to fight. Till that became a power" (p. 328). And Bee tells her, "You're a prisoner of war. May you free yourself" (p. 328).

From the time of her visit with Gildina, Connie does consider herself at war. She identifies the enemy as both the doctors who are experimenting on her and all the others—doctors, police, judges, guidance counselors, social workers, attendants and orderlies, matrons, and EEG technicians—who had a part in locking her up, medicating her, and condemning her. She does find a way to fight back. Having exhausted all possibilities of escape when she is unable to run away while on furlough at her brother's house, Connie returns with the only weapon she can: parathion, the most deadly poison in her brother's nursery. She pays a final visit to Mattapoisett and tells Luciente she plans to kill someone with power over her, who means to do her in. Luciente replies: "Power *is* violence. When did it get destroyed peacefully? We all fight when we're back to the wall—or to tear down a wall" (p. 370). Just after her last interview with the doctors before her scheduled amygdalotomy, Connie puts the parathion into their freshly brewed coffee and kills four of them. She dedicates her "act of war" to her fellow patients, to Claud, and to those who will be born from her best hopes. "At least once I fought and won," she says (p. 375).

To appreciate how Connie has won, one must consider her situation as she does, from a political standpoint. As an individual, she has few options: amygdalotomy, suicide, or an action that results in her lifetime confinement to the violent ward of Rockover State. None of her individual options is desirable. Although it causes her return to Rockover State, poisoning the doctors is at least active, a fighting back that can help make possible Luciente's future instead of Gildina's. By killing the doctors in charge of the dialytrode and amygdalotomy experiments, Connie can ensure that the research will be slowed down, perhaps even stopped. Her act is political. It affirms her individual revolt in a way that may help to bring about a future in which her descendants can affirm their humanity and their individuality. Without her time travel to the two futures, Connie would not have come to political awareness and would not have acted as she did. Only when she contrasts the New York of 2137 with the Mattapoisett of 2137 does she realize her responsibility to do what she can to prevent a future that is worse than her present. The science-fiction form of the novel makes possible an ending that Hacker and others should be able to accept as aesthetically satisfying, an individual solution that is also political.

## Conclusion, 1981

Piercy's ending for *Woman on the Edge of Time* is both provocative and risky. Some readers will be so offended by the ending that they will reject the entire novel. But whatever readers think about Connie's solution—her murder of the doctors—they should not let their reaction allow them to disregard the issues Piercy raises in the novel. Those issues are crucial ones for women and for medicine. Their importance was recognized by Alan A. Stone, the 108th President of the American Psychiatric Association, in his 1980 Presidential Address. Like Hacker and Piercy, Stone knows that individual solutions are not possible without social change. What is necessary, he says, is "a new conceptoin of all our human values and all the paradigms of psychiatry."[9] Piercy said it her way; Stone, his.

Drawing conclusions or implications from fictional evidence is always tricky. But one implication for medical ethics of Piercy's argument seems clear: establishing standards and legal procedures is not enough to produce ethical medical practice. Those who are concerned about medical ethics must extend their concern and their efforts to the larger political arena and work to create a society that makes ethical treatment of all people and patients—regardless of gender, race, or nationality—possible in all spheres of their lives.

## Notes

1. Joanna Russ, "What Can a Heroine Do? Or Why Women Can't Write," in *Images of Women in Fiction: Feminist Perspectives*, ed. Susan Koppelman Cornillon, rev. ed. (Bowling Green, Ohio: Bowling Green University Popular Press, 1973), pp. 3-20.

2. Marilyn Hacker, "Science Fiction and Feminism: The Work of Joanna Russ," *Chrysalis, a magazine of woman's culture*, no. 4 (1977): 67.

3. Ibid.

4. Phyllis Chesler, *Women and Madness* (Garden City, N.Y.: Doubleday, 1972).

5. For an excellent discussion of the conflict between ethos and ethics in medicine, see Larry R. Churchill, "Ethos and Ethics in Medical Education," *North Carolina Medical Journal* 36, no. 3 (January 1975): 31-33.

6. Marge Piercy, *Woman on the Edge of Time* (New York: Fawcett Crest, 1976),

p. 16. All further references to the novel are to this edition and will be cited parenthetically in the text.

7. George J. Annas et al., *Informed Consent to Human Experimentation: The Subject's Dilemma* (Cambridge, Mass.: Ballinger, 1977), p. 181.

8. Sissela Bok, *Lying: Moral Choice in Public and Private Life* (New York: Pantheon Books, 1978), p. 67.

9. Alan A. Stone, "Presidential Address: Conceptual Ambiguity and Morality in Modern Psychiatry," *The American Journal of Psychiatry* 137, no. 8 (August 1980): 891.

# Medical Morals and Narrative Necessity

## DAVID E. WHITE

For opponents of medical innovation, what might be called the "slippery slope strategy" is probably the most popular line of attack. Everyone who has argued about euthanasia is familiar with such arguments as:

Euthanasia as a policy is a slippery slope. A person apparently hopelessly ill may be allowed to take his own life. Then he may be permitted to deputize others to do it for him should he no longer be able to act. The judgment of others then becomes the ruling factor. Already at this point euthanasia is not personal and voluntary, for others are acting "on behalf of" the patient as they see fit. This may well incline them to act on behalf of other patients who have not authorized them to exercise their judgment. It is only a short step, then, from voluntary euthanasia (self-inflicted or authorized), to directed euthanasia administered to a patient who has given no authorization, to involuntary euthanasia conducted as part of a social policy.[1]

Such a strategy has a certain appeal. After conceding that the proposed innovation is not necessarily bad in itself, one simply points out that it might lead to another practice, which is universally condemned. Popular and appealing as the argument may be, it has its detractors. John Ladd ridicules it, and Richard Brandt dismisses it in a line. Glanville Williams complains that "this type of reasoning could be used to condemn any act whatever."[2] In her book, *Freedom to Die*, O. Ruth Russell proposes not just limited euthanasia but limited euthanasia with controls to keep it limited. The controls are an answer to the slippery slope objection.[3] Thus, supporters of such innovation dismiss the argument out of hand,

and critics take for granted its decisiveness. We are, therefore, tempted to believe that the argument is better described as part of one's position than as evidence adduced in its support.

Logicians are no help here; it is plausible applications, not formal structures, that are in dispute: Voluntary euthanasia is merely the first step to involuntary euthanasia. Yes, but only in the sense that walking to the end of the driveway is the first "step" on a trip to China. If I were going to China, I would start out that way, but that I start out that way does not imply that I am going to China. On the other hand, permitting the dissection of corpses was just the first step to experimentation upon and the eventual transfer of organs. It is Robin Cook's *Coma* that carries this trend to its logical conclusion: the murder and the sale of organs to the highest bidder, justified by an appeal to the greatest good for the greatest number. Extrapolative fiction, then, offers the aid we need. Extrapolative medical fiction influences our beliefs about what will happen; it converts possibilities into probabilities. Since our beliefs about what will happen are relevant to our present moral judgments, medical science fiction is also relevant to those judgments.

Medical science fiction, in fact, makes an important contribution to popular thought regarding medical ethics. If the slippery slope strategy is important to popular, as well as scholarly, thinking and if the value of the argument is logically undetermined (instances of it may be valid or invalid), then certain experiments in thought are going to be crucial. We want to know whether the danger is as real as the critics say, or whether it is plausible to expect safeguards as the supporters of innovation maintain. Science fiction as extrapolative thinking helps us to decide whether or not the catastrophic projection is realistic. Because of its moral consequences for the present, such speculation is anything but idle.

This thesis on the value of medical science fiction has two corollaries: first, science fiction writers are too modest in their self-appraisal and their critics are overly presumptuous; and second, the usual explanations of extrapolation in fiction are too vague to be of any use in determining the value of such stories.

In his essay, "Pandora's Box," Robert A. Heinlein confesses to his readers:

I disclaim any intention of prophesying; I wrote that story ["Blowups Happen"] for the sole purpose of making money to pay off a mortgage and with the single intention of entertaining the reader. As prophecy the story falls flat on its silly face—any tenderfoot Scout can pick it to pieces—but I think it is still entertaining as a *story*, else it would not be here; I have a business reputation to protect and wish to continue making money.[4]

What is of concern is not his motivation but his concession that any tenderfoot could pick the story to pieces. Is Alan E. Nourse, practitioner of medicine and science-fiction writer, correct when he claims that science fiction is not "an attempt at prophecy or specific prediction; rather, it is an attempt at rational speculation about the various patterns the future might assume, given what we know about the present"?[5] Or is it true that it is impossible to anticipate all of the factors that will influence an extrapolation, and therefore, as Thomas N. Scortia explains,

science fiction stories are not intended as exercises in prediction even though. . .successful predictions have occurred. In many instances they follow the pattern that engineers know as "exploring the boundary conditions of the function." Very often in such an exercise the writer's purpose is intended as social warning or as satire and he clearly shows in his speculation that he does not believe that the situation he describes will necessarily come to pass.[6]

Since the slippery slope argument previously mentioned may be refuted if it is shown that the possible outcome is merely possible and not likely, science-fiction stories must be predictive if they are to play the moral role that this essay claims for them.

Critics like Andrew Greeley join Nourse and Scotia in suggesting that extrapolation may go one way just as well as another. Greeley even complains that today's science-fiction writers have become more pessimistic in order to be accepted as serious novelists.[7]

Heinlein's claim that predictions are made by weathermen, in contrast to science-fiction writers, is only the start of the analogy.[8] Our concern with medical ethics and innovations is more like a man deciding whether to take an umbrella with him. He does not have to make a prediction per se, but he does act on the presumption that one prediction is correct. When we decide about a medical innovation we implicitly accept or reject the slippery slope opposition, and we accept it, or reject it, because we find the slope more or less slippery, more or less likely. In practice we accept one science-fiction story and reject another, even if we have never read those stories.

There would be little point beyond entertainment in reading extrapolative fiction if extrapolation were mere extrapolation. Heinlein claims that "extrapolation" means "much the same in fiction writing as it does in mathematics: exploring a trend. It means continuing a curve, a path, a trend into the future, by extending its present direction and continuing the *shape* it has displayed in its past performance."[9] The various devices (narrative necessities), perhaps not consciously used, that make medical science fiction into so many counterparts of the various species of slippery slope arguments are *gedankenexperiments*. That is, they can be thought through; the experiment either does or does not go. There could be no such discrimination if one extrapolation were as good as another.

A short catalogue of story summaries, classified according to the kind of narrative necessity used, offers further support for the thesis that medical science fiction can have important consequences for moral choice.

The most straightforward kind of narrative necessity in telling a story is causal necessity. When the slide down the slope is causally determined, the slope is especially slippery. In "The Little Black Bag," C. M. Kornbluth explains that the genus *homo* has bred himself into an impasse:

Dogged biometricians had pointed out with irrefutable logic that mental subnormals were outbreeding mental normals and supernormals, and that the process was occurring on an exponential curve. Every fact that could be mustered in the argument proved the biometricians' case, and led inevitably to the conclusion that genus homo was going to wind up in a preposterous jam quite soon. If you think that had any effect on breeding practices, you do not know genus homo.

There was, of course, a sort of masking effect produced by that other exponential function, the accumulation of technological devices. A moron trained to operate the twenty-first century equivalent of a linotype seems to be a better typographer than a Renaissance printer limited to a few fonts of movable type. This is also true of medical practice.[10]

Kornbluth ends with doctors who can work the tools of the trade (the little black bag) well enough but cannot read words of more than three syllables. In medicine, as elsewhere, the machines do all the work. Certainly it would seem that the burden of proof in this situation is on those who are optimistic enough to expect that a trend, once established, will not continue. There follows a complicated series of events involving time travel and some additional characters, but these are not essential to the point of the story. Eventually the black bag gets into the hands of a discredited doctor who, indeed, is able to work it and seems to be doing well by his patients, but if he can work the bag, so can a layman who has no scruples. The standing condition of human greed is brought into play, and the ending is gruesome.

What about controls? There were controls, but the "policy in such cases was to leave the bag turned on. The things practically ran themselves, it was practically impossible to do harm with them, so whoever found a lost one might as well be allowed to use it.[11] Might as well—until there is a homicide. The controls along the slope can be expected to work only as well as regulatory things work in general.

A comparable state of medical practice is described in Alan Nourse's "Symptomaticus Medicus," but its causes are not made explicit:

It isn't strange that those physicians used their spells and incantations without question, in complete faith. It isn't strange that those same magical methods have been handed down over the centuries from physician to neophyte, in the dark halls of the infirmaries, even as they are today. And yet today in my city we fight a new plague which cannot be checked by the mightiest magical powers we know. . . .

Our magic is failing, our spells grow weaker by the day, and we are helpless to know why, helpless to reinforce them. Who knows the nature of the diseases that plague us? Do any of you? We are like blind men, working in a darkness we do not begin to understand.[12]

One of the strongest proponents of the slippery slope argument on euthanasia, Philippa Foot, uses a psychological theme: "Apart from the special repugnance doctors feel towards the idea of a lethal injection, it may be of the very greatest importance to keep a psychological barrier up against killing."[13] Psychological forces may not seem as formidable as causal forces, but once a psychological barrier has been crossed controls may be even more difficult to establish since voluntary compliance cannot be expected. We are careless in our identification of health and normality. In "Elouise and the Doctors of the Planet Pergamon," by Josephine Saxton, to be unhealthy is normal; the well person is anomalous. Saxton makes it clear that her story has a moral intent, but what that intent is, is less clear. Certainly, Saxton suggests that unless we sort out the conceptual foundations of medical morality, we are vulnerable to moral chaos when what was once distinct but not separate becomes separate and distinct, which is, of course, what happens to health and normality in this story.

In "Transition Team," Charles Sheffield raises a sort of racial question that involves tampering with the reproductive process. Elizabeth S. Lockwood, the narrator, is a doctor who has been called to investigate some difficulties with children who were born in and are living at a space colony.

"All that I knew when I came here," I said, "was that the children in the Colony were feeling terribly lost and unhappy. That was obvious from the things they were writing in school. Then, even before we got here, I noticed an odd thing. You never called them the children—it was always the 'space-borns'. And when I got here I found that the other adult colonists used the same expression."

"Well, Beth, they are space-born—all of them."

"Of course they are, but more than that they are your children. It's not as if some of the children had been born on Earth and you needed to separate the two types for some reason. They were all born here. Oh, I know there's plenty of love and affection, it's not that. I've seen the teachers working with the children, and I've been impressed by them. But I still found it odd that you would refer to them by a different name. I wondered at first if it were their odd appearance—that was the only explanation that I could think of. . . .

"Tom, all your teaching is done by adults, born and raised on Earth, and it has a single viewpoint—a geocentric one. We can't see the world any other way. . . .You even promote standards of beauty based on Earth physique—which must make them feel like freaks."[14]

A proposed control ("they will get the finest care and education") is exposed as no real safeguard. A radical difference in bodily form implies a radical difference in culture, a gap that is not easily bridged even when the technology is high and the heart is pure.

A psychological pattern, in this case the destruction of a human instinct and a way of life, is also a sort of slippery slope.

Clifford D. Simak has his hero of "Huddling Place," Jerome A. Webster, M.D., think about his home and the ancestor who built it:

John J., the first John J., had come after the breakup of the cities, after men had forsaken, once and for all, the twentieth century huddling places, had broken free of the tribal instinct to stick together in one cave or in one clearing against a common foe or a common fear. An instinct that had become outmoded, for there were no fears or foes. Man revolting against the herd instinct economic and social conditions had impressed upon him in ages past. A new security and a new sufficiency had made it possible to break away.[15]

The doctor never goes anywhere since there is no need to go anywhere: "It all was here. By simply twirling a dial. . . ." Webster suffers from agoraphobia:

Habit and mental pattern and a happiness association with certain things—things that had no actual value in themselves, but had been assigned a value, a definite, concrete value by one family through five generations. . . .No wonder other places seemed alien, no wonder other horizons held a hint of horror in their sweep.[16]

While the story line that follows is unnecessarily sensational, the author's point is clear. Webster, an authority on the Martian brain, is the only one who can save the planet's leading philosopher, who is in need of treatment. The Martian philosopher has discovered a concept that will "remake the solar system," that will "put mankind ahead a hundred thousand years in the space of two generations."[17] Webster finally decides to try to overcome his agoraphobia only to discover that his servant, Jenkins, has sent the Martian ship away. Jenkins firmly believed that the doctor would not make a house call to Mars, would not, in fact, even want to be bothered with the request. Once one's character has been established, once habits are entrenched, it may be impossible to act against the set pattern of a life, no matter how great the emergency. The slope continued even though its creator tried to stop it.

Medical innovation may be technological, organ transplants, genetic engineering and mechanical life-support systems, or attitudinal, the acceptance of abortion, the refusal to prescribe placebos, and the willingness to let a dying patient refuse treatment. Critics of any innovation or previously unusual practice often claim that while the practice may seem beneficial in a few isolated cases, in the long run it will prove disastrous because it is merely the first step down a slippery slope, or, to vary the metaphor, the thin end of a wedge. The critics of innovation are, then, predictors of highly pessimistic outcomes. There is an easy answer to all such arguments: deny the prediction. Such denial simply involves arguing that while the disasterous consequences could occur, in fact they will not. As long as we are aware of the dangers, innovators claim, we can institute controls that will prevent voluntary euthanasia, for example, from progressing by degrees to involuntary euthanasia. Critics of innovation counter that the controls will not work, and thus the issue is stalemated. By the rules of logic, there is no good reason for accepting one side over the other. Medical science fiction, however, can be used to break this stalemate. An obvious objection to this thesis is that science fiction is not a reliable guide to what will happen; the stories could be written for or against any medical innovation. The devices used to create narrative necessity, however, make a good story believable because it is plausible, and it is plausible because there is a certain logic to its development. In the stories cited so far the controls that sound effective when proposed are defeated by accident or by the persistence of the baser elements in human nature. The reader is not asked to take someone's word for this pessimistic projection, he is invited to judge for himself after hearing the story.

Thus far the stories have involved causal necessity and the destruction of psychological barriers, but there are other kinds of grease to make the slope slippery.

A full analysis of the techniques of narrative necessity would require a careful discrimination between what can be expressed only in narrative, a story line, and what is illustrated or exemplified in a story, a line of thought. Although this distinction may be very important to the study of literature as philosophy (or philosophy as literature), the thesis proposed here will be sustained if *any* of the techniques mentioned work as suggested.

Sometimes the slippery slope is in reality an appeal to precedent. In the beginning of Heinlein's *Fear No Evil*, the case for brain transfer is made by arguing that the same objections could be raised against any transfers that have already been performed.

The most compelling devices for extrapolation do not introduce anything new. The elements are all existing conditions that are merely combined in a way yet unknown. For this reason, the supernatural and the fantastic do not need to be considered. If the parts can exist and the whole is no more than the sum of its parts, then the slope can be made plausible, and some arguments of this nature can be removed from the list of fallacies.

"The Pain Peddlers," a Robert Silverberg story, provides a fine example. Vicarious pain and suffering on television, high medical costs, game show greed, astronomical fees for screen rights, subservience to popular taste, physicians with dual allegiance, and the bootlegging of entertainment products are well known today. Silverberg combines these elements against the background of popular interest in medicine, especially the gory details.

Two other species of the slippery slope rely on the idea of a continuum. In what might be called the *sorites* device, what seems insignificant by itself is repeated again and again until an enormous change has occurred. For example, one by one doctors stop making house calls "as the tide of automation swept in to do what doctors were no longer needed to do. . . .You swam with the tide or you drowned."[18] This action, innocently repeated, eventually leads to disaster in "The Last House Call," by Alan Nourse.

The continuum idea may also be exploited in the form of a wedge. Once the thin edge has entered, the process continues and grows out of control. The spread of disease is a favorite here, from Nourse's "Plague" to Stephen King's *The Stand*. In both, medical disasters begin by accidents, accidents that are inevitable, given enough time. And in both, the accidents become full-fledged catastrophes because the medical authorities falsely announce that they are under control.

Our medical morals are determined to a large degree by how seriously we take the slippery slope concerns of the critics of innovation. How seriously we take the extrapolation is influenced by the sort of story we imagine. "Neither *Brave New World* nor *1984* will prevent our becoming a planet under Big Brother's thumb," writes Frank Herbert, "but they make it a bit less likely. We've been sensitized to the possibility, to the way such a dystopia could evolve."[19]

My thesis is even stronger than Herbert's, for I feel that science-fiction stories can be decisive in breaking the stalemate found in certain slippery slope projections. This is so because good stories are persuasive; the narrative moves along with a kind of necessity. The science-fiction writer can appeal not only to causal necessity and psychological forces (especially the destruction of psychological barriers), but also to precedent, to the reordering of existing conditions, and to the cumulative effect of small moves along a continuum.

## Notes

1. J. Gay-Williams, "The Wrongfulness of Euthanasia," in *Intervention and Reflection: Basic Issues in Medical Ethics*, ed. Ronald Munson (Belmont, Calif.: Wadsworth, 1979), p. 143.

2. Glanville Williams, *The Sanctity of Life and the Criminal Law* (London: Faber and Faber, 1958), p. 280.

3. O. Ruth Russell, *Freedom to Die* (1975; reprint ed., New York: Dell Publishing Co., 1976).

4. Robert A. Heinlein, "Pandora's Box," in *Turning Points: Essays on the Art of Science Fiction*, ed. Damon Knight (New York: Harper and Row, 1977), p. 239.

5. Alan E. Nourse, "Science Fiction and Man's Adaptation to Change," in *Science Fiction, Today and Tomorrow*, ed. Reginald Bretnor (New York: Harper and Row, 1974), p. 121.

6. Thomas N. Scortia, "Science Fiction as the Imaginary Experiment," in *Science Fiction, Today and Tomorrow*, ed. Reginald Bretnor, p. 144.

7. Andrew Greeley, "Varieties of Apocalypse in Science Fiction," *Journal of American Culture* 2 (1979): 284.

8. Heinlein, "Pandora's Box," p. 238.

9. Ibid., pp. 238-39.

10. Frederik Pohl, ed., *The Best of C. M. Kornbluth*, (New York: Ballantine Books, 1976), pp. 41-42.

11. Ibid., p. 68.

12. Alan E. Nourse, "Symptomaticus Medicus," *Rx for Tomorrow*, (New York: David McKay, 1971), p. 4.

13. Phillipa Foot, "Euthanasia," in *Intervention and Reflection*, ed. Ronald Munson, p. 160.

14. Charles Sheffield, "Transition Team," in *Destinies*, ed. James Baen (New York: Ace, 1978), pp. 74-75.

15. Clifford D. Simak, "Huddling Place," in *Modern Masterpieces of Science Fiction*, ed. Sam Moskowitz (New York: World, 1965), pp. 354-55.

16. Ibid., p. 366.

17. Ibid., p. 368.

18. Nourse, *Rx for Tomorrow*, p. 145.

19. Frank Herbert, "Science Fiction and a World in Crisis," in *Science Fiction, Today and Tomorrow*, ed. Reginald Bretnor, p. 71.

# VIII

# History and Heroes, The Sublime and Changing Theism

In earlier sections of this book, various authors have explored issues and problems of historical importance and have traced the history of their impact. Issues of aesthetics, the special features of science fiction as an art form, historic trends, and culturally conditioned concept formations also have been explored. This section, too, can be considered historical. The chapters within it deal with history itself and the modes of recording events and actions, the history of the aesthetic "sublime" and its place in early science fiction, and the culturally formed concepts of deity and sexism.

The philosophy of history includes studies of how history, events in time and place, are to be understood, and whether or not there is a pattern to those events and the existence of the civilizations in which they happened. Some may seek not just a workable interpretation but a detectable "plan"; others may try to determine whether persons influence events or events influence persons. These concerns interest not only philosophers of history but also sociopolitical thinkers, theorists, and a number of science fiction and fantasy writers and readers.

William Schuyler inquires into the philosophy of history and the place of heroes in history. He examines both different "modes" of history (ways in which history has been structured) and their adequacy. Schuyler cites examples of epic, antiepic, and counterepic modes, noting their strengths and weaknesses. How do they deal with

substantive change, with social development, with those
persons known as heroes? He points out that most persons seem to want, as the notion of history seems to presuppose, an order and cause-effect event structure. What
individuals get, however, is related to the mode they
choose to interpret history.

Concepts, as well as events, seem to have a history. One
such concept, once quite prominent in aesthetics but now
seemingly forgotten, is the sublime. Bart Thurber examines the concept of the sublime, its history, its meaning,
and its influence, especially on science fiction.

Contrary to what may seem to have happened after the
eighteenth century, Thurber believes, the sublime did not
simply disappear. Instead, it appeared in "new, surprising
ways," especially in relation to science and technology.
According to Thurber, the sublime became "*the* crucial
idea" for the development of modern science fiction.
Thurber supports his claim by tracing historic instances
from Shelley's *Frankenstein* through Poe and Doyle to
Verne. The sublime, in other words, became linked with
science, and in Verne it became linked with scientific
*method*. Verne presents science *as* sublime, and in the fusion of these two, Thurber points out, the basis for *science*
fiction was assured.

In chapter 13 Anne Hudson Jones discussed the dominance of paternalism and sexism in our culture and medical practice. Robert Pielke explores an aspect of this issue
that is even more embedded in our historic-cultural roots:
the predominantly masculine portrayal of God in the Judeo-Christian tradition. There is, Pielke holds, a general
thematic similarity between the major themes of feminist
theology/feminist opposition to this masculine God portrayal and the themes of science fiction. Both, Pielke
finds, are qualifiedly atheistic; both reject dualism, recognize portrayals of God as culturally specific, reject transcendence in favor of pantheism or panentheism, and
hold that the old religious world view and its mythology
are "things of the past." He suggests that science fiction
can fill this void, for it can provide, or is providing, a new
mythology that is appropriate for the scientific-technolog-
ical world view that pervades our era and culture.

# 15

## Heroes and History

*WILLIAM M. SCHUYLER, JR.*

In history, observed H.A.L. Fisher, "I can see only one emergency following upon another as wave follows upon wave."[1] He may have been right, but other historians have viewed it as highly structured. The term, after all, is derived from the Latin *historia*, meaning story. Despite developments in this century, we still prefer a story to have a plot and perhaps even a moral. If these elements are not actually present in the course of events, historians have always been willing to supply them. In the hope of illuminating the question, "What are heroes, and how do they fit into history," I shall confine myself in this chapter to history as description.[2]

The best places to find heroes are in epics and fiction modeled (more or less successfully) after the epics. If, however, the epic form, as a dictionary states, celebrates "episodes of a people's heroic tradition" is it history?[3] Tradition, after all, is not the same as history.

But the dictionary definition neglects several important points. First, as far as the people who composed them were concerned, epics were history. Gods, demons, and heroes were real. Second, while some matters, such as theogony or children's stories or medical knowledge, might come down through the oral tradition outside of the epic, it was the epic that determined which events were important and traced what were taken to be causal sequences. Third, as Joseph Campbell has shown, epics have a strong similarity in story line.[4] Finally, when history at last became a distinct genre, it was still heavily influenced by the epic's central postulate that the deeds of individuals were what was important. It is only recently that social and economic forces have been taken into account in writing history.

For these reasons, it seems that epics and epic fiction can tell us something about history. Epics embody world views. If Campbell is right about their story lines, then their world views share important features. It is possible, in fact, to identify an epic point of view and several assumptions required by it about what can happen, how it can happen, and why it can happen.

The first assumption is that history is made by heroes; no one else makes any real difference. It may be a hero's fate to die at the hands of a nonentity, but the nonentity does not affect history because that was the hero's fate.[5] It follows from this that only heroes get to make meaningful choices. Everyone may have free will, but most people and their choices don't matter. In order to bear this burden, heroes are larger than life. Any attempt to portray them as merely human reduces the epic to the level of the picaresque, where, by definition of both genres, history is not made. Fourth, they don't make heroes like that any more, which is a relief to almost all of us. Bards are inclined to attribute this lack to the degenerate times in which they live, but this is disingenuous. Heroes are made, not born; and they are made by bards. The problem with turning a living person into a hero is that he may refuse to stay in character. The bards, then, quite naturally prefer to work with the dead. The descendants of the bards, reporters and public relations consultants, are still at it, as Tom Wolfe shows in *The Right Stuff*.[6]

This means that history is no longer being made. Nothing important can change, because only heroes can make changes, and there aren't any of them left around.

This, however, pinpoints a serious problem that heroes have: they can't *stop* making history. Even if a hero wants to quit he isn't allowed to. No one really believes that Odysseus settled down to a bucolic life after slaughtering his wife's suitors, which is why Kazantzakis could get away with grafting a new ending onto Homer. On a less cosmic level, Sherlock Holmes wasn't even allowed to die, much less retire. For these reasons there is an insatiable demand for sequels.[7]

Since heroes are never allowed to die, retire, or settle down, when they are not actually needed, they are dangerous. In the presence of a satisfactory status quo, the establishment has an overriding interest in getting rid of any existing heroes and preventing the appearance of any new ones. As long as there are no heroes nothing will happen.

In another sense, however, nothing happens even when heroes make history. Heroes act against a static background that does not change no matter what they do. Have they burnt the topless towers of Ilium? No matter; there will always be another challenge. A hero's work is never done, which is another reason why he can't quit. It is no accident that Valhalla, a paradise for heroes, is so designed that its inhabitants spend their days in mortal combat, and the losers are resurrected in time for dinner. History in the epic mode is a record of events without substantive change.

Finally, even culture heroes, who clearly make substantive changes in the status quo, fit into this framework nicely; for the changes they make lead to the status quo current in the epic, and it is this that is regarded as immune to change. The gods punished Prometheus, but they couldn't take back fire. The change was irreversible, and there are no heroes left to make further changes.

If the epic world view is tenable, what happens after the end of the epic? On the other hand, if the epic world view is not adequate, how do we describe events in the terms of whatever different world view we might adopt? While Homer and Snorre Sturleson cannot tell us, fantasy offers some tantalizing clues.

Few authors have faced either of these two questions squarely. E. R. Eddison is one of the few. In his "Letter of Introduction" to *The Mezentian Gate*, he remarks that "A very unearthly character of Zimiamvia is that nobody wants to change it. . . .Zimiamvia is, in this, like the saga-time: there is no malaise of the soul. In that world, well fitted to their faculties and dispositions, men and women of all estates enjoy beatitude in the Aristotelian sense. . .(activity according to their highest virtue)." Accepting the epic world view, Eddison offered an answer to the first question in *The Worm Ouroboros*, which recounts the deadly quarrel between Juss, King of Demonland, and the terrible Gorice XII, King of Witchland.[8]

Gorice is sworn to destroy Demonland. By a fearsome spell, Goldry Bluszco, brother to Juss, is stolen away. Through his arts Juss learns that he must rescue his brother or lose the war against the Witches. He and his cousin Brandoch Daha undertake the long and arduous quest, returning only just in time to smite the forces of Witchland. Gorice is killed when he fails in his attempt to destroy the Demons by another spell, and his generals are victims of treachery.[9] The Demon lords return to the arts of peace, only to find that they are bored. In the end, because they have pleased the gods, they are granted a boon: their great enemies are restored to life and the cycle begins again.[10]

Yet, it is not clear that everything is exactly the same. Surely that would be just as boring. If the cycle is to repeat itself endlessly, even with minor variations, the gods themselves may grow weary of it. And, as Eddison tells us in *The Mezentian Gate*, that is exactly what happens, with the result that He Who is the male principle in the dyad of Eddison's theology decides to die.[11] Even eternal recurrence will not serve for gods and heroes. They will choose to perish, and what will be left?

There are some clues to be found outside of literature. Among the etchings of Giovanni Battista Tiepolo, there are two extraordinary series of *capricci*. Their subjects can be described, but their significance is obscure. In a landscape of ruins, bizarre figures perform mysterious acts. What are we to make of the main figures in "Punchinello Talking to Two Magicians," much less of the subsidiary figures?[12] In writing *The Malacia Tapestry*, Brian Aldiss set out to construct a world in which this etching and several others by Tiepolo would be straightforward realism. Inspired by the Venetian artist, Aldiss created a Byzantine city with strong amalgams of Italy and Serbia.[13]

Ruins and magicians abound in these drawing and prints and in Malacia as well. It is an ancient city, and it is crumbling. The magicians are the priests of a heathen religion that Christianity in its Malacian form has been unable to overcome.[14]

Such a failure is not surprising, for in the epic mode of history no substantive changes are allowed. In Malacia, this is explicit; it is the substance of the Original Curse. Yet, even the city's Supreme Council cannot prevent changes in fashion and taste, as Piebald Pete points out; nor does it wish to. Such changes make no difference.[15]

All of this is of no moment to Perian de Chirolo, Aldiss's narrator and protagonist. Perian likes to think of himself as an actor of some talent and no moral fiber. The story is concerned with his love affairs, which are played out against the backdrop of his professional life. Of these, the most serious is with Armida Hoytola, the daughter of a wealthy family. To woo her, he involves himself with Otto Bengtsohn, who is trying to produce a drama on magic lantern slides with a primitive camera, the Zahnoscope. His involvement gives him access to Armida, whose parents have reluctantly permitted her to take a part in the drama.[16]

Perian glides over the surface of life, amiably unfaithful to all his women, occasionally suffering for it and occasionally tricked into showing a spark of decency. But a terrifying encounter with magicians in a forest changes all of this. Against his will, he is given knowledge, and from it flows a sense of propriety and genuine feeling which are the ruin of his affair with Armida. His life will never be the same, and perhaps he is the better for that.[17]

There are no heroes in Malacia. The Original Curse guarantees this because it forbids change. Perian acts bravely on two occasions, but that doesn't make him a hero, any more than Achilles's donning women's garb and hiding to avoid going to Troy disqualified him as a hero.[18] Culture heroes do not exist, either—the Supreme Council and its agents see to that. They enforce the Curse, although their intervention may be unnecessary. They are always particularly concerned with any new technology, which, if there is in it any potential for change, will be ruthlessly suppressed. Bengtsohn discovers this the hard way; he ends up in pieces in the rivers.[19]

It follows that no history is made in Malacia and no substantive changes can occur. Thus Malacia exemplifies the epic concept of history for a period after the age of heroes. In the book's setting, this situation has existed for over 3 million years.[20] *The Malacia Tapestry* is a truncated epic. It has been shorn of heroes and history by the elimination of its beginnings.

Since the notion of substantive change is crucial to our argument, we must pause to discuss it. We know that some changes occur even in unchanging Malacia; Piebald Pete is the victim of one. And while Eddison has said that no one in Zimiamvia wants to change it, certainly he does not mean mere changes in fashion. It is this implicit distinction that marks the authors as modern. The possibility of substantive change yet to come (short of the end of the world, as in the Norse sagas) has no place in the epic world view.

To understand this distinction between changes that are substantive and those that are not, consider the following examples:

The change from feudalism to capitalism was substantive, because it changed not only the people who had power but the foundation on which that power rested. The first industrial revolution brought substantive change in that people began to live in different places (cities), do different things (work in factories), and the structure and function of the family was reshaped.

Changes in dynasty for the most part are not substantive. When the Yuan Dynasty was replaced by the Ming, the Mongols were driven out and replaced by a Chinese imperial family, but the system of government, and even the members of the bureaucracy, remained the same. No changes in social structure occurred except, of course, that it was no longer necessary to demonstrate respect for Mongols. Similar considerations apply to changes of power in the Soviet Union.

Perhaps we could say that substantive change involves a broad redefinition of the roles played by members of society. While this really only introduces more undefined terms, for present purposes it will serve. With this understanding we can say that no such redefinition has taken place in Malacia for over 3 million years, even though a rare individual may change the role he plays.

Nothing in our records leads us to believe that the world is like this. We see substantive change over periods much shorter than 3 million years, and even in Malacia it is said that the ancestral beasts are dying out. Since their presence is necessary for various religious ceremonies, their extinction would make a substantive change. Still, Perian may be wrong about this. If he is, Malacia is contradicted by our experience. If he isn't, we can take this as an affirmation that time will bring change, even in Malacia and in spite of the Curse. In either case the epic model will fail ultimately to represent the way the world is.[21]

The epic mode, then, is not satisfactory as a universal paradigm for history. It does not explain enough, and it ignores things that need to be explained. Even so, it has had an enormous influence on the writing of history. Standard Chinese historiography never really escaped from it, and Gibbon was not the last Western historian to base his writings on it.[22]

But what else happens in the milieux described by the epics? Samuel R. Delany has given this a lot of thought and suggests some answers in *Tales of Nevèryön*.[23] The answers, however, are not terribly revealing. He offers no hope of discovering what really happens, since "all conclusions are genuinely provisional and therefore inconclusive." While this epigraph is depressing another of his epigraphs states, "If one is always bound by one's perspective, one can at least deliberately reverse perspectives as often as possible, in the process undoing opposed perspectives, showing that the two terms of an opposition are merely accomplices of each other. . . ." By offering an "opposed perspective," Delany can illuminate the deficiencies of the epic mode and give warning against the traps we may fall into in rejecting it. Delany then takes the sword-and-sorcery format and turns it upside down.[24]

The form of *Tales of Nevèryön* is a loosely connected set of stories with recurring characters and stories within stories. There are no heroes in them, for the characters are resolutely human. The stories are set in a period when the inventions of the lock and key, the fountain, money, weaving, writing, public drainage, and other such marvels are still within living memory. Their inventors were human; the inventor of the fountain was a barbarian who made a fortune and drank himself to death.[25]

In "The Tale of Gorgik," a boy is enslaved and sent to the obsidian mines. Grown to muscular adulthood, he is bought by a decadent aristocrat to satisfy her sexual whims. What an opportunity! Of course he cannot take advantage of it, because he lacks the necessary knowledge of court factions and the political and economic principles in operation in what everyone agrees are strange, barbaric, and primitive times. He survives only because he knows his place and stays there. When the Child Empress speaks to him, he is forced to flee for his life, since few will believe that he does not know how to use the leverage this incident gives him.[26]

There is the ring of truth to this, but would Conan, that epitome of a pseudo-epic hero, have acted thus? No, and he would have been killed any number of times if his adversaries were not invariably too stupid to last a week in the places of power they are said to occupy. Certainly Sarg, the only real barbarian prince in the Nevèryön stories, would not get away with any show of resistance after he is enslaved. Rebellious slaves are simply left to die with their arms and legs broken.[27]

The only one in Nevèryön who gets away with uncouth and impetuous behavior is the Suzeraine of Strethi, who is almost universally disliked and is in any case a bore. He gets away with it because he is, after all, an aristocrat, rather than a commoner or a foreigner with no connections.[28]

Conan's implausibility illuminates the conditions under which relatively real heroes appear plausible. However wily Odysseus was, however clever Jason was, neither went alone into danger. Each had his armed crew to back him. Theseus is an exception to this rule, but he was playing a game that had specific rules, not barging into an open-ended situation. Heroes do remarkable things, but they do them in contexts that prevent their opponents from simply slaughtering them out of hand, which usually would be the sensible thing to do. The constraints may be as simple and iron-bound as codes of honor and hospitality. And it is usually very effective for the hero to seduce a princess—at least in epics. Delany suggests, quite correctly, that this is not likely to help unless the princess is a mine of politico-economic information and the hero is in a position to use it.[29] (Medea knew exactly how to discourage pursuit).

Granted that the hero acts in a context and under constraints that are largely pushed into the background of an epic, what does he do? Perhaps he single-handedly attacks a castle and frees his imprisoned lover and all the slaves? Could anyone but a hero manage such a feat? Sarg does it in "The Tale of Dragons and Dreamers." Delany even provides a fairly plausible scenario to show how he could do it.[30]

There are, however, some jarring elements in the story. Sarg's lover is Gorgik, which is a little unusual in the swords-and-sorcery genre. This is the *seventh* time they have gone through this routine. Gorgik has allowed himself to be captured every one of the seven times so that the scenario, the real purpose of which is to free all slaves, can take on its proper form. With only a few minor variations, the castles all have the same plan. The placement of the guards varies hardly at all. Even the slaves react in the same way. The Suzeraine of Strethi, by now a decadent aristocrat rather than an uncouth one, is piqued (no more) by Sarg's interruption of his torture of Gorgik. " 'Oh, not again. Really, this is the *last* time!' " he says, disappearing through a secret door.[31]

This is a classic bonehead plot, as Delany is well aware. Success depends on the opposition doing all the wrong things. While it did take the French a long time to learn that there was no point in having heavily armored knights charge English bowmen, this scenario still strains credulity. For just that reason, the episode tells us something important about heroes. Sarg is not a hero. Thus his success reveals what we feel is necessary for a hero, precisely because we feel the lack of it in Sarg.[32]

Why is the effect of Sarg's deeds on history negligible? The Suzeraine of Strethi escapes. As several people, including slaves, point out, the freed slaves simply will be retaken by slavers or killed. (Spartacus and Nat Turner also failed). In the epic context, heroic deeds at least make history, even though there are no substantive changes. In the context of Nevèryön, heroic deeds do not make history because a different concept of history is in operation. In Nevèryön it is the social forces unleashed by inventions that bring about substantive changes in the world, and history is the record of how things changed. There is no place for heroes in such a context. It follows, then, that heroes are products of a context, specifically, the epic context.[33]

Delany has written an anti-epic, and it is helpful to contrast it with another example of that genre, Pope's *The Rape of the Lock*. Pope made his point by preserving all the epic conventions except for the importance of the subject. He treats a sow's ear as if it were a silk purse, and the joke lies in the manifest incongruity.[34] Delany keeps the subject, but rejects the epic conventions for treating it. By doing so, he is able to show that the silk purse is a sow's ear after all.

Delany's approach, however, is essentially subversive rather than constructive. Although he uses a mode different from that of the epic to demonstrate the epic's weaknesses, it is clear from his deconstructionist epigraphs that he does not claim the mode is superior. Any genuine alternative to the epic mode and world view must lie elsewhere. Perhaps the most radical option is the counter-epic. In the counter-epic, the conventions of the epic mode are not merely supplanted, they are flouted. Charles Lee's "Proem" is a paradigm case. He savages his victims by describing them in obviously bad verse. The barb lies in the fact that the flaws Lee introduces deliberately are exactly those that his victims have unwittingly put into their poems.[35]

Thomas Pynchon's *Gravity's Rainbow* is, among many other things, a counter-epic. Unlike Lee, Pynchon does not use the counter-epic mode to attack targets external to his work. His target (at least one of them) is not just the epic mode but the very possibility of history, which he assails through the story of Tyrone Slothrop.[36]

Slothrop begins with all the stigmata of a hero. He has had a *geas* laid on him in infancy (by the behaviorist Dr. Jamf). He has a remarkable talent. (His sexual encounters during the London blitz accurately forecast where the rockets will fall). Sinister powers (Pointsman and his cohorts of "The White Visitation") are determined to manipulate or destroy him, perhaps both. He neutralizes their agents (Katje and Sir Stephen); he undertakes a quest (for the fabulous 00000 rocket); and mysterious strangers (Blodgett Waxwing, Francisco Squalidozzi, et al.) appear to lend him assistance in his hours of need.[37]

Slothrop has never wanted to be a hero, never thinks of himself as a hero, but what can he do? Heroes are made, and they can't quit; they are the elite, the chosen. By definition they are winners even when they lose. Enzian, however, gives him a spell: *mba kayere*, I am passed over. He must become unchosen, preterite. Because this is a counter-epic, he can do it.[38]

At this point, everything, from the epic point of view, goes haywire. Slothrop's *mana* decays; from hero, he declines to Rocketman, pseudo-comic-book hero, to Plechazunga, giant pig-hero of a village festival. He himself disappears. People cease to notice him. The sinister powers lose interest. What of the *geas*, the quest? We never find out. Those who are passed over do not have such things. Even the author has lost track of him by the end of the book.[39]

If heroes can't quit, how can this happen? The answer is that the epic mode simply ignores most of the world. Only heroes count in epics, but there cannot be an elite, those who are chosen, without a preterite, those who are passed over. The preterite exist, but heroes and bards do not see them.[40]

By resigning from the elite to join the preterite, Slothrop has done something inconceivable from the epic point of view. Heroes can't quit because they cannot *imagine* quitting. The problem is in themselves, not in the world. However, this figure-and-ground relation, which the epic point of view imposes on the world, is not to be found in the world.

Taken to its logical conclusion, this line of reasoning implies that things happen and that is all. H.A.L. Fisher would be more correct than he would like to be, for it isn't history that records one emergency after another, it's chronicles. History carries an implication of an order that is denied in the counter-epic mode. Records of events in this mode are possible, but history is not.

The lesson in Slothrop's story is that nothing is more important than anything else. (Actually, this is just one of a large number of lessons in *Gravity's Rainbow*, many of which contradict each other.) By the same token, this is a counter-dialectical view: there is no pattern or necessity in events that could give history a direction.

The counter-epic point of view is therefore an attack on cause and effect. Without that, or something like it, we cannot learn from the past. Moreover, the foundations of ethics and social justice are undermined: if I believe that my acts do not have consequences, I can act on other people with no thought of the outcome for them. Even the epic world view does better than that. Even as an artificially imposed order, the epic world view is better than no order at all, despite its harsh treatment of the preterite (being passed over has its disadvantages, as any serf could tell you).

An order imposed is still order, which would make history possible, although arbitrary. The problem is that it is They who get to choose what order is imposed, or so Pirate Prentice tells Roger Mexico in *Gravity's Rainbow* after both of them have rebelled against Them. Other possible imposed orders are defined by Them as delusional systems. The only defense is to join Us and take over from Them, says Prentice, for then We get to specify the order that is imposed.[41]

This is a step in the right direction, but it is not a satisfactory solution to the problem. The true solution can be found in Richard Rorty's proposal for dealing with incommensurable discourses.[42]

Rorty holds that while we may be able to predict every event, including human utterances, on the level of describing physical objects, we cannot predict what they will mean, and that includes things that happen to inanimate objects as well as human utterances.[43] Rorty argues that we cannot predict meanings or morals because events may be described objectively and accurately in terms of incommensurable vocabularies: that is, two different ways of talking about something may both be "correct" and yet be irreducible to each other. To say they are irreducible is not to say they are incompatible. Heroes must be lucky or favored by the gods; these amount to the same thing, but they are not the same.[44]

Adopting these views, we do not need to abandon the epic point of view for writing history (or the Marxist point of view) as long as we recognize its limitations. Instead, we must give up the quest for a uniquely correct mode of representing history. There isn't any. We must refrain from complaining that a point of view does not represent something outside its scope. If the epic mode cannot deal with social change and you want to deal with it, you must pick a mode that serves your purpose. The epic mode is not thereby discredited.

The epic mode can tell us what really happened. So can the anti-epic mode and even the counter-epic mode. They will tell us different things about the same events, but that is because no mode can tell us everything. As for heroes, they can exist only in the epic mode and perhaps some of its close relatives. In other modes, the traits ignored or deemphasized in the epic mode become apparent. Heroes are revealed as human beings whose elite status is accidental, not essential, thus disqualifying them as heroes. Yet, this may increase our admiration for them. We expect superhuman feats from someone with superhuman powers, but for someone who is only human to accomplish the same things would be truly prodigious. As such, these deeds deserve to be recorded; for despite the difficulties, history must still be written "in order that. . .the memory of the past may not be blotted out from among men by time, and that great and marvelous deeds. . .may not lack renown."[45]

## Notes

1. H.A.L. Fisher, "Preface," *A History of Europe*, 3 vols. (Boston: Houghton Mifflin, 1935), 1: vii.

2. I would like to thank my colleagues Philip Alperson and Charles Breslin for suggestions that have greatly improved this paper. Brian Aldiss kindly corrected me on several points; and I am indebted to Gail Fleischaker and Emily Spradlin for their assistance in compiling these notes.

3. *The American Heritage Dictionary of the English Language*, s.v. "epic."

4. Joseph Campbell, *The Hero with a Thousand Faces*, 2d ed. (1968; reprint ed., Princeton, N.J.: Princeton University Press, 1972), pp. 245-47.

5. See, for example, Poul Anderson, *The Broken Sword*, rev. ed. (1971; reprint ed., New York: Ballantine Books, 1977), pp. 43, 65. Cf. p. 68.

6. Hesiod, "The Works and Days," *Hesiod*, trans. Richmond Lattimore (Ann Arbor, Mich.: University of Michigan Press, 1959), 11. 108-201. See also Tom Wolfe, *The Right Stuff* (New York: Farrar, Straus and Giroux, 1979), esp. pp. 268-91.

7. Nikos Kazantzakis, *The Odyssey: a Modern Sequel*, trans. into English verse, introd., synopsis, and notes by Kimon Friar (New York: Simon and Schuster, 1958). Rev. John Lamond, D.D., *Arthur Conan Doyle: A Memoir* (1931; reprint ed., Fort Washington, N.Y.: Kennikat Press, 1972), p. 54. Lamond says that Conan Doyle always intended to resurrect Holmes after Reichenbach Falls, but he also mentions the outraged letters the author received. Regardless of Doyle's intentions, there have been plenty of others who were willing to take up where he left off; Nicholas Meyer is one of the more engaging of them.

8. E. R. Eddison, *The Mezentian Gate* ([England]: n.p., 1958), p. xii. E. R. Eddison, *The Worm Ouroboros* (London, 1922; reprint ed., New York: E. P. Dutton, 1952), pp. 57, 106, 387.

9. Eddison, *The Worm Ouroboros*, pp. 54-58, 59, 64, 105-6, 158-206, 267-68, 328-38, 358-68, 413, 416.

10. Ibid., pp. 427-40.

11. Eddison, *The Mezentian Gate*, pp. 171-75, 226-29, 236-40.

12. Aldo Rizzi, *The Etchings of the Tiepolos*, trans. Lucia Wildt (London: Phaidon, 1971), R. 12.

13. Brian Aldiss, *The Malacia Tapestry* (England, 1976; reprint ed., New York: Ace, 1976). The illustrations are R. 5, 9, 11, 12, 13, 19, and 34 (right half), along with *L'Astrologo* by Francesco Maggiotto. E., R. 11, appears on page 311 of Aldiss and is described on pages 308-10. The easily accessible paperback edition does not do justice to the illustrations. The hardcover edition (New York: Harper & Row, 1977) is preferable. Future references will be to the Ace edition.

The temptation to identify Malacia with Venice must be avoided. Nevertheless, Malacia has the same stifling atmosphere that Browning found in the city of Tiepolo:

'As for Venice and her people,
    merely born to bloom and drop,

'Here on Earth she bore her fruitage,
    mirth and folly were her crop;
'What of soul was left, I wonder,
    when the kissing had to stop?

(Robert Browning, "A Toccata of Galuppi's," *The Poetical Works of Robert Browning: Complete from 1863 to 1868 and the Shorter Works Thereafter* [1905; reprint ed., London: Oxford University Press, 1940], pp. 220-21, stanza 14.)

The genesis of the novel is interesting. Aldiss planned a series of twelve short stories set round the Tiepolo etchings. He wrote four; they worked so well that he decided that he must abandon the static frame of the story cycle in favor of the novel format, which is better suited to a more ambitious treatment. (Letter received from Brian Aldiss, 30 October 1981).

14. Aldiss, *Tapestry*, pp. 82-83, 179, 214, 239.

15. Ibid., pp. 25, 315-16.

16. Ibid., pp. 5, 32, 37, 84, 85, 421-22.

17. Ibid., pp. 79-80, 175, 199, 204, 250, 278, 308-13, 392. But Perian's propriety is not ours.

18. Ibid., pp. 136-41, 318-21.

19. Ibid., pp. 22-23, 30, 373, 376, 391.

20. Ibid., pp. 198, 315, 343. Although there is a missing link, it seems reasonable to infer that Desport could not have founded Malacia much later than the battle of Ittssobeshiquetzilaha.

21. Ibid., pp. 76, 119. Aldiss is of the opinion that the curse is wearing off. (Personal interview with Brian Aldiss, 20 March 1981).

22. The annals and biographies form of standard histories does include some material on social and economic institutions, but it clearly gives the most weight to the acts of individuals. See K.H.J. Gardiner, "Standard Histories, Han to Sui," in *Essays on the Sources of Chinese History*, ed. Donald O. Leslie, Colin Mckerras, and Wang Gungwu (Canberra, 1973; Columbia, S.C.: University of South Carolina Press, 1975), pp. 42-52; and Wang Gungwu, "Some Comments on Later Standard Histories," in *Sources*, pp. 53-63. Gibbon habitually speaks of treaties between rulers rather than states and victories of generals rather than armies. See Edward Gibbon, *The Decline and Fall of the Roman Empire*, 3 vols. (London, 1776-1783; reprint ed., New York: Modern Library, n.d.), chap. 56 (vol. 3, pp. 313-41).

23. Samuel R. Delany, *Tales of Nevèrÿon* (New York: Bantam Books, 1979).

24. Gayatri Chakravorty Spivak, Translator's Introduction to *Of Grammatology*, by Jacques Derrida (Baltimore: Johns Hopkins University Press, 1975), quoted in Delany, *Tales*, p. iv.

25. Delany, *Tales*, pp. 153, 160.

26. Ibid., p. 32.

27. Ibid., pp. 122, 136, 148. Robert E. Howard, *Conan the Conqueror* (1935 as *The Hour of the Dragon*; reprint ed., New York: Ace, 1953), pp. 48-49 (barbarian stupidity), 105-6 (civilized stupidity).

28. Delany, *Tales*, pp. 42-43.

29. What Gorgik gets from the Vizerine Myrgot flows from her scheming, not his cunning. He doesn't know enough (ibid., pp. 40-42, 44). He learns, however, and later he knows well enough how to make use of his acquaintance with the Princess Elyne (ibid., pp. 52-53).

30. Ibid., pp. 218-35.

31. Ibid., pp. 218, 219, 224-25, 232, 238, 240.

32. This has happened before to the Suzeraine of Strethi (" 'Oh, not again!' "). Instead of better defense, he put in a secret passage. Of course, it took the French fourteen years (from Agincourt in 1415 to the relief of Orleans in 1429) to catch on. See Fletcher Pratt, *The Battles that Changed History* (New York: Doubleday, 1956), pp. 104-22.

33. Delany, *Tales*, pp. 74-76, 153, 221, 323.

34. Alexander Pope, *The Rape of the Lock*, 2d ed. (1714; reprint ed., Menston, England: The Scholar Press, 1969) pp. 8-9.

35. Charles Lee, "Proem," in *The Stuffed Owl: An Anthology of Bad Verse*, 2d ed. with introduction by D. B. Wyndham Lewis and Charles Lee, 2d ed. (London, 1930; reprint ed., New York: Capricorn, 1962) pp. xxi-xxiv.

36. Thomas Pynchon, *Gravity's Rainbow* (New York: Viking, 1973).

37. Ibid., pp. 48-50, 81-82, 84-86, 215-16, 223-26, 246-48, 262-65, 292, 607-9.

38. Ibid., p. 362.

39. Ibid., pp. 365-66, 376-82, 567-73, 738-42.

40. Ibid., pp. 495, 554-56.

41. Ibid., pp. 637-39.

42. Richard Rorty, *Philosophy and the Mirror of Nature* (Princeton: Princeton University Press, 1979), pp. 315-22.

43. Ibid., pp. 387-88.

44. Ibid., pp. 387-88.

45. Herodotus, *Herodotus*, trans. A. D. Godley, rev. ed., 4 vols. (Loeb Classical Library, rev. ed. of vol. 1, 1926; reprint ed., Cambridge, Mass.: Harvard University Press; London: William Heinemann, 1966), vol. 1, bk. 1, chap. 1, p. 3.

# Toward a Technological Sublime

## BART THURBER

### I

Although the idea of the sublime is ancient, it was applied originally in a strictly technical sense. The integrity of the sentiment or its relation to the author's comprehensive design for the work did not enter into the equation, nor did the question of the reader's response. The sublime was just elevation of style, and most of the ancient rhetoricians (Caecilius, for example, whose own *On the Sublime* Longinus had read) concentrated almost exclusively on rhetoric in order to solve the writer's problem of how to generate lofty sentiments. Certain figures (tropes, metaphors, or a specifically balanced phrase) were felt to be appropriate to this enterprise; others were not.

*Peri Hypsous*, the anonymous first-century treatise on the sublime conventionally attributed to Longinus, was different, however, and far more influential for modern aesthetics. While Longinus also dealt with tropes and figures and technical rhetorical detail, he changed, radically and powerfully, the conventional meaning of the sublime. The sublime is lofty, elevated, supremely noble, but it is also, Longinus wrote, "the echo of a great soul." The sublime for Longinus was not just a matter of following a few simple rules; it was a quality of feeling, a certain magnificent intensity that could not always be taught because it could not always be defined. Longinus named five "sources" of sublimity—great thoughts, noble feelings, lofty figures, diction and arrangement—but the first two, the most crucial, Longinus held, were the result of innate natural capacity and exceeded the limits of the teachable. They may even exceed the limits of the knowable, since the essence of the Longinian sublime is transport: the reader is carried out of himself ("the soul. . .takes a proud flight, and is filled with joy and vaunting"), while the author, if not quite so ecstatic, is at least transported beyond mere rhetorical imitation in an intensity of effort that by definition eludes rhetorical categories.[1]

In Longinus, then, the sublime becomes unconventional. It could seem to exist without an intervening text; it is "a thing of the spirit, a spark that leaps from the soul of the writer to the soul of his reader."[2] It is surprising and dramatic. Since it can elude description, it can be unpredictable, and since it can be unpredictable, it is also, for the first time in Longinus, dangerous.

Longinus did not stress this last point, although it became crucial for later writers. But if the greatest effects in language are sometimes a matter of not obeying rules, what use are the rules? The sublime exceeds and therefore calls into question all convention, all normalcy. At some point it calls the text itself into question, which must obey most of the rules most of the time or be incomprehensible. Longinus recognized that the sublime could tempt a writer into what Shelley called, rather unfortunately, the "impalpable inane," so to those who identified the sublime with the freedom of democracy he argued for the necessity of rules: "It is perhaps better for men like ourselves to be ruled than to be free, since our appetites. . .would set the world on fire with deeds of evil."[3]

As prophesy the sentiment is all too accurate, as more than one French aristocrat discovered in 1789, but it was precisely this dangerous freedom, rhetorical or otherwise, that made the Longinian sublime so deeply attractive to the eighteenth century. Longinus' conservative disapproval of unbridled freedom was far less effective than his own argument for breaking rules, so that his treatise lent powerful impetus to the growing interest in rhetorical and compositional insurrection.

By the middle of the eighteenth century that interest was very strong, particularly in England, and it was in England that Longinus and the theory of the sublime were most eagerly taken up. The writers of the eighteenth century, especially the English, who made major contributions to the theory of sublime naturally adapted the theory to their own concerns. Interest grew in the psychological effect of the sublime, particularly as it was to be found in nature—itself a great change, as there had been no "nature" in Longinus—and in what the sublime could contribute to the English revolt against neoclassical aesthetics, which had come to seem arbitrary. Edmund Burke's *Philosophical Enquiry into the Origin of Our Ideas of the Sublime and Beautiful* (1757) was vastly influential in its own time and later; Burke articulated something of the danger in the Longinian sublime and was the first to suggest that terror, fear, and awe also could be part of the sublime emotion. "Indeed," Burke wrote, "Terror is in all cases whatsoever either more openly or latently the ruling principle of the sublime."[4] He went on to add obscurity, darkness, and power (among others) to his catalogue of sublime effects, and he referred throughout to Milton, *Paradise Lost*, Hell, and Satan as "dark, uncertain, confused, terrible and sublime to the last degree."[5]

In doing all this Burke considerably widened the scope of the sublime. He made possible what Thomas Weiskel has called the negative sublime, which can be disturbing, even alienating.[6] After Burke the sublime was not necessarily ethically positive; it did not need to be ethical at all, much less elevating or uplifting. It went beyond good or evil so it was either good or evil; what mattered was the power, the confusion, and daring in the sublime, all of which explicitly defeated rational expectation in order to amaze and stagger and perhaps even frighten the reader.

The effect of this and related ideas on eighteenth-century thought was profound. Poems like Keat's "Lamia" or "The Rime of the Ancient Mariner" became possible, as well as the art of Blake or Fuseli and the rise of political terrorism and the Gothic novel. It is not an accident that Gothic novels, with their haunted houses, looming precipices, underground dungeons, and satanic but oddly appealing heroes developed in the period 1790-1820. They are the heirs of the Burkean sublime and the best evidence for the continuing influence of the sublime on fiction. Although not at all uplifting and usually quite unconcerned with rhetorical nicety of any kind, eighteenth-century Gothic fiction does offer the reader access to powerful, scarcely controlled emotion and equally powerful protagonists, fatally divided between—as the sublime itself was— good and evil.

By the end of the eighteenth century, the sublime was a powerful idea. Kant had discussed it in the *Critique of Judgement* (1790): Wordsworth had placed it at the center of his experience in *The Prelude* (1805);[7] Byron had praised Burke and the Burkean sublime, and hordes of Gothic novels in cheap cardboard covers attested to its popularity. It is strange, then, that the idea of the sublime disappeared. It is in fact almost inconceivable. Ideas do not just disappear, yet it could be said that this is what happened in the nineteenth century. Victorian aestheticians, Mill or Carlyle or Arnold or Ruskin, almost never used the word, and even when they did, their interest in the socialization of art, or the history of art, or the teaching of art precluded their considering the sublime with anything approaching Burke's seriousness. What happened? Did an entire culture suddenly decide to ignore the sublime? Was it simply a passing fad?

Like all such issues in literary history the problem is complex. The sublime, for example, was assumed in or clearly affected various nineteenth-century versions of romantic transcendentalism. It was part of what Emerson found in nature; it is clearly related to Carlyle's "clothes" philosophy in *Sartor Resartus*, and it is one aspect of what Ahab sought in *Moby Dick*. Still, the sublime is not present *per se* in any of these works. It may have contributed to the look and feel of the ideal, but its potency as an independently serious aesthetic issue was considerably less than earlier. If it is present at all, it is in the background, not the foreground.

Gothic novels, it is true, continued to be written throughout the nineteenth century, and perhaps the sublime survived in its fictonal guise if the idea itself did not. Yet Gothicism itself changed in the nineteenth century. Until the 1890s, when there was a resurgence of interest in Gothicism, fewer strictly "Gothic" works were written than earlier, and those that were seemed noticeably less *outre* than their romantic forebears. *Wuthering Heights* (1847), for example, is Gothic enough in its architecture, its setting, and in its deeply divided, half-human half-inhuman protagonist, but at its end the Gothicism in the landscape is successfully subdued and Heathcliff, the Gothic hero, is dead. Like other Victorian novels *Wuthering Heights* thus celebrates compromise and disciplined submission rather than romantic over reaching. Burke's sublime was indeed becoming less attractive, because it was foreign to all compromise and deeply antisocial.[8]

There are of course other possibilities. It could be argued that because of Baudelaire's fascination with Poe, the sublime was a crucial element in the development of Symbolisme. It could also be argued that the sublime helps to explain the Victorian fascination with coincidence in fiction and perhaps even the development of the idea of the unconscious in Freud. But these ideas are highly speculative and deal with the effects of the sublime, rather than the sublime itself. Freud or Dickens did not translate the sublime into their own terms; the relative primacy of the sublime in their works is equivocal and possibly even secondary.

It is much less equivocal in other areas. The sublime did not actually disappear or become transformed or less significant than it once had been. Rather, it appeared in new and surprising ways, chiefly having to do with science and technology. The sublime became one of the crucial ideas for the development of modern science fiction—perhaps even *the* crucial idea, since it was an example of the mingling of the human and the inhuman, or the familiar and the unfamiliar. In its preoccupation with insurrection, freedom vs. responsibility, moral and ethical relativity, and proud, independent flight toward some unspecified unknown, the sublime is the archetype of much modern science fiction. That the antecedents of science fiction are Gothic has been noticed before.[9] These antecedents, however, could be described with greater accuracy and economy as the sublime, which antedates Gothicism and predicts it. The idea of the sublime helps us to see, moreover, that like the Gothic novel, modern science fiction did not simply come out of nowhere at the beginning of the nineteenth century. It was instead a latter-day adaptation of a centuries-old tradition, modified to suit the concerns of a technological age.

## II

*Frankenstein* (1818) is widely regarded as the first science fiction novel, and not without reason. It links science and technology to the sublime, not merely to Gothicism, and does so in a way that is unforgettable.

It is obvious that the sublime is present in *Frankenstein*: the monster reads *Paradise Lost*, which "excited different and far deeper emotions" in him than his other reading[10] and he compares himself to Adam, but on reflection sees, like innumerable other protagonists of the sublime, that "Satan [is] the fitter emblem" of his condition (p. 130). Furthermore, the monster first meets his maker on the slopes of Mont Blanc, which Mary Shelley's husband had used as an image of the sublime two years previously in "Mont Blanc" ("and when I gaze on thee / I seem as in a trance sublime and strange"). "These sublime and magnificent scenes," Victor Frankenstein says, "afforded me the greatest consolation. . .my slumbers, as it were, waited on and ministered to by the. . .grand shapes which I had contemplated during the day" (p. 96). This is the soothing natural sublime described by Burke and others, but it is followed two pages later by a stunning (and characteristically sublime) reverse. Contemplating the "wonderful and stupendous" vision of Mont Blanc, Frankenstein summons the sublime ("take me, as your companion") and gets immediately the monster. The monster is the sublime personified. He has "superhuman" speed and arouses "rage and horror" in Frankenstein because of his "unearthly ugliness. . .too horrible for human eyes" (p. 99).

The link between this demonic sublime and science is equally clear. M. Walman, a natural philosopher (scientist) at the University of Geneva, describes to Frankenstein what scientists can do:

. . .penetrate into the recesses of nature, and show how she works in her hiding places. . .ascend into the heavens. . . .command the thunders of heaven, mimic the earthquake, and even mock the invisible world with its own shadows. [P. 46]

Frankenstein's reaction is characteristic and curiously predictive of his battles later with the monster:

As he went on, I felt as if my soul were grappling with a palpable enemy; one by one the various keys were touched which formed the mechanism of my being: chord after chord was sounded, and soon my mind was filled with one thought, one conception, one purpose. [P. 46]

All of which leads Frankenstein to attempt to penetrate the sublime, this mysterious, eerie and sulphurous unknown, almost with his bare hands.

One secret which I alone possessed was the hope to which I had dedicated myself; and the moon gazed on my midnight labours, while, with unrelaxed and breathless eagerness, I pursued nature to her hiding places. Who shall conceive the horrors of my secret toil, as I dabbled among the unhallowed damps of the grave, or tortured the living animal to animate the lifeless day. . .I seemed to have lost all soul or sensation but for this one pursuit. It was indeed but a passing trance that only made me feel with renewed acuteness so soon as, the unnatural stimulus ceasing to operate, I had returned to my old habits. I collected bones from charnel-houses; and disturbed, with profane fingers, the tremendous secrets of the human frame. [P. 53]

The Faustian parallels are obvious. Frankenstein, and by implication science itself, penetrates beyond the human, beyond even the living, where no man should go. This first of all mad scientist is fittingly punished for his excessive zeal; the monster reifies sublimity and pursues Frankenstein, until both are locked in a dialectical struggle the ultimate outcome of which is beyond our knowing.

The first stages of Frankenstein's quest, however, *are* knowable. The relationship between science and the sublime in Frankenstein is no mystery. Science *enables* the sublime; it becomes specific, identifiable, palpable. It makes the supernatural natural; it allows Frankenstein to see, hear, and taste, almost, what the sublime feels like. Science is the means to, in Wallace Steven's phrase, "muse the obscure." Here the obscure is, if not exactly clear, at least surely and definitely—and monstrously—"there."

The sublime is not as "there" as it might be in *Frankenstein*, for the novel is weak in specific technological detail.[11] But the link between science and the sublime described in Frankenstein proved enormously fruitful for the nineteenth century in widely different contexts. Carlyle, for example, described his first ride on a train in terms not categorically different from Shelley's:

To whirl through the confused darkness, on those steam wings, was one of the strangest things I have experienced—hissing and dashing on, one knew not whither. . . .We went over the tops of houses—one town or village I saw clearly, with its chimney heads vainly stretching up towards us—under the stars; not under the clouds but among them. Out of one vehicle into another, snorting, roaring we flew: the likest thing to a Faust's flight on the Devil's mantle; or as if some huge steam night-bird had flung you on its back, and was sweeping through unknown space with you, most probably toward London.[12]

Carlyle here responds to the new machine technology, not science proper, but much of nineteenth-century science was closely involved with machine technology and was felt to be so by contemporary artists and writers. Turner's "Pain, Steam and Speed," as Herbert Sussman points out in *Victorians and the Machine*, equates the locomotive, the new "technological sublime" with an older, natural sublime.[13] In America writer after writer, with characteristic optimism, thought of the new technology as even *more* sublime than the older version:

Objects of exalted power and grandeur elevate the mind that seriously dwells on them, and impart to it greater compass and strength. Alpine scenery and an embattled ocean deepen contemplation, and give their own sublimity to the conceptions of beholders. The same will be true of our system of Rail-roads. Its vastness and magnificence will prove communicable, and add to the standard of the intellect of our country.[14]

Not all writers were so optimistic. Just as the sublime itself could seem good, evil, or both, so too could technology and the new science. Henry Adams was frightened by it, Emerson admired it, Dickens found it demonic (especially in *Hard Times*), Thoreau feared and distrusted it, but common to each was a belief in the transcendence of the machine.[15] It was more than the sum of its parts; it was the visible manifestation of invisible, unearthly, and ultimately sublime strength and grandeur.

Nowhere is this link more explicit than in Bulwer-Lytton's late Victorian dystopia, *The Coming Race* (1871). In the company of a mining engineer, the narrator descends through the earth to discover a superior race, the Vril-ya, who possess robots, fly and have in general mastered all the secrets of nature. The narrator's description of the land of the Vril-ya is enlightening:

The view beyond was of a wild and solemn beauty impossible to describe—the vast ranges of precipitous rock which formed the distant background, the intermediate valleys of mystic many-colored herbage. . .the serene lustre diffused over all by myriads of lamps, combined to form a whole of which no words of mine can convey adequate description, so splendid was it, yet so sombre; so lovely, yet so awful.[16]

Clearly this is a sublime landscape, as Brian Aldiss has noticed.[17] It is also highly technological, and this underground technological sublime is the distinguishing characteristic of the master race. "Machinery," the narrator writes, "is employed to an inconceivable extent in all the operations of labor within and without doors" (p. 31). The Vril-ya possess Vril, a magical but still "scientific" substance, which is yet another example of the reified sublime in nineteenth-century science fiction. "There is," the narrator asserts,

No word in any language I know which is an exact synonym for vril. I should call it electricity, except that it comprehends in its manifold branches other forces of nature, to which, in our scientific nomenclature, differing names are assigned, such as magnetism, galvanism, etc. These people consider that in vril they have arrived at the unity in natural energic agencies. . .applied scientifically through vril conductors, they can exercise influence over minds, and bodies animal and vegetable, to an extent not surpassed in the romances of our mystics. [P. 23]

Later Zee, who falls in love with the narrator, impresses him with several good (and scientifically sublime) reasons why he should be careful of falling in love with her.

> Zee inspired me with a profound terror—a terror which increased when we came into a department of the museum appropriated to models of contrivance worked by the agency of vril. . . .She seemed to endow them with intelligence, and to make them comprehend and obey her command. She set complicated pieces of machinery into movement, arrested the movement or continued it, until, within an incredibly short time, various kinds of raw material were produced as symmetrical works of art, complete and perfect. [P. 56]

Indeed, the narrator later asserts, "she rather awed me as angel than moved me as woman."

## III

In these works, the connections between the sublime, machine technology, and contemporary science are explicit, but the idea of the sublime contributes to the development of science fiction in subtler ways as well. The mystery story and early science fiction have in common the sublime; and the existence of a technological sublime can help us to account for the appeal of even so terrible a writer as Jules Verne.

Poe's detective in "The Murders in the Rue Morgue" and "The Purloined Letter," M. Dupin, shares with other nineteenth-century detectives (Dicken's Mr. Bucket, for example, in *Bleak House*) a certain familiarity with sublime depravity. Dupin is a fallen angel, the member of an "illustrious" family now mysteriously ruined. He lives in abject circumstances in a "time-eaten and grotesque mansion," which suits the "rather fantastic gloom" of his temper. He searches out "rare and very remarkable" volumes of forgotten lore and impresses Poe's narrator with the "wild fervour and vivid freshness of his imagination." He stirs, like a vampire, only at night.[18]

But he is also, to use Poe's word, analytic. He does what Victor Frankenstein does. He penetrates to the heart of a sordid, terrible, and in "Rue Morgue" a genuinely hellish set of circumstances, only to emerge with the reified, articulated sublime; but Dupin's reification is a solution, not a monster. When Dupin masters the sublime, he does so with inductive science, which is, as Poe himself asserts, "the *truly* imaginative;" thus he enhances again the possibilities of the sublime for science fiction. The sublime lies in Dupin's explanation, in other words, in the solution of the mystery.[19] Dupin is uniquely able to solve the mystery because he is both a Gothic hero/villain and a wizard of inductive science. He unites the contraries and thus shows, not so much that science and the sublime are affiliated, but that the sublime and scientific *method* are.

This point was crucial for the development of science fiction. Many science-fiction stories to this day are simply elaborations of a mystery, and the pleasure in reading the story lies in seeing the mystery solved accurately and reasonably. But it also lies in seeing the sublime explained, harnessed, articulated, known. This is the appeal of many of Poe's stories, and it is certainly the appeal of two of Poe's direct literary descendents, Sir Arthur Conan Doyle and Jules Verne. Both men acknowledged Poe as a significant influence, both wrote science fiction, and both authors' science fiction functions as Poe's did, placing the method itself, the analytic, at the core of the story.

Doyle's hero, Sherlock Holmes, was modeled directly on Dupin,[20] and shares with him a propensity for dark nights, gloomy phantasy ("I have noticed such a dreamy, vacant expression in his eyes," says Watson in *A Study in Scarlet*), and the special stimulation of crime: "But I abhor the dull routine of existence. I crave for mental exaltation. That is why I have chosen my own particular profession, or rather created it, for I am the only one in the world."[21]

Of course, Holmes is also an accomplished scientist. He is introduced to Watson in *A Study in Scarlet* as one who has just discovered a reagent for hemoglobin. He maintains a complete amateur laboratory, can trace almost any kind of tobacco, and reasons with the precision of a computer. This precision, like Dupin's, enables Holmes to penetrate to the heart of one gruesome, hellish, or diabolical mystery after another, while another man of science, Dr. Watson, can only look on amazed. Watson's problem, like other scientifically trained onlookers in science fiction, is that he is not sufficiently in touch with the sublime to be really scientific. "You would," he tells Holmes in 'A Scandal in Bohemia,' "certainly have been burned had you lived a few centuries ago."[22] Watson's constant limitation is that he would not, which again reinforces the fact that, in Doyle as in Poe, genuine science and the sublime go hand in hand.

However, the relationship between the sublime and the techniques of science is nowhere more decisive than in Jules Verne. Verne was another of Poe's French admirers. He wrote a sequel to *The Narrative of Arthur George Pym* and was indebted to Poe for several ideas.[23] He also wrote the first recognizably modern science fiction, in which he ranged, sometimes *ad nauseum,* over all that was known at the time about geology, biology, archeology, minerology, astronomy, physics, or engineering. His heroes are not always the fervid seekers of the sublime that Dupin and Holmes are (although Nemo, his most memorable character, is), but his science is always persuasive, as modern as possible, and central to his story.

At least it would seem that it is. One question that always arises with Verne is *why* he expected the mass of scientific detail he packed into his stories to seem interesting. He prided himself on his precision, and he was indisputably popular, but vast stretches of *Journey to the Center of the Earth, Twenty-Thousand Leagues Under the Sea* and *From the Earth to the Moon* are little more than guidebooks to what was, even then, conventional science. In Verne there is always a voyage to some unknown, isolated, or otherwise strange place, and in this sense Verne may be said to duplicate Frankenstein's or Dupin's attempt to make the unknown known. Unlike Shelley or Poe or Doyle, he does it with massive detail. Consider the following, in *From the Earth to the Moon*:

A litre of gunpowder weighs about 2 lbs; during combustion it produces 400 litres of gas. This gas, on being liberated and acted upon by a temperature raised to 2,400 degrees, occupies a space of 4,000 litres: consequently the volume of powder is to the volume of gas produced by its combustion as 1 to 4,000. One may judge, therefore, of the tremendous pressure of this gas when compressed within a space 4,000 times too confined. All this was, of course, well known to the members of the committee when they met on the following evening.

"In fact," continued Barbicane, "cast-iron cost ten times less than bronze; it is easy to cast, it runs readily from the moulds of sand, it is easy of manipulation, it is at once economical of money and of time. In addition, it is excellent as a material, and I well remember that during the war, at the siege of Atlanta, some iron guns fired one thousand rounds at intervals of twenty minutes without injury."

"Cast iron is very brittle, though," replied Morgan.

"Yes, but it possesses great resistance. I will now ask our worthy secretary to calculate the weight of a cast-iron gun with a bore of nine feet and a thickness of six feet of metal."[24]

This is remarkable writing; "science" fiction with a vengeance. It is especially remarkable in light of the novel's conclusion: having spent some 110 pages discovering how to get the travelers to the moon, Verne launches them, loses them, and finds them again endlessly orbiting the moon, in a page and a half. He intended a sequel, true, but at first blush this looks like technical barbarism of the worst kind. Verne's entire interest in the story lies in seeing how it might be done; the travelers, the human beings, he leaves quite literally dangling in the breeze. It is perhaps why Lewis Mumford in *The Pentagon of Power* can allude to "the essentially archaic and regressive nature of the science-fiction mind."[25]

This reading of Verne, indeed of all science fiction, however, misses the point. Like his contemporaries, Verne was less interested in sublime emotions than in seeing how the sublime worked. It is out of that interest that the origins of modern science fiction took shape. Verne, however, added something new. He assumed that his readers would find technological detail interesting, not because he was a bad writer, necessarily, but because in Verne science is not like the sublime, nor is it *where* the sublime is, it is assumed to *be* sublime. Verne's contribution was to fuse the two, indissolubly. Whatever scientists do is sublime, for good or evil; technical detail describes nothing beyond itself, but in Verne there is nothing beyond itself for technology *to* describe. It is the process, the science, which is as new, as wondrous, and as powerful in its way as Frankenstein's monster. No wonder Verne had little time for his characters. It was a waste of time from his point of view, because time not spent musing this new, technical obscurity was time wasted on superfluous detail.

## IV

With Verne, modern science fiction had what was required to make the last, critical decision: that science could in any sense be fiction. Before Verne, this was not clear; after Verne, nothing was clearer. That decision, moreover, is inexplicable without the idea of the sublime, which, beginning with *Frankenstein*, attached science and technology to some of the oldest and deepest of human concerns. It is one reason why technology has never been emotionally "cool," despite the wishes of scientists and technocrats. We have been raised on Holmes or Dupin or Frankenstein, and because of them and the sublime, we are accustomed to seeing in science the model of some of our greatest and most powerful aspirations. Our debt to them, to this "regressive" science fiction, is very great.

## Notes

1. All quotations from Longinus are from W. Rhys Roberts' translation of *On the Sublime* (Cambridge: Cambridge University Press, 1899), as reprinted in part in W. Jackson Bate, *Criticism: The Major Texts* (New York: Harcourt Brace Jovanovich, 1970), pp. 62-75.

2. *Princeton Encyclopedia of Poetry and Poetics*, ed. Alex Preminger (Princeton, N.J.: Princeton University Press, 1965), p. 819.

3. Bate, *Criticism*, p. 75.

4. Edmund Burke, *A Philosophical Enquiry into the Origin of Our Ideas of the Sublime and Beautiful*, ed. J. T. Boulton (London: Routledge and Kegan Paul, Ltd., 1958), p. 58.

5. Ibid., p. 59.

6. Thomas Weiskel, *The Romantic Sublime: Studies in the Structure and Psychology of Transcendence* (Baltimore: The Johns Hopkins University Press, 1976).

7. For a discussion of the aesthetic and philosophical importance of the sublime in Wordsworth see M. H. Abrams, *Natural Supernaturalism* (New York: W. W. Norton and Co., 1971), pp. 97-113.

8. That the sublime is antisocial is a point recognized by Immanuel Kant; see *The Critique of Judgement*, trans. J. H. Bernard (New York: Haffner Press, 1951), pp. 116-17, and 139. For the history of the Gothic novel in the nineteenth century, see Montagu Summers, *The Gothic Quest* (1938), Devendra P. Varwa, *The Gothic Flame* (1957), or Robert Kiely, *The Romantic Novel in England* (Cambridge, Mass.: Harvard University Press, 1972).

9. By, for example, J. O. Bailey in *Pilgrims Through Space and Time* (New York: Argus Books, 1947), p. 71; Eric S. Rabkin, *The Fantastic in Literature* (Princeton, N.J.: Princeton University Press, 1976), pp. 182, 186; Brian Aldiss, *Billion Year Spree: The History of Science Fiction* (London: Gorgi Books, 1975), pp. 59-60.

10. Mary Shelley, *Frankenstein* (New York: Dell Publishing Co., 1975), p. 130. All other page numbers for *Frankenstein* refer to this edition.

11. Although Shelley does indicate that she was familiar with the developments in electricity and galvanism, see, for example, "the subject of electricity and galvanism, which was at once new and astonishing to me" (p. 40).

12. James Anthony Froude, *Thomas Carlyle, A History of His Life In London.* (New York, 1884), Volume 1: p. 144. Quoted in Herbert Sussman, *Victorians and the Machine* (Cambridge, Mass.: Harvard University Press, 1976), p. 25.

13. Sussman, *Victorians*, p. 31.

14. Charles Caldwell, "Thoughts on the Moral and Other Indirect Influences of Railroads," *New England Magazine* 2 (April 1832): 288-300. Quoted in Leo Marx, *The Machine In the Garden: Technology and the Pastoral Ideal in America* (New York: Oxford University Press, 1964), p. 195.

15. Both Herbert Sussman in *Victorians and the Machine* and Leo Marx in *The Machine and the Garden* provide more thorough discussions of these attitudes

than I can here. See also Arthur Koestler, *The Ghost in the Machine* (New York: 1977); and Lewis Mumford, *The Myth of the Machine* (New York: Harcourt Brace Jovanovich, Inc., 1970), Volume 1, *Technics and Human Development* and Volume 2, *The Pentagon of Power*.

16. Sir Edward Bulwer-Lytton, *The Coming Race*, in *Works* (Philadelphia: John Wanamaker, 1910), p. 17. All page numbers for *The Coming Race* refer to this edition.

17. Aldiss, *The Billion Year Spree*, p. 93.

18. Edgar Allan Poe, *Forty-Two Tales* (London: Octopus Books Ltd., 1979), p. 566.

19. Cf. Rabkin, *The Fantastic in Literature*, p. 161.

20. William S. Baring-Gould: *The Annotated Sherlock Holmes* (New York: Clarkson N. Potter, Inc., 1967), Volume 1, p. 7.

21. Sir Arthur Conan Doyle, *The Sign of the Four* (New York: Peebles Press, 1975), p. 148.

22. Sir Arthur Conan Doyle, *The Adventures of Sherlock Holmes* (New York: Peebles Press, 1975), p. 2.

23. Cf. Aldiss, *The Billion Year Spree*, p. 106.

24. Jules Verne, *From the Earth to the Moon* (London: Octopus Books, 1978), p. 223. All page references to the novel are from this edition.

25. Mumford, *The Pentagon of Power*, caption from Plate II.

# The Rejection of Traditional Theism in Feminist Theology and Science Fiction

## ROBERT G. PIELKE

It seems beyond dispute today that the portrayals of God in the Judeo-Christian tradition have been overwhelmingly masculine. Not yet settled is how this fact should be understood and what, if anything, ought to be done about it. On one side of this debate are the conservatives who find no difficulty in the situation; on the other side are feminist theologians and their various sympathizers who regard the situation as intolerable. Logically speaking, there is no middle ground. Theological imagery commands either assent or rejection. You are either for him or against him.

The feminist opposition, of course, is not univocal, but there are certain common themes that serve to define the parameters of the movement. When this thematic material is carefully considered, it strongly resembles the thematic material of science fiction.

### Thematic Similarities

The initial caveat in this endeavor should be obvious: within each body of literature there are bound to be exceptions. It would be absurd to claim that all feminist theology and all science fiction exemplify identical convictions. Nevertheless, as roughly identifiable groupings, each one possesses a certain overall unity. The writings discussed here can be clearly acknowledged to be in one category or the other.

#### The Significance of Religion

It seems obvious that both feminist theology and science fiction recognize that religion has had a dramatic influence on the way individuals think and behave. In the introduction to their anthology, *Womanspirit Rising*, Carol Christ and Judith Plaskow observe:

> It is only when the crucial importance of religion, myth and symbol in human life are understood that feminists can begin to understand how deeply traditional religions have betrayed women. . . .Once one recognizes the importance of religion, then an enormous sense of injustice must follow the discovery that religions are sexist and that they continue to exert a powerful influence on society.[1]

In this, the existence of sexism is attributed, in effect, to religion, especially the Judeo-Christian religious tradition. Although science fiction has begun only recently to touch on the issue of sexism, it has always been aware of the pervasiveness of religion. Mary Shelley's *Frankenstein* (often referred to as the first modern work of science fiction) would be incomprehensible without an awareness of the religious conviction that the creation of life was for God alone.[2] Similarly, most dystopian fiction, such as George Orwell's *1984* and Aldous Huxley's *Brave New World*, rests on the state's having displaced religion as the foundation for social stability.[3] Even more obvious are those aliens who are imagined as having god-like characteristics. Arthur C. Clarke's classic, *Childhood's End*, is perhaps the most striking example of the alien as divine.[4] Indeed, the distinction is virtually obliterated in the story. There are in fact numerous examples in which religious beliefs, institutions, and practices form the explicit content of the stories, for example, Moorcock's *Behold the Man*, Miller's *A Canticle for Leibowitz* and Heinlein's *Stranger in a Strange Land*.[5] Finally, the imaginative creation of an alternate world, when thoroughly accomplished, always entails an alternate religion. While it would not be difficult to cite many examples, perhaps the best is Frank Herbert's recently completed *Dune* quartet.[6]

In the introductory essay to Roger Elwood's small anthology, *Strange Gods*, which is devoted to stories about the relationship between religion and science fiction, George Zebrowski writes:

> Theologically oriented science fiction has always had a special interest for writers, readers, and critics. . . .It is not surprising that this is the case. Religion is an integral part of our seven-millennia-plus of recorded history, and whatever an individual's beliefs, or lack of them, this span of influence cannot be overlooked.[7]

Indeed, it has not been overlooked.

## A Critical Attitude Toward the Received Tradition

Feminist theologians oppose the Judeo-Christian tradition in varying ways. Again, Christ and Plaskow have an instructive comment:

> While differing on many issues [feminist theologians] agree that religion is deeply meaningful in human life *and* that the traditional religions of the West have betrayed woman. They are convinced that religion must be reformed or reconstructed to support the full dignity of woman.[8]

Regardless of whether one advocates reformation or total reconstruction, an underlying critical attitude is essential if any real change is to occur. In science fiction, this critical attitude may not be as obvious at first glance, but here too it is an essential component. James Gunn, in his excellent collection of stories "from Gilgamesh to Wells," observes that

> Science fiction could not be written until people began to think in unaccustomed ways. . . .People also had to adopt an open mind about the nature of the universe—its beginning and end—and the fate of man. Science fiction's religion is skepticism about faith. . . .The reasons for this are clear: religion answers all the questions that science fiction wishes to raise.[9]

Although a few writers, C. S. Lewis for example, have used their fiction to reaffirm the fundamental components of the tradition, they are exceptions that only illustrate the overwhelming tendency.[10] Science fiction can only exist in an atmosphere free of traditional restrictions, including, and perhaps especially, religious restrictions.

## Divine Imagery as the Reflections of Culture

A reliance on symbols to express the experience of divinity is unavoidable, but the particular symbols adopted is another matter entirely. Most religious thinkers agree that cultural factors play a large part in determining divine imagery. Feminist theologians have pointed out that the culture in which JHWH's presence was first experienced was overwhelmingly patriarchal. There is no doubt that the "father" symbol is a product of the ancient, Middle-Eastern nomadic culture. They disagree, however, over whether or not it is possible to disentangle successfully the divine content from the masculine form in which it has been presented traditionally. Reformers, such as Carol Ochs in *Behind the Sex of*

*God* feel that it is possible; revolutionaries, like Mary Daly in *Beyond God the Father—Toward a Philosophy of Women's Liberation*, feel it is impossible.[11] The underlying issue is whether or not patriarchy is an essential component of the Judeo-Christian God. While revolutionaries see JHWH's essence as "fatherhood" and all that this implies, for reformers "fatherhood" is merely an accidental feature.

Harlan Ellison, in his *Deathbird Stories*, has suggested the cultural derivation of divine imagery with a thoroughness and savagery unparalleled by any other writer of science fiction or any form of writing. His introductory remarks to the book suggest (albeit fictionally) that a god's existence is contingent on human intentionality: "when belief in a god dies, the god dies." Ellison then goes on to draw the correlation between specific gods and specific cultures, concludng the list with the observation that "perhaps one day soon the time will pass for Jehovah and Buddha and Zoroaster and Brahma. Then the Earth will know other gods."[12] After the introduction, each story deals with the newly emerging gods that are replacing the unsalvageable (and insane) Jehovah, and the culture these gods reflect is not pretty. Even though Ellison has little if anything to say about the status of patriarchy, he obviously shares with feminist theologians a negative attitude toward our culture and the gods it has created.

Other science-fiction writers, while not as explicit as Ellison, have presupposed the cultural origins of divine imagery without self-consciously exploring the idea. Every one of the writings already mentioned would be incomprehensible if a familiarity with the Judeo-Christian tradition could not be assumed. Their portrayals of God, in other words, are dependent for their meaning on culture-specific symbols.

### An End to Dualism

One of the most far-ranging critiques of patriarchal religion involves the rejection of dualism, and Rosemary Ruether is the primary spokesperson for this position:

All the basic dualities—the alienation of the mind from the body, the alienation of the subjective retreat of the individual, alienated from the social community; the domination or rejection of nature by spirit—these all have roots in the apocalyptic-Platonic religious heritage of classical Christianity. But the alienation of the masculine from the feminine is the primary sexual symbolism that sums up all these alienations.[13]

Ruether is actually a reformer, rather than a revolutionary, despite her Marxist strategy for change.[14] Since one of the more radical theologians, Naomi Goldenberg, feels the same way, there is good reason to believe that the rejection of dualism is a common trait among feminist thinkers. Goldenberg believes witchcraft to be the emerging form of feminist spirituality and lists its essential characteristics, one of which is, "*No body and soul dualism.* Witchcraft does not separate the body from the soul and accord one a more lofty destiny from the other.[15] Throughout her book, Goldenberg explores the reasons for this rejection and the various implications of having done so with provocative results.

It should be kept in mind, however, precisely what is being rejected. Dualism is a metaphysical position in which it is maintained that the two irreducible components of reality are matter and mind (or some similar designations). Feminist theologians are interested primarily in the implications of this position, which, most of them claim, entails sex-role differentiation, if not patriarchy itself. It is possible to agree with at least the former and weaker of these two claims, without being committed to the latter, but the point to remember is that the metaphysical position and its implications are two different issues.

Science-fiction writers are by no means univocal on the issue of sexism. On the one hand there are such blatantly sexist writers as Robert Heinlein (in his justifiably famous *Stranger in a Strange Land*), and on the other, such ardent antisexists as Ursula Le Guin (in her equally famous *Left Hand of Darkness*).[16] And—lest it be inferred from this that a writer's biological sex is the sole determinant of his or her position—there are counterexamples. Daniel Keyes's *Flowers for Algernon* (the basis for the film *Charly*) is decidedly nonsexist, while Joanna Russ in *The Female Man* is so angry at the masculine gender that a reverse sexism is alleged to take place.[17] Increasingly, the issue of sexism is being raised and explored in science fiction just as it is in theology.

By its very nature science fiction seems antidualistic despite its occasional thematic material to the contrary. Whatever else it does, science fiction involves us in a certain kind of experience that has qualities strikingly similar (if not identical) to the religious experience.[18] Its major characteristics include the paradoxical feelings of horror and fascination, a sensation of being overwhelmed completely by something wholly other and intrinsically incomprehensible, and the awareness of human insignificance. In this kind of complex encounter, the consciousness of any absolute distinction between mind and matter is totally obliterated no matter what the reality may be. Ideally, it is an ecstatic experience that borders on a mystical union with whatever is felt to be ultimate (a god, the universe, nothingness). More and more now, science fiction provides the means for having this kind of experience, just as religious practices once did and still do for some. It is in this experience that the alienation between the objective world and the subjective self is overcome.

### An End to Transcendence

Even among the more moderate feminist theologians, the concept of a transcendent god is considered hopelessly phallic. The result is something akin to pantheism or panentheism. Carol Ochs, for example, in a section on the nature of the deity, states:

We, all together, are part of the whole, the All in All. God is not father, nor mother, nor even parents, because God is not other than, distinct from or opposed to creation. . . .I do not hold that God is reduced to the natural world but rather that the natural world is divine. God is in the world but is not the world. . . .God contains the world.[19]

Obviously, this conviction is closely related to their rejection of dualism; in fact, the one might actually imply the other.

The same is true of science fiction, for the Ultimate, which it allows us to confront, is always in one way or another its subject matter. No matter how it may be understood and portrayed, it does not exist apart from the reality in which humanity has its existence. This, however, does not in any way lessen its incomprehensibility; the Ultimate is still experienced as something wholly other, but it is experienced as existing within our midst. *The Star Maker* by Olaf Stapledon is an excellent portrayal of the panentheistic conception of God, in which all reality participates in the divine process.[20] Heinlein's *Stranger in a Strange Land* suggests the more traditional pantheism in which God and reality are one and the same. (Those who are enlightened address one another with the phrase, "thou art god.") Less obvious, but no less accurate, examples are those stories in which humanity confronts the unknown, whether in the form of an alien, another planet, a different time, or even something hidden in the depths of the human psyche. In virtually every case, this confrontation produces in the reader or viewer, as well as in the characters, the same experiential qualities previously mentioned. Hence, the transcendental experience pertains to something immanent.

## The Abandonment of a Theos

Literally speaking, all feminist theology is atheistic. Theism is an epistemological position that claims knowledge of God's existence, while
atheism is the knowledge claim of God's nonexistence. It is important
to note, however, that in denying God's existence, feminist theologians
are specifically referring to one and sometimes two features of the traditional Western deity: its maleness, as denoted by the Greek gender
suffix *os*, and its particularity as one being among others. Many feel that
it is possible to have a conception of the godhead that is neither male
nor female, although feminine imagery is a necessary expedient in affecting this change. For these reasons, Elisabeth Fiorenza is convinced
that "maleness is [not] the essence of Christian faith and theology. . . .Yet
this female-matriarchal language ought not to be absolutized if we do
not want to fall prey to a reverse sexist understanding of God. The
Christian language about God has to transcend patriarchal as well as
matriarchal language and symbols."[21] Others regard this feminization
process as the unavoidable and necessarily permanent alternative to a
masculine god. Cults of the Goddess (including various nonsatanic forms
of witchcraft) are manifestations of this radical approach. Their purpose
is "to provide an understanding of reality that validates femaleness and
thus makes possible female—and human—growth and change."[22] Most
revolutionary of all are those who deny God's status as a particular being.
Mary Daly's critical reliance on Paul Tillich, Martin Buber, and Alfred
North Whitehead is a dramatic illustration of this perspective. In one
of her more cryptic and provocative passages, she suggests that our Thou
relationship with Being-in-process should be characterized by referring
to God as verb and not as a noun.[23] Obviously, masculine imagery must
then fall by the wayside.

In both senses of the affirmation, science fiction is clearly atheistic. It
necessarily takes a critical attitude toward the received religious traditions, and this inevitably includes the traditional notions of God. Perhaps
the most obvious examples are those stories in which a virtually omnipotent and/or infinitely mysterious alien stands in the place of a god.
Humans may or may not become privy to this knowledge, but there is
no doubt about the writer's intentions: the traditional God does not exist.
Arthur C. Clarke's *Childhood's End* is typical of this approach. More recently, there have been writings that suggest that the gods are human
inventions, for example Ellison's *Deathbird Stories* and Moorcock's *Behold*

*the Man.* Of course, there are numerous instances in which humans are alone as in Miller's *Canticle for Leibowitz.* Except for C. S. Lewis and a handful of others like him, the rejection of the traditional Judeo-Christian Theos is virtually unanimous.

### Further Similarities

Further similarities should be readily apparent given what has been said already. Among them are certainly the following: an end to traditional worship, which presupposes a sharp subject/object distinction; an affirmation of a "spiritual" dimension to humanity since the *Numinous* is not apart from and different than humanity; a renunciation of homocentrism, for the spark of divinity is present everywhere no matter how it may be understood); and the necessity to express all of these ideas in terms of myth and symbol.

### A Tentative Hypothesis

This thematic similarity is much more than mere coincidence. Science fiction provides us with a new mythology, a mythology ideally suited for the scientific technological world view that has emerged from the wreckage of the old religious world view. There are several related factors that make this hypothesis quite credible.

First, myth and symbol are regarded as vital for the expression of the depth dimension of existence. Although this is an acknowledged truth for a wide variety of thinkers, religious and otherwise, our immediate concern is with feminist theologians. Naomi Goldenberg, for example, adopts the rather widely held perspective that mythmaking is the essential process by which we give meaning to our lives. Her position becomes especially interesting when she predicts an extension of this process to include fiction: "The use of contemporary fiction as a resource for reflection on new gods, images and metaphors for our new [feminine] psycho-religious consciousness will become more prevalent."[24] To date Carol Christ has made the most extensive use of literature in this way, and she finds Doris Lessing's works to be most significant.[25] While not yet given a great deal of attention by feminist theologians, it takes little imaginative effort to see that science fiction is capable of playing this role as well.

Second, the vestiges of traditional religion exist in an alien and often hostile environment. The old religious myths are no longer capable of providing the modern world with a viable meaning. Literally understood, they do not accord with and are consequently rejected by a scientific perspective, neo-evangelicalism and the new religious right notwithstanding. In this inhospitable situation, religion either must assume a militantly defensive posture or conform. In either case, religion cannot exist today and retain the same form as it once did. However, this is not to suggest that "spirituality" is incompatible with a scientific world view. Loren Eiseley's *Immense Journey* is a vivid example of how a scientific thinker can manifest "religiousness" apart from "religion."[26] And so, I would argue, is much of science fiction. What has changed is not the human need to express a depth dimension but the *manner* of its expression. And this is precisely the thrust of feminist theology.

Third, the scientific world view is pervasive; its influence cannot be avoided or ignored. Yet this does not mean that we should accept its presence with unmixed and unqualified gratitude. Although few of us would wish to return to a prescientific age, we must recognize that science and technology have produced as much harm as good. Science fiction has always recognized this, and has often adopted an antiscientific posture. Feminist theologians, albeit indirectly, have been just as vociferous in their criticisms. Mary Daly argues that phallic morality has been responsible for war, genocide, and rape, including the rape of the earth.[27] And phallic morality is nothing other than crass technical reasoning, which gives no thought to anything but the accomplishment of immediate ends. Scientists need not think this way, but too often they do.

Thus, given the decline of traditional religious imagery as the means to express the "spiritual" dimensions of humanity in a scientific age, what could be more natural than for science fiction to assume this role. These are the same factors that have given rise to feminist theology. The next stage in this development no doubt will be a merger of some kind: feminist theologians writing science fiction, or science fiction writers adopting the content of feminist theology.

## Notes

1. Carol P. Christ and Judith Plaskow, eds., "Introduction: Womanspirit Rising," *Womanspirit Rising: A Feminist Reader in Religion* (New York: Harper & Row, 1979), p. 3.

2. Mary Shelley, *Frankenstein*, ed. M. K. Joseph (London: Oxford, 1969).

3. George Orwell, *1984* (New York: Harcourt, Brace & World, 1963); and Aldous Huxley, *Brave New World* (New York: Harper, 1946).

4. Arthur C. Clarke, *Childhood's End* (New York: Ballantine, 1953).

5. Michael Moorcock, *Behold the Man* (New York: Avon, 1970); Walter Miller, Jr., *A Canticle for Leibowitz* (New York: Bantam, 1976); and Robert Heinlein, *Stranger in a Strange Land* (New York: Berkley, 1961).

6. Frank Herbert, *Dune* (New York: Ace, 1965); *Dune Messiah* (New York: Berkley, 1969); *Children of Dune* (New York: Berkley, 1976); and *God Emperor of Dune* (New York: Putnam, 1981).

7. George Zebrowski, "Whatever Gods There Be: Space-Time and Deity in Science Fiction," in *Strange Gods*, ed. Roger Elwood, (New York: Pocket Books, 1974), p. 9.

8. Christ and Plaskow, *Womanspirit Rising*, p. 1.

9. James Gunn, ed., "Introduction," *The Road to Science Fiction: From Gilgamesh to Wells* (New York: Mentor, 1977), p. 2, 3.

10. For example, C. S. Lewis' *Out of the Silent Planet* (New York: Macmillan, 1943), *Perelandra* (London: John Lane, 1942), and *That Hideous Strength* (New York: Collier, 1965).

11. Carol Ochs, *Behind the Sex of God* (Boston, Mass.: Beacon, 1977); and Mary Daley, *Beyond God the Father* (Boston, Mass.: Beacon, 1973). See also *Gyn/Ecology: The Metaethics of Radical Feminism* (Boston, Mass.: Beacon, 1978).

12. Harlan Ellison, *Deathbird Stories* (New York: Dell, 1975), pp. 13, 14.

13. Rosemary Ruether, "Motherearth and the Megamachine: A Theology of Liberation in a Feminine, Somatic and Ecological Perspective," in *Womanspirit Rising*, ed. Christ and Plaskow, p. 44. See also *Liberation Theology* (New York: Paulist Press, 1972) and *New Woman/New Earth* (New York: Seabury Press, 1975).

14. Carter Heyward, "Ruether and Daly: Theologians Speaking and Sparking, Building and Burning," *Christianity and Crisis* 39, no. 5 (April 2, 1979): 66-72.

15. Naomi R. Goldenberg, *Changing of the Gods: Feminism and the End of Traditional Religions* (Boston, Mass.: Beacon, 1979), p. 111.

16. Heinlein, *Stranger in a Strange Land*; and Ursula Le Guin, *Left Hand of Darkness* (New York: Ace, 1969).

17. Daniel Keyes, *Flowers for Algernon* (New York: Bantam, 1970); and Joanna Russ, *The Female Man* (New York: Bantam, 1975).

18. See my article, "Star Wars vs. 2001: A Question of Identity," in *Selected Preceedings S.F.R.A. Conference, 1978*, ed. Thomas J. Remington (Cedar Falls, Iowa: University of Northern Iowa, 1979), pp. 178-200; and in *Extrapolation* (Summer 1983).

19. Ochs, *Behind the Sex of God*, p. 137.

20. Olaf Stapledon, *The Star Maker* (Baltimore, Md.: Penguin, 1972).

21. Elisabeth Schussler Fiorenza, "Feminist Spirituality, Christian Identity and Catholic Vision," in *Womanspirit Rising*, ed. Christ and Plaskow, pp. 137, 139.

22. Christ and Plaskow, "Creating New Traditions," in *Womanspirit Rising*, ed. Christ and Plaskow, p. 194.

23. Daly, *Beyond God the Father*, pp. 33-34.

24. Goldenberg, *Changing of the Gods*, p. 118.

25. Carol Christ, "Spiritual Quest and Women's Experience," in *Womanspirit Rising*, ed. Christ and Plaskow, pp. 228-45.

26. Loren Eiseley, *The Immense Journey* (New York: Random House, 1957).

27. Daly, *Beyond God the Father*, pp. 114-22, 174-78.

# Further Reading

## Chapter 1. Philosophy and Science Fiction

Clareson, Thomas D. *Many Futures, Many Worlds: Theme and Form in Science Fiction.* Kent, Ohio: Kent State University Press, 1979.

Knight, Damon, ed. *Turning Points: Essays on the Art of Science Fiction.* New York: Harper & Row, 1977.

Lem, Stanislaw. *Solaris.* Translated by Joanna Kilmartin and Steve Cox. New York: Berkley Publishing Co., 1971.

———. *The Cyberaid.* Translated by Michael Kandel. New York: Avon Books, 1976.

———. *The Futurological Congress.* Translated by Michael Kandel. New York: Seabury Press, 1976.

———. *A Perfect Vacuum.* Translated by Michael Kandel. New York: Harcourt Brace Jovanovich, 1979.

Miller, Fred D., Jr., and Smith, Nicholas D., eds. *Thought Probes: Philosophy Through Science Fiction.* Englewood Cliffs, N.J.: Prentice-Hall, Inc., 1981.

Rose, Lois, and Rose, Stephen. *The Shattered Ring: Science Fiction and the Quest for Meaning.* Richmond, Va.: John Knox Press, 1970.

Stapledon, Olaf. *Sirius.* Baltimore, Md.: Penguin Books, 1964.

———. *Odd John.* New York: Berkley Publishing Co., 1965.

———. *Last and First Man* and *Star Maker.* New York: Dover Publications, Inc., 1968.

## Chapter 2. Science Fiction and Emerging Values

Aldridge, Alexandra. "Scientising Society: The Dystopian Novel and the Scientific World View." Ph.D. dissertation, University of Michigan, 1978.

————. "Brave New World and the Mechanist/Vitalist Controversy." *Comparative Literature Studies* 17, 2 (1980): 116-32.

————. "Popular Futurism: Soft Thinking in Hard Times." *Michigan Quarterly Review* 20, 3 (1981).

Burtt, E. A. *The Metaphysical Foundations of Modern Science.* 2d. ed., 1924. Reprint. New York: Doubleday, 1954.

Capra, Fritjof. *The Tao of Physics.* New York: Bantam Books, 1975.

Hillegas, Mark. *The Future as Nightmare: H. G. Wells and the Anti-Utopians.* New York: Oxford University Press, 1976.

Le Guin, Ursula K. *The Dispossessed.* New York: Harper & Row, 1974.

Roszak, Theodore. *The Making of a Counter Culture.* New York: Doubleday, 1969.

Samuelson, David."Studies in the Contemporary American and British Science Fiction Novel." Ph.D. dissertation, University of Southern California, 1969.

"Science Fiction on Woman—Science Fiction by Women." *Science Fiction Studies* 7 [Part 1], 20 (March 1980).

Shelley, Mary. *Frankenstein.* 1818. Reprint. New York: Dell, 1975.

Suvin, Darko. "On the Poetics of the Science Fiction Genre." *College English* 34, 3 (1972): 372-82.

Thompson, William Irwin. *Passages About Earth.* New York: Harper & Row, 1973, 1974.

Wagar, W. Warren, *H. G. Wells and the World State.* New Haven: Yale University Press, 1961.

"Women and the Future." *Alternative Futures* 4, 2-3 (1981).

Wood, Michael. "Coffee Break for Sisyphus." *The New York Review of Books*, 2 October 1975, p. 3.

## Chapter 3. Cosmological Implications of Time Travel

Allen, Thomas Benton. *The Quest: A Report on Extraterrestrial Life.* Philadelphia: Chilton Books, 1965.

Angeles, Peter. *The Problem of God.* Columbus, Ohio: Charles E. Merrill Publishing Co., 1974.

————. *Critiques of God.* Buffalo, New York: Prometheus Books, 1976.

Asimov, Isaac. *Extraterrestrial Civilization.* New York: Crown Publishing, 1979.

————. "Science and the Mountain Peak." *The Skeptical Inquirer* 5 (Winter 1980-81): 42-51.

Barnhart, Joe E. *Religion and the Challenge of Philosophy.* Totowa, N.J.: Littlefield Adams, 1975.

Blanshard, Brand. *Reason and Belief.* London: Allen & Unwin, 1974.

Bracewell, Ronald Neubold. *The Galactic Club: Intelligent Life in Outer Space.* San Francisco: W. H. Freeman, 1975.

Cloud, Preston. *Cosmos, Earth and Man.* New Haven: Yale University Press, 1978.

Dwyer, Larry. "Time Travel and Changing the Past." *Philosophical Studies* 29 (1975): 341-50.

Flew, Antony, and MacIntyre, Alasdair. *New Essays in Philosophical Theology.* New York: Macmillan, 1955.

Fulmer, Gilbert. "Animistic and Naturalistic World Views." *Religious Humanism* 11 (1977): 36-39.

———. "The Concept of the Supernatural." *Analysis* 57 (1977): 113-16.

———. "Understanding Time Travel." *Southwestern Journal of Philosophy* 1 (1980): 151-56.

———. "Time Travel, Determinism, and Fatalism." *Philosophical Speculations in Science Fiction and Fantasy* 1 (1981): 41-48.

Horwich, Paul. "On Some Alleged Paradoxes of Time Travel." *Journal of Philosophy* 72 (1975): 432-44.

Hoyle, Fred. *Astronomy and Cosmology: A Modern Course.* San Francisco: W. H. Freeman, 1975.

Hume, David. *The Natural History of Religion.* Edited by J. E. Root. Stanford, Calif.: Stanford University Press, 1957.

Huxley, Julian. *Religion Without Revelation.* New York: Mentor, 1958.

Jastrow, Robert. *God and the Astronomers.* New York: Norton, 1978.

Kaufman, William J. *Reality and Cosmology.* New York: Harper & Row, 1973.

Kolenda, Konstantin. *Religion Without God.* Buffalo, N.Y.: Prometheus Books, 1976.

Koyre, Alexandre. *From the Closed World to the Infinite Universe.* New York: Harper & Row, 1958.

Lepp, Ignace. *Atheism in Our Time.* Translated by Bernard Murchland. Toronto: Macmillan, 1964.

Lewis, David. "The Paradoxes of Time Travel." *American Philosophical Quarterly* 13 (1976): 145-52.

McVittie, George Cunliffe. *Fact and Theory in Cosmology.* New York: Macmillan, 1961.

Motz, Lloyd. *The Universe: Its Beginning and Ending.* New York: Scribner's, 1975.

Neilsen, Karl. *Scepticism.* London: Macmillan, 1973.

Pap, Arthur. *An Introduction to the Philosophy of Science.* New York: Free Press of Glencoe, 1967.

Rescher, Nicholas. *Scientific Explanation.* New York: Free Press, 1970.

Russell, Bertrand. *Religion and Science.* New York: Oxford University Press, 1961.

Scriven, Michael. *Primary Philosophy.* New York: McGraw-Hill, 1966.

Shapley, Harlow. *The Stars and Man: The Human Response to the Expanding Universe.* Boston: Beacon Press, 1964.

Smart, William Marshall. *The Origin of the Earth.* Cambridge: Cambridge University Press, 1953.

Weinberg, Steven. *The First Three Minutes: A Modern View of the Origin of the Universe.* New York: Basic Books, 1977.

## Chapter 4. *Siddhartha and Slaughterhouse Five* (A New Paradigm of Time)

Werth, Lee F. "Some Second Thoughts on First Principles." *Philosophy in Context* 4 (1975): 78-88.

———. "Principles and Orders," *Philosophy in Context,* supplement to vol. 4. (1975): 57-66.

———. "Normalizing the Paranormal." *American Philosophical Quarterly* 15, 1 (January 1978): 47-56.

———. "Tachyons and Yogons." *Darshana International* 18, 2 (April 1978): 66-77.

———. "The Untenability of Whitehead's Theory of Extensive Connection." *Process Studies* 8, 1 (Spring 1978): 37-44.

———. "On Again, Off Again." In *Philosophers Look at Science Fiction,* edited by Nicholas D. Smith. Chicago: Nelson-Hall, 1982, pp. 21-45.

## Chapter 5. Nature through Science Fiction

Amis, Kingsley. *New Maps of Hell: A Survey of Science Fiction.* New York: Harcourt, Brace & Co., 1960.

Anderson, Poul. "Garden in the Void." In *Exploring Other Worlds,* edited by Sam Moskowitz. New York: Collier Books, 1963.

Berger, Harold L. *Science Fiction and the New Dark Age.* Bowling Green, Ohio: Bowling Green University Popular Press, 1976.

Bester, Alfred. "Adam and No Eve." In *Famous Science Fiction Stories: Adventures in Space and Time,* edited by Raymond J. Healy and J. Francis McComas. New York: Modern Library, 1957.

Brunner, John. *The Sheep Look Up.* New York: Ballantine Books, 1973.

Callenbach, Ernest. *Ectopia.* Berkeley, Calif.: Banyan Tree Books, 1975.

Christopher, John. *No Blade of Grass.* New York: Avon Books, 1957.

Clark, Hohn D. "Minus Planet." In *Before the Golden Age: A Science Fiction Anthology of the 1930's,* vol. 3, edited by Isaac Asimov. New York: Doubleday, 1974.

Davidson, Avram. "Or All the Seas With Oysters." In *The Arbor House Treasury of Modern Science Fiction,* compiled by Robert Silverberg and Martin H. Greenberg. New York: Arbor House, 1980.

Finney, Jack. *The Invasion of the Body Snatchers.* New York: Dell, 1978.

Hamilton, Edmond. "Devolution." In *Before the Golden Age: A Science Fiction Anthology of the 1930's,* vol. 3, edited by Isaac Asimov. New York: Doubleday, 1974.

Harrison, Harry. *Deathworld.* In *The Deathworld Trilogy* by Harry Harrison. New York: Berkley Books, 1976.

Herbert Frank. *Dune.* New York: Chilton Book Co., 1965.

———. *Hellstrom's Hive.* New York: Bantam Books, 1972.

Hoyle, Fred. *The Black Cloud.* New York: Signet Books, 1969.

Huxley, Aldous. *Brave New World*. Reprint. New York: Harper & Row, 1969.

Kapek, Karel. *War With the Newts*. Translated by M. Weatherall and R. Weatherall. New York: Bantam Books, 1959.

Klass, Morton. "In the Beginning." In *Apeman, Spaceman*, edited by Leon E. Stover and Harry Harrison. New York: Doubleday & Co., Inc., 1968. Reprint. New York: Berkley Publishing Co., 1970.

Le Guin, Ursula K. *Rocannon's World*. New York: Ace Books, 1966.

Lewis, C. A. *Perelandra*. Reprint. New York: Macmillan Paperbacks, 1965.

Meek, S. P. "Submicroscopic." In *Before the Golden Age: A Science Fiction Anthology of the 1930's*, vol. 1, edited by Isaac Asimov. New York: Doubleday, 1974.

Russell, Eric Frank. "Symbiotica." In *Famous Science Fiction Stories: Adventures in Space and Time*, edited by Raymond J. Healy and J. Francis McComas. New York: Modern Library, 1950.

Sheckley, Robert. "Shape." In *The Arbor House Treasury of Modern Science Fiction*, edited by Robert Silverberg and Martin H. Greenberg. New York: Arbor House, 1980.

Stapledon, Olaf. *Star Maker*. Reprint. Baltimore, Md.: Penguin Books, 1972.

Suvin, Darko. *Metamorphoses of Science Fiction: On the Poetics and History of a Literary Genre*. New Haven: Yale University Press, 1979.

Vance, Jack. *Son of the Tree*. New York: Ace Books, 1964.

———. *The House of Iszm*. New York: Ace Books, 1954.

———. *The Blue World*. New York: Ballantine Books, 1966.

Verne, Jules. *The Mysterious Island*. Reprint. New York: Airmont Publishing Co., Inc., 1965.

Voltaire, F.M.A. "Micromegas." In *Voltaire: Candide and Other Writings*, edited by Haskell M. Block. New York: Modern Library, 1956.

Weinbaum, Stanley G. "The Parasite Planet." In *Before the Golden Age: A Science Fiction Anthology of the 1930's*, vol. 3, edited by Isaac Asimov. New York: Doubleday, 1974.

Wells, H. G. *The Time Machine*. In *Seven Science Fiction Novels of H. G. Wells*. New York: Dover Publications, 1950.

———. "A Story of the Stone Age." In *Twenty-Eight Science Fiction Stories of H. G. Wells*. New York: Dover Publications, Inc., 1952.

Wyndham, John. *The Day of the Triffids*. New York: Doubleday & Co., 1951.

## Chapter 6. Teleology of Human Evolution for Mentality?

Corning, William, and Balaban, Martin, eds. *The Mind: Biological Approaches to Its Functions*. New York: Interscience Publishers, 1968.

Fox, Michael. *Integrative Development of Brain and Behavior in the Dog*. Chicago: University of Chicago Press, 1971.

Gazzaniga, Michael, and Blakemore, Colin, eds. *Handbook of Psychobiology*. New York: Academic Press, 1975.

Gould, James, and Gould, Carol Brant. "The Instinct to Learn." *Science 81* 2, 4 (May 1981): 44-50.

Johanson, Donald, and Edey, Maitland. *Lucy: The Beginnings of Humankind*. New York: Simon & Schuster, Inc., 1981.

Jolly, Clifford, and Plog, Fred. *Physical Anthropology and Archeology*. 3d ed. New York: Alfred A. Knopf, 1982.

Lorenz, Konrad. *Man Meets Dog*. Baltimore, Md.: Penguin Books, 1965.

Matthews, L. Harrison. *The Natural History of the Whale*. New York: Columbia University Press, 1978.

Rensberger, Boyce. "Facing the Past [Neanderthals *not* Brutish-looking]." *Science 81* 2, 8 (October 1981): 40-50.

Ridgway, Sam. *Mammals of the Sea: Biology and Medicine*. Springfield, Ill.: Charles C. Thomas Publisher, 1972.

Sarnat, Harvey, and Netsky, Martin. *Evolution of the Nervous System*. New York: Oxford University Press, 1974.

Trumler, Edward. *Your Dog and You*. New York: Seabury Press, 1973.

## Chapter 7. *Star Trek*: A Philosophical Interpretation

Asherman, Allan. *Star Trek Compendium*. New York: Simon & Schuster, 1981.

Berger, Albert I. "Science Fiction Fans in Socio-Economic Perspective: Factors in the Social Consciousness of a Genre." *Science-Fiction Studies* 4 [Part 3] (November 1977): 232-46.

Blair, Karen. *Meaning in Star Trek*. New York: Warner Books, Inc., 1977.

Bretnor, Reginald, ed. *Science Fiction: Today and Tomorrow*. New York: Harper & Row, 1974.

―――. ed. *Modern Science Fiction: Its Meaning and Its Future*. Chicago: Advent Publishers, Inc., 1979.

Clareson, Thomas, ed. *The Other Side of Realism*. Bowling Green, Ohio: Bowling Green University Press, 1971.

Gerrold, David. *The World of Star Trek*. New York: Ballantine Books, 1973.

Irwin, Walter, and Love, G. B. *The Best of Star Trek*. New York: Signet, 1978.

Lectenberg, Jacqueline; Marshak, Sandra; and Winston, Jean. *Star Trek Lives: Personal Notes and Anecdotes*. New York: Ballantine, 1975.

Lem, Stanislaw. "On the Structural Analysis of Science Fiction." Science-Fiction Studies 1 [Part 1] (Spring 1973): 26-33.

Roddenberry, Gene. *Star Trek: The Motion Picture, A Novel*. New York: Pocket Books, Inc., 1979.

Russ, Joanna. "Towards an Aesthetic of Science Fiction." *Science-Fiction Studies* 2 [no. 6] (July 1975): 112-19.

Sackett, Susan. *Letters to Star Trek*. New York: Ballantine, 1977.

Spinoza, Baruch. Ethics, Book 4 "Of Human Bondage." Translated by William Hale White. 3d edition revised by Amelia H. Stirling. London: Duckworth, 1889.
Trimble, Bjo. *Star Trek Concordance*. New York: Ballantine,1976.
Turnbull, Gerry. *A Star Trek Catalog*. New York: Grosset & Dunlap, 1979.
Whitfield, Stephen. *The Making of Star Trek*. New York: Ballantine, 1968.

## Chapter 8. There Are No Persons

Cornman, J. *Materialism and Sensations*. New Haven: Yale University Press, 1971.
———. *Perception, Common Sense, and Science*. New Haven: Yale University Press, 1975.
Dennett, D. *Brainstorms*. Cambridge: M.I.T. Press, 1978.
Descartes, René. *Meditations on First Philosophy*. In vol. 1 of *The Philosophical Works of Descartes*. 2 vols. Translated by Elizabeth S. Haldane and G.R.T. Ross. New York: Dover Publications, 1955. [Republication of 1931 corrected edition.]
Eddington, A. *The Nature of the Physical World*. Ann Arbor: University of Michigan Press, 1963.
Gazzaniga M. *The Bisected Brain*. New York: Appleton-Century-Croft, 1970.
Halverson, W. *A Concise Introduction to Philosophy*. New York: Random House, 1981.
Rorty, R. *Philosophy and the Mirror of Nature*. Princeton: Princeton University Press, 1979.
Rosenthal, D. *Materialism and the Mind-Body Problem*. Englewood Cliffs, N.J.: Prentice-Hall, 1971.
Sagan, C. *The Dragons of Eden*. New York: Ballantine Books, 1977.
Sellars, W. *Science, Perception and Reality*. New York: Humanities Press, 1963.
Smart, J. *Philosophy and Scientific Realism*. New York: Humanities Press, 1963.

## Chapter 9. Bounded by Metal

Asimov, Isaac. "The Bicentennial Man." In *The Best Science Fiction of the Year #6*, edited by Terry Carr. New York: Holt, Rinehart & Winston, 1977, pp. 333-79.
Beer, Andrew. "Robots with Human Traits." Presentation at *Robotics Futures Conference*. Long Island University, Brooklyn Campus, 26 April 1980.
Dick, Philip K. "Man, Android and Machine." In *Science Fiction at Large*, edited by Peter Nichols. New York: Harper & Row, 1976, pp. 200-224.
Knight, Damon. "An Annotated 'Masks.'" In *Those Who Can: A Science Fiction Reader*, edited by Robin Scott Wilson. New York: New American Library, 1973, pp. 212-31.
Phillips, Peter. "Lost Memory." In *Themes in Science Fiction*, edited by Leo P. Kelley. New York: McGraw-Hill, 1972, pp. 343-53.

Warrick, Patricia "Images of the Man-Machine Intelligence Relationship in Science Fiction." In *Many Futures, Many Worlds: Theme and Form in Science Fiction*, edited by Thomas D. Clareson. Kent, Ohio: Kent State University Press, 1977, pp. 182-223.

## Chapter 10. Metaphor As a Way of Saying the Self in Science Fiction

Cottle, Thomas J., and Klineberg, Stephen L. *The Present of Things Future*. New York: Free Press, 1974.

Haynes, Felicity. "Metaphoric Understanding." *Journal of Aesthetic Education* 12 (April 1978): 99-115.

Kaminsky, Jack. *Language and Ontology*. Carbondale: Southern Illinois University Press, 1969.

MacCormac, Earl R. *Metaphor and Myth in Science and Religion*. Durham, N.C.: Duke University Press, 1976.

Percy, Walker. *The Message in the Bottle*. New York: Farrar, Straus and Giroux, 1975.

Scholes, Robert. "The Roots of Science Fiction." In *Science Fiction: A Collection of Critical Essays*, edited by Mark Rose. Englewood Cliffs, N.J.: Prentice-Hall, 1976, pp. 46-56.

## Chapter 11. Language Fragmentation in Recent Science Fiction

"Absurdist SF." In *The Science Fiction Encyclopedia*, edited by Peter Nichols, pp. 15-16. Garden City, N.Y.: Doubleday & Co., 1979.

Burke, Kenneth. *Language as Symbolic Action*. Berkeley: University of California Press, 1973.

Huntington, John. "Science Fiction and the Future." In *Science Fiction: A Collection of Critical Essays*, edited by Mark Rose. Englewood Cliffs, N.J.: Prentice-Hall, 1976, pp. 156-66.

Scholes, Robert, and Rabkin, Eric. *Science Fiction: History, Science, Vision*. New York: Oxford University Press, 1977.

## Chapter 12. Medium and Message in Ellison's "I Have No Mouth, and I Must Scream."

Brady, Charles J. "The Computer as a Symbol of God: Ellison's Macabre Exodus." *Journal of General Education* 28 (Spring 1976): 55-62.

Ellison, Harlon. *Alone Against Tomorrow*. New York: Macmillan, 1970.

Jennings, Edward M., ed. *Science and Literature: New Lenses for Criticism*. Garden City, N.Y.: Doubleday Anchor Books, 1970.

MacLeish, Arnold. "Why Do We Teach Poetry?" *Atlantic* 197 (March 1956): 48-53.

McLuhan, Marshall. *Understanding Media: The Extensions of Man.* New York: McGraw-Hill, 1964.

Scholes, Robert. *Structuralism in Literature.* New Haven: Yale University Press, 1974.

———. *Structural Fabulation.* Notre Dame: University Press, 1975.

## Chapter 13. Feminist Science Fiction and Medical Ethics: Marge Piercy's *Woman on the Edge of Time.*

Annas, George J., et al. *Informed Consent to Human Experimentation: The Subject's Dilemma.* Cambridge, Mass.: Ballinger, 1977.

Annas, Pamela J. "New Worlds, New Words: Androgny in Feminist Science Fiction." *Science-Fiction Studies* 5 [part 2] (July 1978): 143-56.

Barber, Bernard. *Informed Consent in Medical Therapy and Research.* New Brunswick, N.J.: Rutgers University Press, 1980.

Bok, Sissela. *Lying: Moral Choice in Public and Private Life.* New York: Pantheon Books, 1978.

Chesler, Phyllis. *Women and Madness.* Garden City, N.Y.: Doubleday, 1972.

Churchill, Larry R. "Ethos and Ethics in Medical Education." *North Carolina Medical Journal* 36, 3 (January 1975): 31-33.

———. "Physician-Investigator/Patient-Subject: Exploring the Logic and the Tension." *The Journal of Medicine and Philosophy* 5, 3 (September 1980): 215-24.

Hacker, Marilyn. "Science Fiction and Feminism: The Work of Joanna Russ." *Chrysalis, A Magazine of Woman's Culture* 4 (1977): 67-79.

Khouri, Nadia. "The Dialectics of Power: Utopia in the Science Fiction of Le Guin, Jeury, and Piercy." *Science-Fiction Studies* 7 [part 1] (March 1980): 49-60.

Olemedo, Esteban L., and Parron, Delores L. "Mental Health of Minority Women: Some Special Issues." *Professional Psychology* 12, 1 (February 1981): 103-11.

Pearson, Carol. "Women's Fantasies and Feminist Utopias." *Frontiers* 2, 3 (Fall 1977): 50-61.

Piercy, Marge. *Woman on the Edge of Time.* New York: Fawcett, Crest, 1976.

———. "Dear FRONTIERS." Letter. *Frontiers* 2, 3 (Fall 1977): 63-64.

Russ, Joanna. "What Can a Heroine Do? Or Why Women Can't Write." In *Images of Women in Fiction: Feminist Perspectives,* edited by Susan Koppleman Cornillon. Revised ed. Bowling Green, Ohio: Bowling Green University Popular Press, 1973, pp. 3-20.

Spitzer, Therese. *Psychobattery: A Chronicle of Psychotherapeutic Abuse.* Clifton, N.J.: Humana Press, 1980.

Stone, Alan A. "Presidential Address: Conceptual Ambiguity and Morality in

Modern Psychiatry." *The American Journal of Psychiatry* 137, 8 (August 1980): 887-91.

Winslade, William J. "Ethical Issues." In *Psychiatric Research in Practice: Biobehavioral Themes*, edited by E. A. Serafetinides. New York: Grune & Stratton, 1981, pp. 227-40.

## Chapter 14. Medical Morals and Narrative Necessity

Abe, Kobo. *Inter-Ice Age 4*. New York: Knopf, 1970.

Ballard, J. G. *The Drowned World*. New York: Berkley, 1962.

————. *The Burning World*. New York: Berkley, 1964.

————. *The Crystal World*. New York: Farrar, Straus & Giroux, 1966.

————. *The Impossible Man*. New York: Berkley, 1966.

————. *The Subliminal Man*. In *The Best Short Stories of J. G. Ballard*. New York: Holt, Rinehart & Winston, 1978.

Bax, Martin. *Hospital Ship*. New York: New Directions, 1976.

Bradbury, Ray. "A Medicine for Melancholy." In *Vintage Bradbury*. New York: Random House, 1965.

Conklin, Groff, and Fabricant, Noah. *Great Science Fiction Stories about Doctors*. New York: Colliers, 1963.

Crichton, Michael. *The Andromeda Strain*. New York: Knopf, 1969.

————. *The Terminal Man*. New York: Knopf, 1972.

Del Rey, Lester. *Nerves*. 1942. Expanded edition. New York: Ballantine, 1956.

Dickinson, Peter. *The Green Gene*. New York: Pantheon, 1973.

Dickson, Gordon. *The R-Master*. New York: J. B. Lippincott, 1973.

Doyle, Arthur Conan. *The Poison Belt*. London & New York: Hodder & Stoughton, 1913.

England, George Allan. "The Man With the Glass Heart." In *The Fantastic Pulps*, edited by Peter Haining. New York: St. Martin's, 1975.

Fisher, Lou. "Bloodstream." In *Epoch*, edited by Robert Silverberg and Roger Elwood. New York: Berkley, 1975.

Haldeman, Jack. *Vector Analysis*. New York: Berkley, 1978.

Harness, Charles R. *The Rose*. New York: Berkley, 1953.

Hawthorne, Nathaniel. "Rappaccini's Daughter." 1844. Reprint. In *The Road to Science Fiction #1 From Gilgamesh to Wells*, edited by James E. Gunn. New York: Mentor, New American Library, 1977, pp. 180-208.

Keller, David H. *Life Everlasting and Other Tales of Science, Fantasy, and Horror*. Newark, N.J.: Avalon, 1947.

Keyes, Daniel. *Flowers for Algeron*. New York: Harcourt, Brace & World, 1966.

Kornbluth, C. M. "The Little Black Bag." In *The Best Science Fiction Stories of C. M. Kornbluth*. London: Faber, 1968.

Leinster, Murray. *Doctor to the Stars*. New York: Pyramid Books, 1971 [c. 1964].

————. *S.O.S. from Three Worlds*. New York: Avon Books, 1967.

Matheson, Richard. *I Am Legend*. New York: Fawcett, 1954.

———. *What Dreams May Come*. New York: Putnam's, 1978.

Nourse, Alan E. *Star Surgeon*. New York: McKay, 1960.

———. *The Mercy Men*. New York: McKay, 1968.

———. *Rx for Tomorrow: Tales of Science Fiction, Fantasy and Medicine*. New York: David McKay, 1971.

———. *The Bladerunner*. New York: McKay, 1974.

———. "Extrapolation and Quantum Jumps." In *The Craft of Science Fiction*, edited by Reginald Bretnor. New York: Harper & Row, 1976.

Page, Thomas. *The Hephaestus Plague*. New York: Bantam, 1975.

Pohl, Frederik. *Man Plus*. New York: Random House, 1976.

———. *Gateway*. New York: St. Martin's, 1977.

Sheffield, Charles. "Transition Team." In *Destinies*, edited by James Baen. New York: Ace, 1978.

Silverberg, Robert. "The Pain Peddlers." In *Windows into Tomorrow*. New York: Hawthorn, 1974.

Simak, Clifford D. "Huddling Place." In *Modern Masterpieces of Science Fiction*, edited by Sam Moskowitz. New York: World, 1965.

Stewart, Fred M. *The Methuselah Enzyme*. New York: Arbor House, 1970.

Strete, Crain. *The Bleeding Man and Other Stories*. New York: William Morrow, 1977.

White, James. *Hospital Ship*. New York: Ballantine, 1962.

———. *Star Surgeon*. New York: Ballantine, 1963.

———. *Major Operation*. New York: Ballantine, 1971.

———. *Monsters and Medics*. New York: Ballantine, 1977.

Winter, J. A. "Expedition Polychrome." In *Gates to Tomorrow*, edited by Andre Norton and E. Donaldy. New York: Atheneum, 1973.

Wolfe, Bernard. *Limbo*. New York: Random House, 1952.

Wyndham, John. *The Chrysalids*. In *America: Re-birth*. New York: Ballantine, 1955.

Yarbro, Chelsea Quinn. *Time of the Fourth Horseman*. Garden City, N.Y.: Doubleday, 1976.

## Chapter 15. Heroes and History

Aldiss, Brian. *The Malacia Tapestry*. London: Jonathan Cape, 1976. 1st American edition: New York: Harper & Row, 1977.

———. Personal Interview. 20 March 1981 (Schuyler).

———. Letter to Wm. M. Schuyler. 30 October 1981.

*The American Heritage Dictionary of the English Language*. Boston: Houghton Mifflin, 1970.

Anderson, Poul. *The Broken Sword*. Revised ed. 1971. Reprint. New York: Ballantine Books, 1977.

Asimov, Isaac. *Foundation*. New York: Gnome Press, 1951.

————. *Foundation and Empire*. New York: Gnome Press, 1952.

————. *Second Foundation*. New York: Gnome Press, 1953.

Browning, Robert. "A Toccata of Galuppi's." In *The Postical Works of Robert Browning: Complete from 1863 to 1868 and the Shortest Works Thereafter*, 1905. Reprint, London: Oxford University Press, 1940, pp. 220-21.

Campbell, John. *The Hero With a Thousand Faces*. Princeton: Princeton University Press, 1972.

Delany, Samuel R. *Tales of Nevèryön*. New York: Bantam, 1972.

Derrida, Jacques. *Of Grammatology*. Translated by Gaytri Chakravorty Spivak. Baltimore, Md.: Johns Hopkins University Press, 1976.

Dray, William R., ed. *Philosophical Analysis and History*. New York: Harper & Row, 1966.

Eddison, E. R. *The Mezentian Gate*. [England]: n.p., 1958.

————. *The Worm Ouroboros*. 1922. Reprint. New York: E. P. Dutton, 1952.

Fisher, H.A.L. "Preface." *A History of Modern Europe*. 3 vols. Boston: Houghton Mifflin, 1935. Vol. 1.

Gibbon, Edward. *The Decline and Fall of the Roman Empire*. 3 vols. 1776-1783. Reprint. New York: Modern Library, n.d. Vol. 3.

Herodotus. *Herodotus*. Translated by A. D. Godley. 4 vols. Rev. ed. Loeb Classical Library. 1926. Reprint. Cambridge, Mass.: Harvard University Press, 1966. Vol. 1.

Hesiod, "The Works and Days." In *Hesiod*, translated by Richmond Lattimore. Ann Arbor: University of Michigan Press, 1959.

Howard, Robert E. *Conan the Conqueror*. 1935 as *The Hour of the Dragon*. Reprint. New York: Ace, 1953.

Kazantzakes, Nikos. *The Odyssey: A Modern Sequel*. Translated by, with introduction, synopsis, and noted by, Kimon Friar, New York: Simon & Schuster, 1958.

Lamond, John D.D. *Arthur Conan Doyle: A Memoir*. 1931. Reprint. Fort Washington, N.Y.: Kennikat Press, 1975.

Lee, Charles. "Proem (From the Cacohymniad, Book I.)" In *The Stuffed Owl: An Anthology of Bad Verse*. 2d ed. Edited with Introduction by D. B. Wyndham Lewis and Charles Lee. 1930. Reprint. New York: Capricorn, 1962.

Leslie, Donald O.; McKerras, Colin; and Gunwu, Wang, eds. *Essays on the Sources of Chinese History*. Columbia, S.C.: University of South Carolina Press, 1975.

Pope, Alexander. *The Rape of the Lock*. 1714. Reprint. Menston, England: The Scholar Press, 1969.

Pratt, Fletcher. *The Battles That Changed History*. New York: Doubleday, 1956.

Pynchon, Thomas. *Gravity's Rainbow*. New York: Viking, 1973.

Rizzi, Aldo. *The Etchings of the Tiepolos*. Translated by Lucia Wildt. London: Phaidon, 1971.

Rorty, Richard. *Philosophy and the Mirror of Nature*. Princeton: Princeton University Press, 1978.

Said, Edward W. *Beginnings: Intention and Method*. New York: Basic Books, 1975.

Wolfe, Thomas. *The Right Stuff*. New York: Farrar, Straus & Giroux, 1979.

## Chapter 16. Toward a Technological Sublime

Abrams, M. H. *The Mirror and the Lamp*. Oxford: Oxford University Press, 1953.

———. *Natural Supernaturalism*. New York: Norton, 1973.

Aldiss, Brian. *Billion Year Spree: The History of Science Fiction*. London: Transworld Publishers, Ltd., 1975.

Amis, Kingsley. *New Maps of Hell: A Survey of Science Fiction*. New York: Harcourt, Brace & World, Inc., 1960.

Bailey, J. O. *Pilgrims Through Space and Time*. 1974. Reprint. Westport, Conn.: Greenwood Press, 1972.

Burke, Edmond. *A Philosophical Enquiry Into the Origins of Our Idea of the Sublime and Beautiful*, edited by J. T. Boulton. London: Routledge & Kegan Paul, Ltd., 1958.

Chase, Richard. *The American Novel and Its Traditions*. New York: Doubleday, 1957.

Doyle, Sir Arthur Conan. *The Annotated Sherlock Holmes*. Edited by William S. Baring-Gould. New York: Clarkson N. Potter, 1967.

Franklin, H. Bruce. *Future Perfect: American Science Fiction of the Nineteenth Century*. New York: Oxford University Press, 1966.

Green, Roger Lancelyn. *Into Other Worlds: Space Flight in Fiction, From Lucian to Lewis*. New York: Arno Press, 1975.

Kant, Immanuel. *Critique of Judgement*. Translated by J. H. Bernard. New York: Haffner Press, 1951.

Ketterer, David. *New Worlds for Old: The Apocalyptic Imagination, Science Fiction and American Literature*. Garden City, N.Y.: Doubleday, Anchor, 1974.

Kiely, Robert. *The Romantic Novel in England*. Cambridge, Mass.: Harvard University Press, 1972.

Koestler, Arthur. *The Ghost in the Machine*. New York: Macmillan, 1968.

Longinus. *On the Sublime*. Translated by W. Rhys Roberts. Cambridge: Cambridge University Press, 1899.

Marx, Leo. *The Machine in the Garden: Technology and the Pastoral Ideal in America*. New York: Oxford University Press, 1964.

Moskowitz, Sam. *Explorers of the Infinite*. Westport, Conn.: Hyperion Press, 1963.

Mumford, Lewis. *The Pentagon of Power*. Vol. 2. *The Myth of the Machine*. New York: Harcourt, Brace Jovanovich, 1970.

Nicholson, Marjorie Hope. *Voyages to the Moon*. New York: Macmillan, 1948.

Rabkin, Eric. *The Fantastic in Literature*. Princeton: Princeton University Press, 1976.

Sussman, Herbert. *Victorians and the Machine: The Literary Response to Technology.* Translated by Richard Howard. Ithaca, N.Y.: Cornell University Press, 1975.

Tropp, Martin. *Mary Shelley's Monster: The Story of Frankenstein.* Boston: Houghton Mifflin, 1977.

Weiskel, Thomas. *The Romantic Sublime: Studies in the Structure and Psychology of Transcendence.* Baltimore, Md.: Johns Hopkins University Press, 1976.

Wolfe, Gary K. *The Known and the Unknown.* Kent, Ohio: Kent State University Press, 1979.

## Chapter 17. The Rejection of Traditional Theism in Feminist Theology and Science Fiction

Christ, Carol P., and Plaskow, Judith, eds. *Womanspirit Rising: A Feminist Reader in Religion.* New York: Harper & Row, 1979.

Daly, Mary. *Beyond God the Father.* Boston: Beacon Press, 1973.

Elwood, Roger, ed. *Strange Gods.* New York: Pocket Books, 1974.

Eiseley, Loren. *The Immense Journey.* New York: Random House, 1951.

Goldenberg, Naomi. *Changing of the Gods: Feminism and the End of Traditional Religion.* Boston: Beacon Press, 1979.

Gunn, James, ed. *The Road to Science Fiction #1: From Gilgamesh to Wells.* New York: Mentor, New American Library, 1977.

Ochs, Carol. *Behind the Sex of God.* Boston: Beacon Press, 1977.

Pielke, Robert. "Stars Wars vs. 2001: A Question of Identity." In *Selected Proceedings, S.F.R.A. Conference 1978.* Cedar Falls: University of Iowa Press, 1979.

# Index

# About the Contributors

ALEXANDRA ALDRIDGE is the founder and coeditor of the quarterly journal, *Alternative Futures*. She has written and lectured extensively on futurism and currently is writing a book about Aldous T. Huxley, D. H. Lawrence, and Rational Mysticism. In 1972-1973 she lectured, with John W. Aldridge, on recent trends in American literary culture at a number of European institutions for the State Department. Dr. Aldridge is presently associate professor of interdisciplinary technology at the College of Technology at Eastern Michigan University and director of the master of Liberal Studies in Technology graduate program, which she helped to design.

ROSEMARIE ARBUR is associate professor of English at Lehigh University in Bethlehem, Pennsylvania. Her essays on American and British Romanticism, literary theory, English pedagogy, the literature of women, and science fiction have appeared in several scholarly works and journals. Her book, *Leigh Brackett, Marion Zimmer Bradley, Anne McCaffrey: A Primary and Secondary Bibliography*, was published in 1982. Professor Arbur's recent scholarship has focused on the relationship between feminism and science fiction and on the "hard science" in science fiction.

DOROTHY ATKINS teaches composition and nineteenth-century British literature at Loras College in Dubuque, Iowa. As well as being an authority on *George Eliot and Spinoza*—her book explains how Spinoza's philosophy influenced the Victorian novelist—Professor Atkins has published essays and presented papers on nineteenth-century literature and science fiction in general.

JOANN P. COBB is associate professor of Humanities and English and Chairwoman of the Department of Humanities and Social Sciences at Parks College, St. Louis University. She has degrees in literature and philosophy. Her articles have appeared in *Enlightenment Essays* and *Philosophy and Literature.*

RICHARD DOUBLE is assistant professor of philosophy at Old Dominion University in Norfolk, Virginia. He also has taught at Seton Hall University, Trenton State College and East Carolina University. He received his Ph.D. from Rutgers in 1977. Dr. Double has contributed articles to *The Southern Journal of Philosophy, Teaching Philosophy, The Journal of Critical Analysis, Philosophy and Phenomenological Research, Philosophical Studies* (Ireland), and *Philosophy Research Archives.*

ADAM J. FRISCH is assistant professor of English at Briar Cliff College, Sioux City, Iowa, where he has been teaching since 1978. Dr. Frisch received his B.A. in English from the University of Michigan in 1967, his M.A. from the University of Washington at Seattle in 1968, and his Ph.D. in English from the University of Texas at Austin in 1977. His professional memberships include the Modern Language Association, the Popular Culture Association, and the Science Fiction Research Association.

GILBERT FULMER is associate professor of philosophy at Southwest Texas State University in San Marcos. He recieved his B.A. in philosophy from Rice University in 1966 and his Ph.D. in philosophy from Rice University in 1972. His dissertation, *Wittgenstein, Relativism, and Reason,* won Rice's annual award for the best thesis, the John W. Gardner Award in Humanities. Dr. Fulmer has published articles in such journals as *Rice University Studies, Analysis, Journal of Value Inquiry, The Personalist,* and *Philosophical Speculations in Science Fiction and Fantasy.*

ANNE HUDSON JONES is associate professor of literature and medicine at the Institute for the Medical Humanities of the University of Texas Medical Branch in Galveston. She has published articles on ethics in medical and scientific writing and practice, on women in science fiction, and on literature and medicine. She is presently completing a reader's guide to the fiction of Kate Wilhelm and writing a book on medicine and the physician in American popular culture. She is also a founding editor of the journal *Literature and Medicine.*

TED KRULIK teaches English at Bushwick High School in Brooklyn, New York, where he is instituting a course in science fiction. He has recently published an article in *Extrapolation* on "Teaching Science Fiction in the Classroom." His essay, "Reaching for Imortality: Two Novels of Richard Matheson," appeared in *Critical Encounters II*, edited by Tom Sinclair (Frederick Unger Publications). Mr. Krulik is now working on a literary study of the works of Roger Zelazny.

PHILIP A. PECORINO is associate professor in the Social Science Department of Queensborough Community College, City University of New York. He received his Ph.D. from Fordham University. Dr. Pecorino is president of the American Assoication of Philosophy Teachers, vice president of the Eastern Division of the Community College Humanities Association and has chaired the executive committee of the Long Island Philosophical Society. He is on the editorial boards of *Aitia*, a two-year college philosophy-humanities journal, and the *Philosophy Teacher's Handbook*.

ROBERT G. PIELKE received his Ph.D. in social ethics from Claremont Graduate School in California in 1973. Through his participation in both popular culture associations and various professional philosophical groups, he has been able to blend a collection of phenomena into a meaningful whole. Although he hopes to devote more time to his writing interests, Dr. Pielke now teaches part-time in the philosophy departments of California Poly State University in Pomona and at LaVerne College. He is author of *Rock Music: A Philosophical Appraisal*.

PAUL RICE, a widely published poet, teaches contemporary literature and creative writing at the University of North Carolina at Ashville. He is a specialist in the literary applications of metaphor and a science fiction fan of long standing. He is presently working on a series of papers treating the fiction of David Lindsay.

WILLIAM M. SCHUYLER, JR. is associate professor of philosophy at the University of Louisville (Belknap Campus). He completed his graduate work in mathematics at the University of Illinois and did his graduate work in philosophy and the history of science at Princeton University.

BARTON D. THURBER received his B.A. from Stanford University and his Ph.D. from Harvard University. He is currently associate professor of English and chairman of the English Department at the University of San Diego. Dr. Thurber is at work on a science fiction novel called *Twenty Eighty Four*, a "history," he states, "of the next hundred years, which is unfortunately only ambiguously sublime."

FRANS VAN DER BOGERT is professor of philosophy and religion at the Appalachian State University in Boone, North Carolina. He received his B.S. in philosophy from Swarthmore College in 1963 and his Ph.D. in philosophy from Cornell University in 1973. Dr. van der Bogert's activities include membership in a number of professional organizations. He is on the steering committee and Board of Directors, and serves as Executive Director of The American Association of Philosophy Teachers. He is a member of the editorial board of *The Philosophy Teacher's Handbook* and editor of *Philosophy Teaching Abstracts*. In addition to frequent presentations at conferences and meetings and regular contributions to *Philosophy Teaching Abstracts*, Dr. van der Bogert has published articles in such works as *Teaching Philosophy* and the *APA Newsletter on Teaching Philosophy*.

LEE F. WERTH is associate professor of philosophy at Cleveland State University. He has a continuing interest in the philosophy of space and time and in metaphysics. Dr. Werth's articles on time have been published in the *American Philosophical Quarterly, Process Studies*, and elsewhere. In 1981 Dr. Werth edited the science fiction and philsoophy issue of *Philosophy in Context*.

DAVID E. WHITE is associate professor and chairman of the Department of Philosophy at St. John Fisher College in Rochester, New York. He received his B.S. in philosophy from Colgate University in 1969 and his M.A. and Ph.D. degrees from Cornell University in 1973. Dr. White maintains membership in a wide range of professional organizations. His articles have been published in such sources as the *International Journal of Philosophy of Religion* and *Second Order*.

**About the Editor**

ROBERT E. MYERS is Professor and Chairman of the Department of Philosophy at Bethany College in West Virginia. He is the author of *Jack Williamson: A Primary and Secondary Bibliography* and of articles which have appeared in *Agora, Teaching Science Fiction, Philosophers Look at Science Fiction,* and *Science Fiction Writers.*